A Seas

In The Sun

Peter Haworth

Published by Dawber Publishing

ISBN 978-0-9563353-3-3

Cover photo: The day after Burnley's Wembley triumph, the victorious players celebrate on an open top bus tour of Burnley and acknowledge the cheers of the ecstatic crowds.

Cover prepared by Craig Lightowler.
Printed by Dolman Scott Ltd

CONTENTS

Dedicated to my wife Julie

IN recognition of her understanding and patience during the last 12 months of a 'work in progress,' and the best part of 30 years of silent teas on a Saturday night after another traumatic afternoon at Turf Moor.

Wembley 2009 gave her an insight into just how much this club means to me and many thousands of fellow Clarets.

Thanks Julie for the sustaining brews and encouragement.

Acknowledgments

TO Tony Dawber, without whom this book would never have gone to print.

To all my friends and colleagues who acted as unwitting contributors through their conversations, texts and emails.

To Dave Thomas for his encouragement, suggestions and continued interest.

To the 'Clarets Mad' website, an invaluable source of information and indicator of the fans' feelings.

To the sports department at BBC Radio Lancashire for their full match commentaries of away games, which through no fault of their own, brought so much grief. Particular thanks for their uncanny knack of creating goals for the opposition with their careless remarks such as "That's unusual for a Burnley game, 0-0 at half time."

But most importantly, to Burnley Football Club for being the inspiration for this work and a major influence on 50 years of my life.

FOREWORD

THE ups and down of life in the Premier League.

What was one quote at the start of the 2009-10 season?

"It's not going to be easy –going into the unknown. But the challenge of competing against the very best is the reward."

When the Clarets booked their place in the top flight of English football after that pulsating day at Wembley, everybody connected with the club was in dream land.

"When will we play at Old Trafford? I hope it's not in November cos I've booked a holiday in the Canaries." "And what's going to happen if we get the Big Four first up? In consecutive weeks? We could be looking down the barrel at the end of August!" "Who are we going to sign?" "What about the new kit?" "The Turf is having a spring clean."

The reality was kicking in. The excitement, the conjecture, the speculation of being involved in one the greatest global sports events of the 21st Century.

Time for reflection as well. I remember Alan Hansen coming to a Q&A in the James Hargreaves Stand back in 2008. "Will Burnley ever get back in the top league, Alan?" asked a diehard fan.

Hansen scoffed.

"Afraid not. It's all about money these days and Burnley don't have any," was the Scotsman's reply.

But is it?

Burnley folk and Burnley FC are made of sterner stuff. Didn't he know the club almost went out of existence in 1987? But that loyal stalwart Brian Miller steered the club through their lowest point. And from that moment on there was only one way to go – upwards. Every Burnley fan hoped, expected, anticipated, prayed that one day they would see their favourites once again compete at the very top level.

It happened. But how?

Because Burnley Football Club is very special. The heart keeps pumping throughout all the turmoil and disappointments. And will always live on.

Peter has captured those key moments brilliantly. His recollections will bring a smile and a cheer to many thousands of Claret fans.

It is one man's personal record of a truly momentous football season.

Enjoy.

Martin Dobson

Former Burnley player and England international

INTRODUCTION

IT'S May 25, 2009, and for myself and fellow followers of Burnley Football Club, our beloved Clarets, it's a date with destiny.

What can reduce a happily married and – well, in my opinion anyway - reasonably intelligent man of 57 summers to a sweating, nail biting, nervous wreck? A Coca-Cola Championship Play Off Final at Wembley, the recently rebuilt, no expense spared national soccer stadium, is the easy answer to that one.

In households all over Burnley, Pendle, Rossendale, probably every county in England, many in Scotland, Wales, Northern Ireland, the Republic of Ireland, and indeed many countries in the world, similar tortured souls can be found on this fateful day.

After 33 years exiled in the soccer wilderness of the Football League, we now unbelievably sit 90 minutes away from the Promised Land, El Dorado, or the Barclays Premier League as it is more commonly known.

Incredible is the only word to describe the magnificent season that had gone before and led us to this often dreamt about but never realistically imagined scenario.

In typical Burnley fashion the 2008/9 campaign, that started with much pre-season optimism after an unusual summer for the Clarets of incoming transfer activity and a series of victories in meaningless friendlies, quickly turned sour.

The first two league games resulted in two thumping defeats, 4-1 away and 0-3 at home, to relatively unfancied opposition, and the fans' familiar rollercoaster was under way. Four games in and there were still only two points on the board, and many of us diehards steeled ourselves for the long, hard relegation battle which looked to be ahead.

However, sandwiched between these games, we had managed two victories in the early stages of the Carling Cup against lower league opposition to lift the spirits slightly. A home draw in the next round against Premier League opposition in the shape of Fulham gave the team the opportunity to put one over the big boys, which they duly took to give the fans something to cheer.

Then, steadily from mid-September to early November, the league form improved, and with only two defeats to high flying opposition in 12 games, the Clarets found themselves sitting a very creditable fifth in the table.

Under the guidance of popular and relatively new manager Owen Coyle, the team had developed an attractive, attacking style of play that was beginning to win admirers beyond Turf Moor.

That defeat of Fulham had come courtesy of a late winner from Jay Rodriguez, a teenage Burnley lad and a product of our improving youth system. And importantly, it resulted in a mouth-watering fourth round draw, an away tie at 'moneybags' Chelsea.

What happened on that fantastic night of November 12 as the Clarets, not content to be cannon fodder, matched and sank the mighty Chelsea on their home turf, lit the blue touch paper and sent the side on a remarkable journey.

Suddenly the players grew in stature and self-belief and, packed with quality and an indomitable team spirit, the smallest squad in the Championship became a force to be reckoned with.

The subsequent conquest of a young but highly rated Arsenal side, 2-0 at Turf Moor, led to an epic two legged Carling Cup semi-final against Tottenham Hotspur. And the fact that the Clarets came back from a three goal deficit only to see the Londoners agonisingly snatch victory two minutes from the end of extra time only served to strengthen their resolve.

From mid-November, the league form had continued to flourish with only one defeat in eight games and on Christmas Eve the Clarets sat fourth in the table, six points from an automatic promotion place after just over half the season.

*"For the first time in years I'm certain Burnley are going to make the play offs, and it wouldn't surprise me one bit if they finish in the Premier League". - **Jimmy McIlroy, Burnley Legend. December 12, 2008.***

Heady days, but in their own inimitable fashion the team then managed to lose five straight league games on the bounce and slip to ninth position and out of touch with the top two.

However, in between the losses, the FA Cup campaign had begun and we were at it again. QPR were dispatched after a third round replay and Premiership opposition were next up as the Clarets were drawn away to West Bromwich Albion.

After ending the league famine on the last day in January with a home win over Charlton, the Clarets comprehensively put out West Brom 3-1 in a replay at Turf Moor, and once more Wembley beckoned.

On to the fifth round, and Arsenal were the opponents for the second time this term, this time though at their own, newly minted super stadium, the Emirates. Unfortunately on this occasion, against a strong in-form team and in front of a crowd of more than 57,000, we couldn't raise our game and went down 0-3.

Dreams of Wembley, so cruelly snatched away in the Carling Cup and now in the FA Cup, were over for us this term.

Or were they? Not so for these vintage Clarets and a manager who had the ability to make his team believe anything was possible.

An impressive and totally uncharacteristic Burnley finish to the season saw them lose only twice in the next 15 games, but even this run left them needing victory in the final match at home to Bristol City to confirm a play off place.

Yet right on cue, we turned in a majestic performance, running out 4-0 winners, and for the first time ever we were in those Championship play offs.

For many fans this would have been enough to cap a tremendous season in which the team had already played 58 games, more than any other team apart from Manchester United, while incredibly using only 23 players in the process.

Not for the Clarets the luxury of 'parachute' payments to boost the coffers and fund transfer window signings. Average attendances, despite the thrilling soccer, still remained amongst the lowest in the Championship, and in monetary terms the Clarets were paupers.

But they had something that money could not buy, a unity of purpose and an iron will that drove them on. The supporters, as their own belief began to grow, became a part of this unity and the bond between manager, team and supporters became almost tangible.

From perennial underdogs, we had become the team to fear and nobody relished meeting Burnley in the play off semi-finals.

The unfortunate task fell to Reading, who in the early part of the season had looked formidable as they played a fluent, attacking brand of football that looked set to carry them to automatic promotion, but had then fallen away badly in the closing stages, finishing just one place above us in fourth.

A tight encounter at the Turf was won by a late Graham Alexander penalty to give us a slender but vital advantage to take to the away leg.

We expected and got a severe testing in the first half of that second leg, but we reached half time at 0-0, and it was there to be had.

Whatever Owen said to his troops at half-time was surely the most inspirational team talk ever, as early in the second half two superb strikes from Martin Paterson and Steve Thompson put the game beyond Reading's reach.

The unbelievable had happened and we were going to WEMBLEY.

We had been exhorted to "Dare to Dream," and this became the slogan visible everywhere around the town and in the local press. Well, we dared to dream and our dreams were on the verge of coming true with just one obstacle, Sheffield United, standing in our way.

A town with a population of less than 100,000 souls, and an average home attendance below 14,000, managed to sell out its full allocation of 36,000 tickets in five frenzied days, and the 'March on Wembley' was on.

And so to May 25, 2009.

It dawns in Burnley as a brilliant, sunny, uplifting day, and for every one of those 36,000 and many more left at home, that was they way it would stay for weeks.

Another super strike from Wade Elliott, worthy of winning any final, coupled with a below par performance from our opponents, means the Clarets run out deserved 1-0 winners, and the world turns claret and blue.

Burnley men don't cry, they like to think they are as hard as nails, but in an outpouring of unrestrained joy, grown men who should know better are shedding buckets of tears. And the women, who are harder than nails - just joking, girls - are crying too.

A mixture of disbelief, relief, adulation, euphoria and every other emotion imaginable engulfs one half of Wembley Stadium as the other end is already vacated by disillusioned Blades.

Never in my 50 years of supporting the Clarets have I witnessed anything like it. My wife and daughter, who have accompanied me on the trip, and my long suffering friends and fellow Clarets are stunned almost speechless. Whatever happens from now I will take the final scenes at Wembley to the grave with me and go a happy man.

13

This once great Lancashire cotton and mining town, which long ago lost its major industries and was down on its luck, has at last regained something powerful and unstoppable, namely its pride.

Against all the odds we have triumphed, and I have to say with some style, and that is and always has been the Burnley way. Once again we have won back our seat at the top table, and whether it be short or long-lived, boy were we going to enjoy it.

"I just thank God so much that I am blessed to be a part of this team and this magnificent final day. This team has just been magnificent. Look at these fans, what an awesome day, what an awesome day. - **Clarke Carlisle, Man of the Match, Coca-Cola Championship Play Off Final. May 25, 2009.**

Just minutes after that final, and inspired by the stupendous efforts of all at Burnley FC and the magnificent supporters worldwide, I resolved to mark the occasion in some way. People who know me think I always have plenty to say, and would prefer I didn't, so for them and anyone else interested, I decided to write a diary of our season back in the big league, our incredible adventure.

True to form, before the fans had chance to escape the carnage that is the Wembley car park, national bookmakers were installing our manager Owen Coyle, known as God to some, as favourite for the newly vacated manager's post at Scottish giants Celtic.

Hold tight. It's all set to be another rollercoaster ride.

JUNE

A New Era Dawns

IT'S early June and Owen Coyle, or OC as he is now commonly known, is away with his family on holiday in Florida.

Despite his attempts to reassure the Burnley public, speculation is still rife in the media that he is a leading contender for the vacant Celtic post. A town waits nervously hoping for the Scots to pinch some opposition team's boss then we can all sleep easy again. Tony Mowbray of West Bromwich Albion seems to have emerged as the front runner, for which we are all truly grateful.

The atmosphere in the town remains buoyant and the effect of the play off victory on community morale is immense. Two weeks on and the flags continue to fly from bedroom windows and passing cars.

There must be some real commercial opportunities here if the club and its suppliers can react swiftly enough and stock the Clarets Store with merchandise. The annual holidays are just a few weeks away and the chance to wear the colours with pride in far flung destinations is too good to miss this year.

After suspending season ticket sales during the play offs, the club announce they are back on sale from Monday, June 8 and that prices are frozen.

An indication of the fever gripping the fans is the queue outside the ticket office early in the day. There is an almost blind panic to snap up the 7,000 or so remaining tickets. No half filled stadium and sterile atmosphere at Turf Moor next season.

My daughter Stephanie queues for eight hours in the blazing Burnley sun. At the end of her ordeal she has just an application form, an envelope, a raffle ticket, an empty stomach and a full bladder to show for it.

Hopefully, after completing this physical and mental challenge, she will be successful in her ticket quest, but there is no guarantee. In order to have the chance to even sit in the same stand as myself, she has to purchase a season ticket, even though she may not be able to attend a number of games as she continues her studies in Liverpool.

Suddenly, from having seats to give away, we have a stadium which is under capacity for current demand. How quickly things can change, and how strong the attraction of the Premiership.

In the local press, for whom the whole play off push has been a life saving bonanza, with ever bigger 'pull out' sections to celebrate each victory, operations director Brendan Flood explains what the transfer policy will be.

We are to buy British and go for targets in the 20 to 24-year-old bracket. This way we hopefully don't upset the strong bond that holds the team together as there will be no megastars on huge and divisive salaries.

The youth of these players additionally means they will have resale value, and this will be essential for us as we look to wheel and deal. This strategy seems to meet with agreement with the fans who have total faith in OC and the directors.

On the same day, Real Madrid announce the signing of the Brazilian playmaker Kaka from AC Milan for the princely sum of £56 million. Within two days, Manchester United accept an £80 million offer from the same club for Cristiano Ronaldo. Good riddance to the guy, a great player but an ego the size of Australia. The world has gone mad.

Starved of proper football for the last two weeks, I turn my attention to 2010 World Cup qualification. England already occupy a comfortable qualifying position in their group and next up are two games against Kazakhstan and Andorra. What an appetising prospect.

I can't see the Kazakh game as I have no Setanta subscription, but then again as they are about to go bust, it would appear neither has anybody else. The game ends in a predictable 4-0 England win after a few early scares, and we head home for the daunting challenge that is Andorra.

What is the point of having these football nonentities in the World Cup, as realistically they wouldn't survive at League Two level?

The minnows are duly despatched in an embarrassingly easy 6-0 victory, in which they don't even muster a shot at goal, and the result leaves England needing just one more win to secure qualification for the final stages in South Africa next summer.

The Andorra game does give me the opportunity to have a look at some of next season's opposition players. How will our defence cope with the power of Wayne Rooney, the pace of Theo Walcott, and the height of Peter Crouch?

Against Andorra they look awesome, but then again so would I. Clearly it's impossible to learn anything from this mismatch, so no need to start worrying yet.

Don't football fans do the strangest and most childish things? I have recently taken to sending wind up emails to work colleagues of different soccer persuasion, notably Blackburn Rovers and Manchester United, in claret and blue font. I type the email and then painstakingly change the font colour on alternate words. I have to say the result is quite appealing.

The recipients have entered into the spirit of things by replying in the colours of their own teams, though this is somewhat easier for them in that blue/white and red/white combinations don't need alternate words changing. Wouldn't life be simpler if we played in black and white?

On the whole, supporters of even our most bitter rivals Rovers have been very complimentary of our achievement in gaining promotion. I think the brand of skilful attacking football and desire to try and win every game has earned the admiration of many neutrals and even the old enemy.

Of course, they usually then qualify their compliment by adding: "It will be an easy six points for us next season". We'll see.

The office where I work is a veritable jamboree of Lancashire soccer supporters. There is one Bolton, one Preston, and one and a half Rovers fans. The half is Jilly, who foolishly married a Rovers supporter and that unfortunately taints her.

I now have a bit of a problem with my relationship to the Preston fan, Edward. Most of last season we were allies against the Roverites, but now I find in my newly elevated status I am beginning to look down on him. My non-stop gloating has got to him so badly he has now removed the Deepdale desktop background from his computer, this after I likened it to a Subbuteo stadium.

All those years of being the butt of the jokes changed with one sweet strike of Wade Elliott's boot. Revenge is sweet.

By June 11, the club have announced nine pre-season friendlies. These follow a similar pattern to last season with a three game tour of the USA, two games in Scotland, away matches at League Two sides Accrington Stanley and Bradford City, plus a game at Chester City, newly demoted from the Football League.

The solitary home fixture so far announced is against League One Leeds United. How the mighty are fallen. Not long ago, our Yorkshire rivals were in the Champions League, but now they are about to start their third season in League One.

When I consider the relative positions of Leeds and ourselves, and the available resources of the clubs, my faith in God is somewhat restored. I have met many Leeds fans over the years and most have had an unbelievably arrogant attitude and misplaced belief that they are superior to our little club. How good is it now to see the tables turned and the Clarets in the ascendancy.

I don't think you would find many of our fans so quick to belittle the opposition, though this is probably due to the fact that although we are founder members of the Football League and have a glorious history, with much of it played in the top division, we have of late had many lean years.

In my time supporting the Clarets I have seen them win the Division One Championship in 1959/60 and at the other end of the spectrum, survive demotion from the Football League on that memorable afternoon in May 1987, a day always referred to in Burnley folklore simply as 'the Orient game.' We are also one of the few clubs to have won the Championship of all four divisions of the Football League.

It's fair to say then that our supporters have had the rough as well as the smooth. We know what it's like to struggle, and these seasons in the wilderness have made our fans more appreciative of any success that comes our way. We also know that for a club of our size, success is often quite short-lived, so we make the most of it while it's there.

I believe the games at Accrington and Chester, both clubs currently in serious financial difficulties, is our attempt to assist those less fortunate in their hour of need, knowing our magnificent travelling support will significantly bolster the takings.

Owen Coyle seems to view the trip to the USA as a good team bonding opportunity and with a number of new signings to 'bed in,' this will be vital.

However, some of the messageboard posters on 'Clarets Mad,' an independent fans' website, feel the games against lower league teams are not sufficiently challenging and that we should be testing ourselves against sterner opposition ahead of our Premiership campaign. The contra argument is that pre-season is more about improving fitness levels, shaping a team and tactics and building confidence. I agree with the latter.

Two games are planned in Scotland as OC returns to his spiritual homeland. First up are Kilmarnock of the Scottish Premier League, not usually high fliers but who should provide a decent workout. Then it's on to St Johnstone in Perth, the club from whom we poached OC on the eve of the Scottish League Challenge Cup Final to which he had guided them.

The Saints have had another great season, culminating in promotion to the Scottish Premier League, so the loss of OC doesn't seem to have affected them too badly. Their boss Derek McInnes is being linked with the soon to be vacant post at West Brom as the managerial merry-go-round continues.

Changed days at Turf Moor. From not having two ha'pennies to rub together, the club now has riches it could only dream of. I have seen estimates on the value of winning promotion to the Premier League of between £30 million and £60 million. Whatever it is, I doubt the club seriously expected to be in this position so quickly.

Now the dilemma. What do we spend it on?

Everywhere you look, there is a legitimate claim to some of the cash. Money is needed for new players, increased salaries, essential work at the ground to meet Premier League regulations, stadium redevelopment, and improvements to the training facilities at Gawthorpe with a view to further improving youth development.

Without doubt, some money will have to be set aside for incoming transfers and to fund the salaries of loan signings if we are to make any sort of attempt to retain our new status. The current squad is too small and lacking in quality in key areas to meet the demands of a Premiership season.

Whilst during the tremendous cup runs of last season, we were able to raise our game for these one-off occasions, next season every game will be a cup final. It's unlikely we will find ourselves against opposition fielding weakened teams as qualifying points for lucrative Champions League places will be up for grabs.

However, we have to be sensible in our approach on players and not get tied in to long contracts and big salaries should the bookmakers' prediction of a quick return to the Championship come to fruition.

Brendan Flood has already indicated that some money has to be spent on improving media facilities and the PA system and estimates a total of £1.2 million. Major ground redevelopment plans are already in place, but these have been 'credit crunched' – haven't we all? – and will stay on hold this season till we see what happens regarding league survival.

The favoured option for spending a further chunk of cash seems to be the development of the Gawthorpe training ground, aiming towards an Academy quality facility.

After many years of running down the once famous youth policy at the club, there now seems once again to be a growing realisation of the importance of developing our own talent. In recent years the club have brought through promising talents such as Richard Chaplow, Chris McCann, Kyle Lafferty and Jay Rodriguez, with Alex MacDonald seriously expected to be the next breakthrough player.

There is no doubt the sale of Lafferty to Glasgow giants Rangers last summer provided the funds to kick start the promotion season, with the cash raised helping to bring in Martin Paterson, Kevin McDonald and Chris Eagles.

Because of its relatively small size, the club will always be in a position where it has to wheel and deal in the transfer market and the continuing development of new young talent will be key to this strategy.

Investment in the Gawthorpe facility seems to be a prudent step forward and with the youth set up in good hands, the strategy will hopefully pay handsome dividends in the not too distant future.

Of course, what is not mentioned in the public debate of how to spend the new riches is the position regarding the repayment of director loans.

It is no secret that the club has only been kept going in recent years by the generosity of Barry Kilby, Brendan Flood, and to a lesser extent the other directors in funding revenue shortfalls by way of loans. In addition, the wolf has been kept from the door by the sale of Turf Moor and Gawthorpe to a company associated with Barry Kilby and other directors.

The club currently enjoys a 99 year lease on the ground and Gawthorpe at annual rates believed to be £303,000 and £30,000 respectively. The total amount of loans to the club are believed to be in the region of £6 million, and these attract an annual interest rate, allegedly of £420,000. Incorporated in the terms of the sale of the ground is an option to repurchase by the club at a fixed rate of £3.4 million.

It would be interesting to be able to read the chairman's mind as to what realistic prospect he felt there was of these loans ever being fully repaid before the incredible events of Spring 2009 culminating in promotion. My suspicion is that he would have considered it highly unlikely.

However, here we are, and once again on the horns of a dilemma.

Should the directors grab the cash and take repayment of the loans fearing a plunge back into the abyss of the Championship? Should they repurchase the ground, putting ownership back with the club and easing some of the fans' unrest that such a major asset was ever externally owned?

If ever there was a good time for such actions, this must be it. However to do so would account for much of the new money coming into the club and seriously weaken its position to compete.

Only the fullness of time and a sight of the balance sheet will reveal the outcome of this dilemma, but we are grateful that the people running the club are honourable gentlemen and, just as importantly, Burnley supporters like ourselves.

Wednesday, June 17 is a big day in the soccer calendar as the eagerly awaited new season fixture list is announced. I have an early morning optician's appointment, and following this as I drive on to work, Radio Lancashire's 10am news announce the Clarets' first fixtures.

We kick off with an away game at Stoke City on August 16, which with no disrespect to our opponents is hardly a game to set the pulse racing.

But then close on the opener's heels is a midweek home game against Manchester United, Premier League Champions and beaten Champions League finalists. That's more like it.

As I get into the office I click the Internet straight on and see the next three fixtures are Everton home, followed by Chelsea and Liverpool away. Bloody hell. What a baptism of fire. Four of last season's top five in the first five games. Well, we asked for it and now we've got it.

I look for the other key fixture but am beaten to it by the half Roverite Jilly, who informs me the game at Deadwood Park is October 17 with the return at the Turf on March 27. Oh well, that should give us some time to get into our stride before we settle some old scores.

I always like a home game on Boxing Day. It gives me the chance to get out of the house after a long day indoors on Christmas Day. It's also a good excuse for a couple of liveners in the pub before the game. And this year doesn't disappoint with a home match against local rivals Bolton that should make for a lively atmosphere.

My daughter has a soft spot for Arsenal, but there's no game with them till December.

We finish the season with a home game to Tottenham Hotspur by which time we will know if we have clinched the Premier League title or are heading back from whence we came. I suppose there's a slight chance it could be neither.

I think it's fair to say that the early season games, daunting though they are, have only heightened the fans' eager anticipation of the coming season. Bring it on.

Speculation continues about potential new signings and some, like Rhys Williams and Russell Anderson, last season's loanees from Middlesbrough and Sunderland respectively, seem possible. Others such as Damien Duff and Luis Boa Morte are highly unlikely.

However, this is the time every year when transfer conjecture reaches fever pitch and this time that is the case even more so for us as for once we appear to be likely big players in the market. Everybody suggesting names appear to have contacts in the know that have 'tipped them the wink,' but my suspicion is that most of them are made up by bored hairdressers in between clients.

The longer it goes before any signings are made, the more ridiculous become the names and the greater the sense of panic that we will be left behind in the player chase. Same thing every season, but realistically nothing much happens till the end of June and the fans will just have to be patient.

OC is back from holidays now and will be lining up his targets. And the manager states his position in no uncertain terms.

"I'm not going to get involved in speculation about transfers because it just leads to frustration for everybody," he says. "Some rumours will be a load of nonsense and what I can assure the fans is when I have news regarding players they will have it from me first. Unless any speculation is confirmed by me, then they can take it as being a load of nonsense."

On Thursday, June 18, we announce the first signing of the summer.

Not a player, better than that. Owen Coyle commits himself to the club till the end of the 2012/13 season. In the short time since he joined Burnley in November 2007, OC has had a massive impact, and the fans can now breathe a collective sigh of relief.

He has won the respect of people both inside Turf Moor and amongst his fellow managers and players in the wider soccer community. He manages the club with great dignity, professionalism, and sense of purpose. Unusually for a football manager, he always seems to say the right thing, and I don't believe I can recollect him ever slagging off the opposition.

There is a growing belief that Owen is very special and destined for great things. Obviously in the modern game contracts are often not worth the paper they are written on, but it is believed that a substantial compensation clause is inserted in this contract to deter predatory clubs.

Meanwhile on the office front, relationships hit a new low with the PNE fan. He emails me, completely unprovoked, a picture of a British National Party rosette and claims it is the new Burnley FC badge. I can only assume this is some vague attempt at humour linked to the election of a BNP councillor for Padiham and Burnley West in the recent Lancashire County Council poll.

I retaliate with a picture of Robbie Blake, dropping his shorts to reveal his 'Bad Beat Bob' underpants, and tell him it is a gesture to the PNE fans. For some reason he takes exception to Robbie's rear end appearing in his face on his computer screen. Looks like its war now.

However, Friday, June 19 is a black day in the office. My full blown Rovers adversary and long time target of my jibes is made redundant. It's a cruel business is redundancy, especially for a guy just turning 40 and with children. Over the years we have sniped at each other at every opportunity, but that has all changed in a matter of minutes.

Colin is another victim of the recession brought on by the credit crunch and this year alone I have lost more than 50 colleagues, many of whom I have worked with for almost 20 years, in similar fashion.

The bankers, whose ill advised money lending has brought about this disaster on decent, hard working people, should be bloody ashamed, but I doubt for one minute they feel any remorse. We wish Colin luck as he clears his desk for the last time, but I have to qualify it by pointing out the luck bit does not apply to the Rovers.

News breaks over the weekend of a substantial seven figure bid for Swansea striker Jason Scotland, but we are informed by the Welsh side's chairman that the two clubs' valuations are miles apart. We are believed to have offered around £1 million and they value the player at £3 million which seems a bit on the high side for a player of 30 with no Premier League experience.

It's all part of the usual transfer game and if we want him badly enough I am sure there will be a further attempt by the club to meet somewhere in the middle. As usual there is much debate concerning the player's merits on the Clarets Mad messageboard, with many for and against.

I must confess to being very impressed by what I saw of him last season in the Championship, and he scored twice in the Swans' 2-0 victory at the Turf. A total of 53 goals in the last two seasons, albeit at lower levels than the Premiership, and his strength and touch suggest he might be worth a punt if the price is right.

A further plus is the fact that he has played previously for Owen Coyle in Scotland, so the manager knows what he is getting. There are suggestions we may face competition from Wigan, who have recently appointed ex-Swans manager Roberto Martinez as their new boss, so we will wait and see.

As the end of June approaches and with it the expiry of players contracts, the rumour mill kicks into overdrive. Added to the players previously mentioned are Everton's Danish right back Lars Jacobsen, England under 21 wingers Andrew Driver and Adam Johnson, who play at Hearts and Middlesbrough respectively, Sheffield United centre back Matt Kilgallon and a Nigerian International centre back called Rabiu Ofolabi who has been playing his football in France and is now out of contract. Any or all of the first three would be most welcome but I'm not sure about the Nigerian as he is a complete unknown.

However, as usual the club completely stump everybody's predictions on the first signing by announcing they have agreed a fee with Derby County for right back Tyrone Mears. At the time Mears is away on holiday but is expected back in the next week for discussions on terms.

Well, nobody saw that one coming. Mears has enjoyed Premiership experience with West Ham and Derby County, and played last season on loan at Marseille whom he joined in controversial circumstances. At 26 years of age and with experience and pace he seems to tick the right boxes.

However he already has a history of a number of clubs under his belt and has in the past been injury prone. But as one of his previous clubs was Preston, we trust Graham Alexander has been able to advise Owen Coyle as to the player's suitability and temperament.

Undoubtedly the full back positions would be areas that we are looking to strengthen so Mears could be the first piece in the jigsaw. The fee is rumoured to be in the region of £750,000 to £1 million.

Thursday, June 25. Another day, another rumour.

This time it's the giant Celtic centre back Bobo Balde. According to the player himself, he is wanted by Burnley and has an unconditional offer to join them. Birmingham, he claims, are also interested and are set to offer him a two year contract dependent on a successful trial with them.

Again this is not the sort of player that fits the profile outlined by Brendan Flood and OC. At 33 years of age, and having played very little football in the last two seasons for Celtic who have been trying to offload him, he would hardly appear to be a likely target. The player is reputed to be on wages of £28,000 a week and when his contract expires at the end of the month is set to collect a £1 million loyalty bonus.

There is as yet no mention of this from the club itself, so as OC says, if he doesn't confirm it then it is nonsense.

As I get ready to leave the office for home at five, I sneak a quick look at Clarets Mad to see yet another name has entered the frame.

This time it is Newcastle defender David Edgar, who is out of contract and reputed to be unhappy with the terms of his new offer.

The Newcastle press indicate that it is more than speculation and expect him to sign for the Clarets. Aged 22 and capable of filling centre back and right back berths, this guy is more like the kind of target we are believed to be pursuing. However, because of his age he would not be available free on a Bosman transfer and a fee would have to be involved.

No more names crop up on Thursday, but Friday's Burnley Express brings the news that Mears has cut short his holiday in Marbella and flown back for a medical at Turf Moor. He is either very keen to join the 'incredible adventure' or his euros are running out and he has heard the sun is shining in Burnley this week.

This seems a very positive action from the player, indicating his desire to be a part of the fairy tale we hope is about to unfold. Perhaps at 26, he realises that if he is to make a serious impact at the top level, now is the time to do it.

Later in the day other media sources suggest Edgar is also having a medical at the club. Watch this space.

It's now 17 days since my daughter queued for her season ticket and she has still had no notification from the club on the outcome of her application. I have not been unduly worried as on checking my bank statement I can see my cheque has been cashed, so I have assumed everything to be OK.

I decide to ring the club and find out what seat has been allocated. Big mistake. I nearly have a heart attack as the young chap handling my inquiry proceeds to search his computer for the information, but to no avail.

He decides that it will be best for him to further investigate without me holding on a premium rate phone line. I agree wholeheartedly, and he promises to ring back. An uneasy few minutes passes as I absentmindedly try to tackle my bangers and mash, and then hey presto, he rings to confirm all was a big misunderstanding due to a spelling error.

He confirms she has a seat in the James Hargreaves Upper Stand, Block NU4 as requested, not particularly close to me but good enough. Phew! My daughter remains on holiday in Zante blissfully aware of my trauma. It must be great to be young and carefree. I wish I could remember.

Sunday. Always a good day for transfer rumours in the press and this one doesn't fail to deliver.

The Clarets are reported to have made a record breaking bid of £2.75 million for the Hibernian and Scotland striker Steven Fletcher. At 22, he has more than 50 goals to his name in around 190 appearances. We are believed to be facing competition from Blackburn Rovers and Celtic for this highly rated young player.

At the same time, reports are circulating that we have bid £1.75 million for the Sheffield Wednesday striker Marcus Tudgay. This guy scored four times against us in last season's Championship games between the two sides as he singlehandedly attempted to derail our promotion run. OC is clearly determined this will not happen again by attempting to sign the player and prevent him going to any other Premier League club and wreaking havoc against us.

Then to round off a hat trick of striker connections, the name of Jermaine Beckford of Leeds United is thrown into the mix. He is a prolific scorer at lower league level with 47 goals in 84 games for Leeds, but could he do it at the top level?

So now we are linked to four strikers, Scotland, Fletcher, Tudgay, and Beckford. It's to be hoped they don't all come, there won't be enough pegs in the dressing rooms.

Bang on cue, Owen's new charges begin to check in at Turf Moor.

On the last day of June the first to sign on the dotted line is Mears and the fee, declared as £500,000 plus add ons, seems a reasonable sum to pay.

Then in the early evening, Fletcher is announced as the second capture and the fee, reported at £3 million, shatters the previous Burnley record which was believed to be the £1.5 million we shelled out for Chris Eagles and Martin Paterson.

These two signings are swiftly followed on July 1 by Edgar from Newcastle United. As the player is under 24, a fee will be involved and this will be set by tribunal unless the clubs can come to an agreement.

The Clarets are again linked with Andrew Driver and are rumoured to have offered £2 million for the player, while a lesser known name and another Scottish target is reputed to be James McCarthy of Hamilton Academical, an 18-year-old midfielder capped at youth level

33

by the Republic of Ireland. We are believed to have offered £1 million for McCarthy who made his first team debut at the age of 15.

Both bids are reported to have been rejected, and we await further developments as if these players are indeed targets, negotiations will surely follow.

Just over five weeks have elapsed since that fateful day at Wembley, and they have passed in a blur. Not one day seems to have gone by without some major story coming out of, or concerning, Burnley FC in not only the local but also the national media.

Such is the power of the Premier League and the grip it has on the nation's fervent football fans. It is indeed the only place to be, and even more so for us after such a long absence from the top flight and the flirtations with disaster.

At the end of June we stand on the dawn of a new, exciting, slightly frightening era, but one we will enter full of hope and pride. Up the Clarets.

JULY

A New Way

THERE is no doubt that having seen the initial signings for the Premiership campaign, it is clear Burnley are attempting a new way to survive and prosper in the big time.

Traditional wisdom has it that the only way to stay up is by spending big and going for players with Premiership experience. These types of player tend to be in the later stages of their career and command not only large fees but also equally large wages, and they demand lengthy contracts as they see their playing careers reaching the plateau before they decline. Inevitably, the only way this player's value can go in terms of him being a saleable asset in perhaps two years is downwards.

This is clearly not a realistic option for a club such as Burnley. Instead, the declared strategy by the directors and management is to recruit young, hungry players on their way up and with something to prove.

This type of player, if successful at the club, can then potentially become a profitable source of income, with the potential fee they may command helping to set up a conveyor belt of talent passing through the club.

Additionally, in most cases this type of player does not come with an over-inflated ego and is therefore much more manageable and capable of being moulded into the team structure, which is after all what the game is about.

I am not too sure that even if Burnley had the untold riches of a Chelsea or Manchester United, the big spending route is the one they would choose to take. It just wouldn't fit with the club's image and position at the heart of its community.

Not for Burnley superstar soccer mercenaries here for the cash only. OC has said there is no place here for these types, they have to come because they want to play.

The population of this largely working class town, a product of the Industrial Revolution, could not identify with the money grabbers. They have been spoilt by great players like Jimmy McIlroy, Jimmy Adamson and countless more who were prepared to give their all and who actually cared about the club.

From its heyday as the biggest weaving town in the country, the long decline of the town and the loss of its major industries has left the population at times little to be proud of but its football club. From its foundation through the glory days of the 1960's and beyond, the club has built a history of which it and the town view with justifiable pride.

If I am on holiday and I am asked where I live, invariably the mention of Burnley immediately evokes glowing memories and tributes to the town's football club, even from complete strangers who have never seen the place. It is indeed the most famous thing in the town and as such is a prized asset to its inhabitants.

Previous manager Adrian Heath once commented how refreshing it was to see when he passed through the town that all the kids wore Burnley shirts, not Manchester United, Chelsea, or Liverpool. It is the heart and soul of the town and without the football club it would lack any form of identity and be as cheerless a place as the artificially created new towns are.

Funnily enough, success on the field is often mirrored by an upturn in fortune for the town and this promotion seems to have coincided with such a feeling about the place. After many years of decline and neglect, suddenly Burnley is seeing inward cash flow at an unprecedented rate.

Major housing regeneration schemes, new health and sport facilities, and now the new campus of the University of Central Lancashire are all serving to promote a better image of the town. We are starting to link Premier League to 'premier town' and a new air of positivity abounds.

The location of the stadium, within walking distance of the town centre and surrounded by housing, is far removed from the trend of building new stadiums out of town, on the fringes of retail developments and with good motorway links.

The ground has decayed in times of hardship and improved in times of prosperity. It is a living organism. And hopefully it is about to embark on another major growth phase to bring the club confidently into the 21st century.

Owen Coyle, with one of the smallest budgets in the Championship and in a division containing many large city and ex-Premiership teams, proved that not only could clubs like Burnley compete, but that they could also triumph.

I believe this must be an inspiration for all the smaller clubs below the Premier League, showing that it can be done, and it should be the rallying call in many a pre-season talk between managers and their playing staff.

I think among the wider football community there is a strong desire that 'Burnley's incredible adventure' will be successful and will restore some financial sense to a game that is spiralling rapidly out of control. What lies ahead for the Clarets is a true 'David and Goliath' battle, so get ready you 'big guns' for what is coming your way.

How refreshing to hear of a selfless act of generosity by a relatively highly paid professional sportsman. How much more so when that person is none other than the Clarets' new record signing Steven Fletcher.

Often when players leave clubs, it is with a degree of acrimony, but not apparently in this case with the chief executive of Fletcher's former club Hibernian wishing him well in his career and thanking him for being a terrific player for them. Fletcher is then reported to have made the magnificent gesture of donating half of his £250,000 signing on fee to youth development at Hibs.

I can think of many players on much higher salaries and astronomical signing on fees for whom such a gesture would never enter their heads. Well done Steven for attempting to put something back into the club that discovered and developed his talent, and then allowed him to play at the top level. It looks like Owen's judgement of character is once again spot on.

The weekend of July 4/5 is quiet on the transfer speculation front. Clarets Mad run the story that Andrew Driver and James McCarthy remain targets, but apart from that nobody new seems to be linked.

With the first pre-season friendly at Bradford City now just a week away, perhaps we will see more activity this week. It's likely OC will want to get players in early to work on team bonding and try out different formations, and the upcoming trip to the USA gives him just such opportunities.

Elsewhere in the Premiership, transfer activity also seems slow, and the majority of the action is not unsurprisingly coming from the two other promoted teams, Wolves and Birmingham. They seem to be favouring the traditional approach on transfers, but I can't help thinking that Wolves' reported purchase fee of £6.5 million for Kevin Doyle is a bit high.

Birmingham are reported to be tracking Patrick Viera at a substantial fee and no doubt huge wages. Viera is exactly the type of player the pundits think is required, but great player that he is or has been, he is at the wrong end of his career and his appetite for a relegation dogfight may well be questionable.

The most unexpected transfer of the pre-season has to be that of Michael Owen to Manchester United from relegated Newcastle. Although no fee is involved as the player is out of contract, his wages and recent history of injury problems seemed to have ruled him out as a target for any of the big four clubs.

United, reeling from the loss of Cristiano Ronaldo and Carlos Tevez, presumably feel that they can re-ignite his career, and surely if he can't score goals for them with the number of chances that they should create, then he is finished at the top level. Let's just hope he doesn't get into his stride until after August 19.

I don't know whether all footie fans have pre-match rituals that ensure their team's success, but I suspect many do. Mine even extend to taking action during the course of the game to influence the result.

These days I am more restrained but I have found that wearing my Clarets 'More Than 90 Minutes' wristband on my right wrist with the wording facing downwards has been particularly effective in the latter stages of the promotion run. This trick I will definitely take with me into the new season.

Another ploy I have developed when things are not going well during the game is to put my hat on, or alternatively take it off. I have tried the same trick with my glasses but I find this counterproductive as I then can't see, though sometimes this is an advantage.

In the good old days things were much simpler. When the Bee Hole terracing occupied what is now the Jimmy McIlroy Stand, I developed the habit of having a lucky step to stand on. If we scored whilst I was standing on this step I was unable to move from it and had to remember the precise location for the next game. If we conceded a goal, I then had to move to a different one.

My mates also joined in this futile exercise, to the point where if it was a high scoring game we could develop what almost became a line dancing or step aerobic routine. All seater stadiums have taken a lot of harmless pleasure away from the fans.

Our ultimate weapon if things were going badly, and in the days when everybody smoked, was for a large number of us to simultaneously light our cigarette lighters in an attempt to momentarily blind the opposition keeper and create a goal. I don't recall it ever working but it was a good excuse to have a fag.

In addition, in those days what you ate for lunch on match days could also influence the result of a game. We once had a particularly good victory after I consumed Marks and Spencer mince beef pie, chips and beans at the home of one of my friends. Therefore, every Saturday home game for some time after would see four or five hungover teenagers devouring this delicacy at his house, cooked and paid for by his mother, before the pre-match pints. Happy Days!

Monday, July 6, and it's back to work after the weekend. To a man, and woman, my colleagues are all of the opinion we should work two days and have a five day weekend. Perhaps one day it will come.

A quick check of the media rumours suggest that we are set to take a French trialist, Fabrice Pancrate, who is available on a Bosman free transfer from Paris St Germain. He is allegedly a pacy 29-year-old winger previously linked with potential loan deals at Hull City and Everton.

Tuesday, July 7. Hooray, it's my birthday, and what a present. The company I work for and which has been in administration since April 1 is bought by the current managing director and once again we are about to take the textile world by storm. We have some orders, all we need now are some raw materials, some more workers, and some spare parts. In short, we need some money.

I won't worry. I have stopped doing that some time back. Each month's salary is one nearer to my retirement, when hopefully I can pursue a new career as an author.

Anyway, the buy out is a good start to the day so I look to see who the Clarets will deliver up as my birthday signing, and therefore become my lucky player. A check with Clarets Mad, the font of all knowledge on such matters, shows it looks like the Andrew Driver saga is set to drag on, our bid and his club's valuation being still some way apart.

However we are reported to be taking a 20-year-old defensive midfielder from Valencia on a season long loan. He is a Nigerian by the splendid name of Stephen Sunday, one of a family of seven all born on different days of the week, one of his brothers being Man Friday, a loyal servant.

Only joking. He has previously had loan spells at Real Betis and Osasuna in Spain and has dual Spanish and Nigerian nationality so a work permit would not be an issue. He has already represented Spain at under 20 level, and would appear to be being lined up as cover for Graham Alexander in the holding midfield role.

Friday, July 10 and I scour the Burnley Express for any snippets of news on the transfer front. I always feel the local media know a lot more than they let on as they are in fear of upsetting the club by divulging news before it is ready for release. The trick therefore is to try and read what is between the lines, and to see what is not said sometimes rather than what is.

Having tried my technique, I conclude that Friday will be a dull day on the transfer front, although interestingly enough Pancrate, the Frenchman from PSG who it was firmly believed was coming on trial, would appear not now to be doing so. Does this mean he doesn't fancy us, or is a deal to sign a winger already lined up? I note Driver is believed to be on holiday in the Caribbean and wonder if we are awaiting his return to announce his capture.

Owen Coyle is reported to be looking forward to the upcoming game at Bradford but feels we will be a bit rusty due to the match coming so early. He announces his intention to give 22 players 45 minutes each at both Bradford and Morecambe, assuming this is acceptable to the opposition and the referees.

He seems well pleased with his three new players and thinks they have been openly welcomed by the rest of the squad and are settling in nicely. The fans for their part are more interested in which pubs they should use for the pre-match booze up in Bradford.

So much for my Pancrate theory. Saturday's Daily Mail reports he won't be joining the Clarets as he didn't realise he was coming for a trial.

Clarets Mad reveals he turned up believing he was coming for a medical ahead of a deal. Apparently he said he couldn't train for insurance reasons and at that point we pulled the plug. It looks like we have got out of that one nicely as he doesn't look like our cup of tea at all. Stoke and Hull are said to be interested in him, and the best of luck to them.

More interesting for me was an article by Dave Thomas, author of such memorable tomes as "It's Burnley Not Barcelona" and "Russians Don't Land Here." In a short piece on Clarets Mad reviewing the magnificent end to last season, Dave revealed how serious the financial situation had once again become at Turf Moor.

In the closing weeks of the season, the club had been perilously close to going into administration and once again only through an input of cash by four directors, Messrs. Kilby, Garlick, Griffiths, and Sullivan, had this disaster been avoided.

Without these guys taking the gamble with their own hard earned cash, none of what we are about to see would have been possible. In fact, the very existence of the club itself would have been in serious jeopardy. What a debt all of us who claim to be supporters of this great club owe these people, so let's hope with our new found riches we can repay them for their support in the club's hour of need.

So to the first match up, and many Clarets are set to make the pilgrimage to West Yorkshire to see us take on Bradford.

Not me though, as I am booked on a cruise leaving Southampton in one week's time to celebrate a milestone birthday for my long suffering wife. I have to attend to more mundane matters like selecting my wardrobe and last minute adjustments to it, such as a complete overhaul so as not to offend my fellow passengers.

My last trip to Bradford I recall ended with a last minute winner for the Clarets that caused my mate to eject his mobile phone involuntarily from his pocket and deposit it halfway down the stand. Pre-match pints in the Bradford Arms, packed with Clarets, and an extremely inefficient turnstile system obviously not used to seeing many fans are my recollections of that day.

Our opponents have in the not too distant past enjoyed two seasons in the Premier League, 1999/2000 and 2000/2001, but now wallow in League Two. Their first season in the Premiership saw them finish 17th, just avoiding the drop with a last game win over Liverpool.

Unfortunately this was followed by the second season where they never really looked like escaping and finished bottom. A huge financial gamble to try and secure their status had failed, resulting in three relegations and two financial collapses in six years.

This is exactly the trap that we must avoid at all costs. In 2001 City paid Italian star Benito Carbone £40,000 a week, twice the cost of a house near the ground. The club had an unsustainable wage bill and virtually all the fixtures and fittings at Valley Parade had been sold to leasing companies, including the seats the fans sat on. Even the captain David Wetherall had been bought by a finance company and leased to the club.

Why did we have to end the season on May 25? As that campaign drew to a close we were unbeatable and could I'm sure have gone on to lift the Champions League trophy. But today we lose at Bradford City.

Oh the shame of it. I can see the headlines now in the Bradford Telegraph & Argus – 'Premiership new boys humbled by plucky Bantams.' Plucky Bantams? Are they some sort of oven ready chicken?

The Clarets made the short trip to our Yorkshire rivals with a squad of 20, with Chris Eagles and Chris McCann, who were reported to have picked up knocks in training, not being risked. More than 2,000 fans made the trip to have a look at the new signings and no doubt confidently expected our superior class to tell.

I tried to get some radio coverage of the game but the best I could manage was Joe Wilson on BBC Radio Lancashire who I think informed us just twice of the score during the whole of the afternoon. However Joe was in good form and the sun was shining.

The programme took the form of a record request by phone or text, interspersed with cricket reports on the Test and also Lancashire's game at Old Trafford. Being in a good mood, I thought I would request "One Day Like This" by Elbow for all Clarets.

Joe had confirmed that all requests would be played as long as they had the record, so I sat back in the garden and waited for it, only to be told by Joe that we would be having Jon Bon Jovi next and then Elbow "sort of." Intrigued, I listened for news of what was coming, and he then related the tale that unfortunately we could not have the track as he had borrowed the studio disc, took it home and forgot to bring it back.

He confirmed how brilliant it was and to make amends played a Radio Lancashire trailer which featured it as the backing, saying it was the next best thing. You don't get treated like that on national radio. It was certainly different and at this point I should have known the wheels were going to come off that day.

Reports seem to suggest a pretty typical meaningless pre-season affair with multiple team changes during the course of the game. We had

46

started like an express train and deservedly led on 12 minutes through Graham Alexander from Robbie Blake's set up.

Midway through the half, Bradford equalised against the run of play, at which point we again turned up the heat. A second goal was apparently inevitable and it came, as it so often does, to the team on the back foot. Half time 2-1 down, and that's the way it stayed throughout a poor second half.

A review of fans' comments on Clarets Mad seemed to confirm a highly promising 45 minutes for record signing Steven Fletcher and good combination between him and Martin Paterson. Diego Penny at last managed to see some first team action, coming on for the second half in place of 'The Beast,' and while largely unemployed managed one magnificent save. Even the mysterious Dutchman Remco van der Schaaf got almost 30 minutes on the pitch, which was probably almost as much as he managed all last season. All in all not much to be learned from this leg loosener which was more an exercise of increasing fitness and getting a feel of the ball again.

Tuesday, July 14, and the Clarets confirm the fourth signing of the summer with the capture of Hamilton Academical's left back Brian Easton. The player is capped at under 21 and Scotland B level and very clearly fits the criteria already outlined for transfer targets. The fee is reported as an initial £350,000 rising to possibly £700,000 with add-ons.

Willie McKay, the player's agent and interestingly also Tyrone Mears' representative, was quoted as saying: "He is a strong, fast, 6ft 2in left back and there's not many of them about." The player had made clear his desire to follow Steven Fletcher in the Scots exodus to join Owen Coyle's Turf Moor 'gathering of the clans.'

Richard Eckersley, a 20-year-old right back, has rejected terms at Manchester United and is rumoured to be a target. What a disastrous summer for Sir Alex Ferguson, having lost Ronaldo, Tevez and now Eckersley. He is believed to be looking for more first team opportunities and is reported to have already turned down a move to Championship 'loadsamoneys' Queens Park Rangers.

OC is hopeful of further signings before the Clarets leave for the USA on Thursday and delivers a nice line to the press. "There's nothing concrete yet. Whether anything comes to fruition before we go to the States remains to be seen, but we're certainly trying. We'll probably know better at the start, the middle or the end of the week." Almost worthy of Stan the Man, that one.

So after game one, we move swiftly on to the once popular seaside resort of Morecambe or, as it was known in its heyday, Bradford-by-the-Sea, when the population was swelled by 100,000 holidaymakers in the 'Wakes' weeks.

The town, birthplace of comedian Eric Morecambe and butt of many jokes, is very much a newcomer to the Football League. The Shrimps, formed in 1920 but with most of their history in non league, play their football at Christie Park, named after former club president JB Christie, who purchased the ground for them.

They were promoted to the Football League in 2007 after beating Exeter City in the Conference play off final in front of a 40,000 crowd at Wembley - boy, do we know how that feels - after losing to Dagenham & Redbridge at the same stage in 2003.

The game turns out to be more to our liking than Saturday's run out at Bradford as goals from Paterson and the again impressive Fletcher around the quarter hour mark put us firmly in the driving seat. The two strikers again linked effectively, setting up each other's goals and showing good pace and understanding.

OC made the customary multiple changes at half time and during the game, but there was little change to the pattern of play. Fletcher grabbed a second thanks to good work by Joey Gudjonsson, and the Clarets continued to make chances until the final 20 minutes when the game went off the boil. Our hosts claimed a consolation goal but the game ended with the score at 3-1.

The returning McCann played the first half, while Eagles had the full game and produced a man of the match performance. Last pre-season started with defeat in Carolina, USA in the first game followed by an impressive run of results. Let's hope we are set to repeat the same pattern again.

Wednesday brings news of an unusual possible recruit for us. Ecuadorian striker Fernando Guerrero, 19, is set to link up with the Clarets in California for a trial. The player is currently with Castilla, the reserve team of the famous Spanish aristocrats Real Madrid, and has currently been back in Ecuador on loan to Emelec. He was brought up in Spain, so it is to be hoped there will be no work permit problems if anything develops from the trial.

Sheffield Wednesday are reported to be angered by our approach for Marcus Tudgay, suggesting we have made a derisory offer for the player. They claim to have a verbally agreed contract extension that has now been jeopardised by our intervention and the actions of the player's agent.

Owls chairman Lee Strafford's cheap parting shot was: "From my perspective, we want to go into the future with Marcus and see him fulfil his potential playing in the Premier League with Sheffield Wednesday, a club which is widely regarded as one that can sustain a position in the top division."

Oooh! Now that's a bit below the belt. I think he should appreciate that to sustain a position you first have to achieve it, and the Owls look a long way off that at the moment.

What crime are we supposed to have committed? As far as I can see we have offered what we deem a fair price for the player. We have not broadcast the offer which is down to them and the player's agent.

This sort of thing happens every day in football and we ourselves have been on the receiving end of it in recent years with the sales of Robbie Blake to Birmingham and Andy Gray to Charlton Athletic. Sheffield Wednesday need to grow up over this one, after all if they don't like the offer they are perfectly within their rights to reject it.

Whilst the player is a decent sort at Championship level he is unproven at a higher one and there are many other players who would fit our requirements. Personally I think the player doubts Wednesday's ability to make a serious challenge and would like a shot at the top level, though that now seems unlikely to be with us.

Later on Wednesday morning, the Clarets announce the capture of their fifth summer signing, the previously rumoured Richard Eckersley. It's difficult to keep up with all this activity and another youngster means we may need to open a crèche at Turf Moor.

The signing now means we have some serious competition for places in both full back berths. The squad is now taking shape and most of the signings are in place ready for Thursday's departure for California.

It's a long time since we have had such incoming transfer activity in the summer and the level of spending for Burnley is astronomical, though it pales into insignificance when compared to Manchester City. They have now recruited Gareth Barry for £12 million, Roque Santa Cruz for £18 million, Carlos Tevez for £26 million, and are about to sign Emmanuel Adebayor for £25 million.

In addition, they are still pursuing Chelsea and England captain John Terry at God knows what price. The whole thing is ludicrous and will surely kill the game before long. Their manager Mark Hughes must be odds on favourite for the sack if City don't win the title by Christmas.

Thursday brings a bit of an intriguing twist to the Guerrero trial with the media reporting that OC is prepared to pay £2 million for him if the trial is successful. There also seems to be considerable confusion as to where he is currently playing and at what level. Apparently he is no longer with Castilla and is believed to be back in Ecuador playing at one level below their top division.

It seems unlikely that OC would be mentioning sums like this before he has had a chance to evaluate the player, and I think there is a good deal of media invention here. Even if he is the next Ronaldo, there must be question marks about his ability to integrate with the rest of the squad in terms of both background and language. However I imagine the idea will be to room him with Diego Penny when he links up in the States as they will at least share a common language.

Sadly this week sees the passing of two gentlemen who in their different ways have both been Claret heroes, namely former player Tommy Cummings and director Ray Griffiths.

Cummings was a part of the magnificent Division One Championship winning team of 1959-60, and an FA Cup finalist in 1962. A centre half with the Clarets over many years, he played 479 games and scored three goals. At an average of almost a goal every 160 games, he could hardly be described as a prolific scorer, but in that tally he scored what many regard as the best goal ever seen at Turf Moor, in a match against Newcastle United in 1952. Tommy brought pleasure to many thousands of Clarets by his exploits on the pitch and was fortunate to be a part of a team which was probably the greatest in our long history.

Equally a Claret hero in an unsung way, Griffiths was a self made businessman whose generosity funded the club through the lean years and even as recently as April he was still putting his money in to keep the club afloat. What a pity he did not live long enough to see his team play in the 'Promised Land,' but I am sure he will look down from above with some satisfaction that he in no small way made the dream possible.

An article in Friday, July 7's Burnley Express entitled "Psychic's help for Clarets to stay up" catches my eye. It goes on to claim a psychic who has received widespread acclaim in the UK and

USA for his ability to predict, bring good luck to and support a number of high profile celebrities and sports teams is backing the Clarets to stay in the Premier League. The article claims whoever Dean 'Midas' Maynard chooses to support goes on to achieve great things and that this season we are the 'chosen ones.'

Dean says: "I am a down to earth normal lad who has an uncanny ability to produce results, and I am positive that it will continue with Burnley staying in the Premier League come May. I hope that the club takes a chance with me, as they just never know what it might do for their upcoming season".

I don't quite get that last sentence. Is he proposing the club sign him on and pay him or has he picked us because he likes us? Last season Dean backed Stoke City, who are interestingly enough our first opponents. So much for loyalty, then.

Well, the team are off to the USA and I am about to set off on the long drive to Southampton to meet up with the cruise ship. I'm hoping I can keep in touch with what's happening Stateside and I'm sure in this technological age that will be possible via the ship's Internet facilities.

First game up is VC Fusion, followed perhaps though not yet confirmed by a behind closed doors game with David Beckham's LA Galaxy, the tour being rounded off with a match against Portland Timbers.

On Wednesday, July 22, I've been cruising only four days but it's strange how quickly the mind turns back to football matters. Today we visit Alicante and I find myself looking for a football stadium while on an open top bus tour. I don't see one but the 'Plaza del Torres' is prominent. I wonder if they have a team and assume a city of this size must have, but I don't recall the name amongst the Spanish giants.

Tomorrow is Barcelona and they don't come much bigger than that. I did notice on the 'welcome aboard' photo boards a fellow Claret resplendent in her new shirt, so there are some civilised people aboard this ship after all.

There's also a young lad wearing a Bury shirt. How good to see he is not blindly following the big club crowd but supporting his local team. Good lad. Up the Shakers.

My daughter, who I suspect is missing us more than she lets on, texts me with the score from the first USA match, 5-0 to the Clarets. The Internet café on the ship looks a bit pricey so I will have to wait and pick up the details on my return.

After an exhausting and hot day in Barcelona with just a glimpse of the Nou Camp from the bus, we arrive on Friday in Cannes. What a lovely place and a veritable millionaire's playground. The Bentleys, Porsches and Lamborghinis are out in serious numbers. We spot a white Lamborghini and wonder what Chris Eagles is doing here when he should be in California.

As usual, I sweat profusely while all around me the beautiful people maintain their cool and style. What is it with English people and heat? Why do we become dripping lobsters at the first sign of temperatures hitting the 70s?

Mind you, I'd like to see these preening Frenchies on a January night at Turf Moor. The tables would be turned then.

As we leave Cannes, I phone my daughter to get a report on how my home grown tomatoes which I have entrusted to her care are faring. She doesn't seem to have killed them yet but there's still a week to go. I ask her to check Clarets Mad for news and reports of the proposed LA Galaxy game, and she promises to text back on Saturday or Sunday.

As the ship turns in the bay at Cannes and heads for Livorno, our port for Florence, I think how lucky I am to make this trip while looking forward to Premier League soccer all in the same year. Yes, 2009 is truly a vintage year for the Clarets.

Leaving Rome after a day of culture, mind blowing beer prices and sweltering heat, I am once again reminded of home. My wife and I both overhear a conversation on the coach with exotic sounding place names such as Slack, Heptonstall, and Hebden Bridge littering the chat, and then the clincher: "We come from Burnley." At this point I take the opportunity to introduce ourselves as fellow Burnleyites, and of course our travelling companions are also Clarets. One is an acquaintance of Kiko, our rising star Jay Rodriguez's father.

Every conversation I have had or overheard on this trip concerning football, with fans of many clubs, has been complimentary to the Clarets on their fantastic achievement and wishing us all the best.

Not much forthcoming from Stephanie regarding footy news but eventually after a day in Alghero, Sardinia, I get the text that tells me we have beaten Portland Timbers on penalties after a 2-2 draw over 90 minutes. She also reveals reports of a rejected £500,000 bid for Norwich midfielder Daryl Russell, a player we have previously been linked with.

Also, Sheffield Wednesday are apparently refusing permission for us to talk to Tudgay, presumably as we don't meet their valuation.

On Saturday, August 1, we return to Southampton ready for the drive home. After a round trip of 4,386 nautical miles at an average speed of approximately 20 knots, and taking in eight ports, we return to learn that we have managed a 2-2 draw at Accrington Stanley. The game is only saved with two goals in the last seven minutes and the conclusion is that jet lag has been our undoing.

The trip up from Southampton is made in dreadful weather conditions with persistent rain. Welcome home indeed. As I get in range of Radio Lancashire I tune the car radio in for score updates on our only home pre-season friendly, against League One Leeds United.

My old mate Joe Wilson cheerily informs me that the latest score is 0-1 but says little else. I look at my watch. Only half time, plenty of time to sink 'em in the second half. But not so, as nearing home he informs me the score is 0-2, and then rapidly changes it to 1-2.

OC is far from impressed with the performance and admits: "It was there for everyone to see, it's not the performance we're looking for that's for sure. All credit to Leeds, I thought they passed the ball well. We played in fits and starts, bits and pieces but not anywhere near the fluency or quality that we're looking for. I want them to get the fitness from it, but all in all I was disappointed with the performance, no doubt about it. We've said before, results aren't important - far from it - but it's always nice when you do get them along with performances. But we got neither."

So it's now two defeats to lower league Yorkshire neighbours in Leeds and Bradford. It's not what we expected, but everybody consoles themselves with the fact that they're only friendlies, with no points dropped.

My mind starts to drift back to Dean 'Midas' Maynard, and I wonder if it's not too late to get him on board.

A quick glance at the local press confirms Tudgay is staying with Wednesday, but we do seem to have a strong interest in the young Ecuadorian Guerrero. The 19-year-old linked up with the club in the USA, playing both fixtures and making a big impression. There is some cautious talk about a deal, and we await developments.

It turns out the LA Galaxy game didn't go ahead, and neither did the game at Chester due to their financial problems. Oh, and Alicante does have a team but a not very successful one. They must prefer fighting the bulls.

AUGUST

A New Season

AS the team prepare to set off for Scotland and the final two warm up games, I find for the first time I am beginning to get some uneasy feelings about the coming season.

Perhaps this is as a result of the latest two disappointing friendly performances at Accrington and at home to Leeds, but suddenly a bit of my confidence is ebbing away. The size of the task ahead as we rapidly approach the big kick off has now started to darken some of the euphoria that followed the Wembley triumph.

My worst fear is that we start badly, as we have in recent seasons, and take some heavy beatings from the top teams who we meet in the early fixtures. The effect this will have on the morale and confidence of a young team could have devastating consequences for the season.

Then again, it might just be post-holiday blues brought about by my return to work. Let's get two convincing wins in Scotland, coupled with the capture of a signing or two, and then things will look a bit rosier.

However, conversations with work colleagues and business associates confirm it's not just me that's getting edgy. It's easy to see why the doubts are creeping in when you look at the size of our budget compared with the established Premier League sides, and worryingly it also pales into insignificance compared to our promoted partners Wolves and Birmingham.

Have we bitten off more than we can chew? Only time will tell and that time is approaching fast.

When I think about it though, are the doubts any worse than they were last season or would have been this season if we were still in the Championship? No, I don't think they are, because before last season I don't think most fans would realistically have backed us as promotion candidates when you looked at the strength of the league on paper, and similarly this time round the Championship will be just as tough a league to escape from, upwards at least.

Fortunately, the game isn't played on paper, nor is it won or lost in bookmakers' offices, and last season Burnley proved that the total was greater than the sum of the parts. We hope and pray this will again prove to be the case, and that OC's activity in the transfer market has been as shrewd as it has been previously.

On the sixth day of August, appropriately enough our sixth signing is announced, with the young Ecuadorian Guerrero signing on a one year loan. The deal was originally expected to be a straight purchase, but providing safeguards have been put in place regarding the transfer fee should we wish to buy at the end of the period, this seems a more sensible arrangement.

The lad is only young at 19 and coming into a very alien environment in terms of language and culture. He has only been here a couple of days and finds himself heading for Scotland, a land of mutilated language, midges and Irn Bru. But if he can survive that, his chances of acclimatising and becoming the megastar we all hope for will be greatly enhanced.

The loan deal greatly reduces the gamble on both sides. For the club, if he can't cut it in the top league there is no long term commitment, and for the player if he finds Burnley and England not to his liking he can head for home. I think we need to give the lad some TLC, find him a pretty Burnley lass and educate his palette to fish and chips, then we'll see him flying down the flank leaving defenders in his wake.

So much for two convincing wins in Scotland, as we lose both games 0-1. A bizarre Clarke Carlisle own goal derails us at Kilmarnock and a penalty is our undoing at St Johnstone.

Fernando gets a 15 minute run out at Kilmarnock and a second half against the Saints, and favourably impresses the travelling Clarets fans. However, we finish the friendly programme with two wins, two draws and four defeats, including three losses in the last three games.

All the matches were against what I think most fans would class as inferior opposition, so the results split the supporters into two well defined groups.

There are the doom and gloom merchants who see the pre-season form as indicative of a torrid time to come, particularly with the testing early season fixtures. Then there are the more laid back fans who see the results as unimportant and the games as purely fitness exercises.

I am not too sure that we can glean anything about the starting line up at Stoke from the last game at St Johnstone as OC left out the contingent of Scots who are selected for this week's World Cup qualifier against Norway in Oslo. I think these three, Graham Alexander, Steven Fletcher and Steven Caldwell, who has been recalled to international duty after a long absence, will be likely starters at Stoke.

Three more of our young Scots are called up for their country's Under 21 training camp, namely Kevin McDonald, Brian Easton and Alex MacDonald, who is currently on loan to Falkirk until January to enable him to get more first team experience.

Six call ups for Scottish national squads certainly show the improving calibre of player that we are now able to attract. However, I can't help thinking that the week prior to the start of the Premier League season is not a great time to play World Cup games and I hope if our players are selected they get through the games injury free.

Summary of pre-season friendly results

Bradford City (away) - lost 1-2 (Alexander).

Morecambe (away) - won 3-1 (Fletcher 2, Paterson).

Ventura County Fusion USA (away) - won 5-0 (McCann, Eagles, Fletcher (pen), Guerrero, McDonald K).

Portland Timbers USA (away) - drew 2-2 after 90 minutes. (Caldwell, Thompson). Won 4-2 on penalties (scorers Eagles, Gudjonsson, McDonald K, Elliott).

Accrington Stanley (away) - drew 2-2 (Blake, Thompson).

Leeds United (home) - lost 1-2 (Edgar).

Kilmarnock (away) - lost 0-1.

St Johnstone (away) - lost 0-1.

With the Premiership season now less than a week away, the media build up is getting into full swing. I notice in the football section of today's Mail on Sunday there is a two page article entitled "Can Burnley Survive?"

I read it to see if they can but find the article doesn't really offer any conclusions and is mostly just a regurgitation of the history of the town and the club. It's the sort of thing I could have written myself. In fact I have done and you have already read it.

In the Piers Morgan column on the final page of the same newspaper, he makes 20 predictions about the coming season, one of which is that Burnley will be relegated with Hull and Wolves. How I would love to see us prove this pompous, arrogant Arsenal supporter wrong and look forward to seeing another brace from Kevin McDonald nestling in the back of the Gooners' net.

Good old Jeff Stelling, presenter of Sky Sports Soccer Saturday and celebrity fan of the 'Monkey Hangers' Hartlepool United, seems to have a soft spot for the Clarets. Perhaps that's because of his affiliation to another team of perennial underdogs, or maybe, as is rumoured, his wife is a Claret, but whatever the reason, in an article for skysports.com he gives us some welcome encouragement.

The stars of Soccer Saturday were asked to gaze into their crystal balls and give their views on what to expect in season 2009/10, and Jeff duly obliged by nominating us as his surprise package. In his own words: "I think Burnley could finish fourth bottom – which would surprise a lot of people. You look at their squad on paper and it's the weakest in the Premier League by some way and they've got an incredibly low income compared to a lot of the clubs, but I really believe Owen Coyle is a fantastic manager.

"The fact they came up last season, albeit by the play-offs, after playing so many matches with such a tiny squad – and playing such good football in the process – really impressed me. He's not quite a Tony Mowbray figure either, Burnley will knock it around, but there's a steeliness about them at the back and they'll put a foot in when needs be. Everybody has written them off, but I think they could be this year's Stoke. They'll play in a different way, but they'll achieve the same end product in staying up".

That's more like what we wanted to hear. All the so-called experts writing us off before we kick a ball can have a very negative effect on confidence and we need to have the same belief that we had when tackling the big boys last season if we are to achieve survival.

Despite Jeff's optimistic words, the Daily Mail of Monday, August 10 in its pull out guide "The Big Kick Off" has five of the eight Sportsmail big name journalists tipping us for the drop. Chief sports writer Martin Samuel, in his main piece, wonders if "the romance of Burnley's arrival can possibly have, against the odds, a happy ending. Hull City's did last season - it even ended with a song from Phil Brown, the manager - but Burnley's grand history affords them the greatest appeal."

Elsewhere in the guide are Jamie Redknapp's "Ten to Watch" and in amongst them is none other than Wade Elliott.

Jamie comments: "I watched this lad at Bournemouth and he has a tremendous engine and can run all over the field. If Burnley fall short and don't quite make it, Wade will stay in the Premier League because other clubs will take him. He scored the goal to take them up and plays wide midfield or through the middle."

Further favourable comment comes from Andy Townsend. When asked who will be the surprise packages, he replies: "Little old Burnley - as long as their spirit remains strong and their confidence doesn't get shattered by defeats that will inevitably come. I think Owen Coyle can keep them up.

"If they thought the Championship was physical, then they are in for a shock. They will now be playing against quicker, more powerful, more gifted players who can snap you in two **and** play."

In Tuesday's Burnley Express, Owen Coyle comes out fighting with the declaration that no one scares us, and insists the Clarets will be competitive as they look to ram the pundits' predictions down their throats.

Looking forward to one of the most exciting times in the club's history he said: "It doesn't faze us. We know that we can put a team out there that can compete and one that can pass and move the ball. We love playing with wide players and we'll look to win games by playing that type of football.

"We're playing in the best league against some of the best players and indeed best teams in world football. As much as people think it's a privilege to be there, it is, but we've earned it and we have to make sure we retain that status, and we'll do our utmost to do it."

Fighting talk indeed Owen, and just what the dressing room needs to hear at 2.45pm on Saturday.

On the same day as Owen's rousing call, we are linked in the Daily Mirror with a move for Reading's Cameroon international central defender Andre Bikey. Now this is an interesting one as this is the player who was sent off near the end of the play off semi final first leg tie at Burnley.

After having a relatively easy afternoon against the Clarets' strike force, late in the game and for some inexplicable reason, he decided to haul back Steven Thompson who had turned him inside the box. The resulting penalty was duly put away in customary fashion by Graham Alexander and the Clarets had an unlikely lead.

Shortly afterwards he managed to get in a tangle with Robbie Blake and suffered a rush of blood, culminating with him stamping on Robbie in full view of the referee who duly produced the red card and waved him on his way.

What followed was I think the most monumental strop I have ever seen at a football game. Waving his arms wildly and eyes blazing like a madman, he attempted to remove his rather too tight shirt over his head. Unfortunately it stuck and he became more demented in his attempts to free himself. Eventually it came off and he hurled it to the ground before disappearing up the dressing room tunnel, much to the amusement of the crowd.

There ended Mr Bikey's season, and also Reading's hopes as they missed their colossus in the second leg. The Mirror article claims the player has a get out clause in his contract if any team offers £3 million, and there are reports Burnley are set to test the water with a £2.5 million offer.

The general consensus amongst the fans is that he would be a great addition to the squad as he is big, strong, courageous and a good header of the ball. The downside appears to be his temperament but the fans' utter belief in OC's godlike qualities convinces them that he will be able to tame the beast. Again we are left to wonder on whether the move will become reality as there is no comment from the club.

What a coincidence. After Jeff Stelling gives us a vote of confidence, who should we draw in Round Two of the Carling Cup? None other than the 'Monkey Hangers' themselves. A very good result for Hartlepool, an away win after extra time at Coventry, rewards them with a home tie against one of the big guns. I bet that's got Jeff nervous.

It will be interesting to see how we approach this competition this year with Premiership survival uppermost in our thoughts. After last season's heroics in this cup, I think OC will still be very interested in a good run again and wouldn't expect us to be fielding seriously weakened teams. However, we may take the opportunity to blood one or two of the newly turned professionals in the early stages.

Clarets Mad are reporting that the Bikey situation is perhaps closer to a deal than we think and suggest a fee has been agreed and that the player may be a Claret before we leave for Stoke. However, in any case he would be ineligible to play until probably the Everton game as he serves out his suspension for those antics at Turf Moor.

On the same day there is good news with the announcement of new contracts being signed by two of our young home grown players, Chris McCann and Jay Rodriguez. Both have agreed new contracts tying them to the club till the summer of 2011. I must confess to being a little puzzled by the short term of these new contracts but I assume it is related to the uncertainty about our ability to remain in the Premier League and the effect that relegation would have on our finances.

Of our three Scottish players on World Cup duty in Oslo, Alexander and Caldwell make the starting line up while Fletcher is an unused substitute. The Scots suffer a heavy 4-0 defeat as Caldwell's brother Gary is sent off for two bookable offences, and worse still Steven is substituted in the second half after a booking.

The media are reporting that he was taken off through injury, citing a groin strain. If this is the case then we already have a serious problem at centre back for the first game because if Caldwell is out, Clarke Carlisle is the only fit specialist in that position.

New signing David Edgar, who would have been in contention, sits out a one game suspension carried forward from last season's final game in Newcastle colours while Michael Duff, who would also have been a candidate, has an ankle injury and has not played since the American tour. It looks like we may have to employ Stephen Jordan as a makeshift centre back, and although he has played there before it is not ideal, particularly as it is likely we will face the dangerous and physical pairing of James Beattie and Ricardo Fuller, both of whom have given us problems in the past.

So at last it's Friday, August 14 and the eve of our great adventure.

After 33 years of pain, suffering, and almost extinction, we are about to step out unbelievably again in the top flight. How do I feel? Bloody nervous but excited is the answer to that.

67

The hype and media coverage particularly in this final week have been incredible and just underline the importance of Premier League status. The week is capped off by the showing on BBC1, albeit only in the North West, of a documentary presented by celebrity fan Alastair Campbell entitled 'Burnley are Back,' and those three words just about sum it all up. In the words of the Burnley Express front page article of the day, "Bring it on."

Game 1 – Saturday, August 15, 3pm – Stoke City – Away

IT'S a bit of a novelty for the Premier League, a 3pm kick off time, but for old timers like me, that's the traditional start time for league soccer.

Nowadays, particularly in the Premier League, the television companies dictate the start times for many games with Saturday lunch and tea time kick-offs, Sunday lunch and 4pm starts, and even Monday night games.

Today though, we are going to start our "season in the sun" at the proper time and 2,900 lucky Clarets, from the 36,000 that were at Wembley, will see the lads back where they belong.

We have a good record against Stoke at the Britannia Stadium, with two wins, one draw and one defeat in the last four games there, and this gives us some hope of a decent start.

Probably not to our liking is the long ball style of play adopted by our opponents, who play a very physical game with a major attacking ploy being the phenomenal long throws of Rory Delap. I think it's fair to say that Stoke are a fairly atypical Premier League side and we won't encounter this style often this season.

My fear is that we tend not to defend well in this type of game, with the exception of the home game against Sheffield United last season where we mopped up everything they launched at us and gave them a footballing lesson.

The trick with these sides is not to give them throw ins anywhere near the line of the penalty area. This we must avoid at all costs to restrict the aerial bombardment. 'The Beast' Brian Jensen will have to be at his most decisive in coming for the ball and using his not inconsiderable frame to dominate his goal area. It will be no place for faint hearts.

At kick off time I take up my customary position in the back garden. The conditions are cloudy and blustery, but not too unpleasant as I seat myself under the drying towels on the line.

I cast my mind back to last season at this time when I was confidently and eagerly anticipating the opener at Sheffield Wednesday, and a sudden dread comes over me. In that game, we went two down in the space of about three minutes and were overwhelmed 4-1. Please not the same again.

The game seems to get off to a reasonable start and whilst we aren't creating much, we seem to be getting our share of the ball and don't seem too troubled defensively. As expected, Jordan is in at centre back for the injured Caldwell, with Mears being favoured at right back over Eckersley. The formation is 4-1-4-1 with Alexander protecting the back four and Fletcher the lone striker.

As the game progresses we start to hear more about long throws raining in from Delap as I feared, and on 19 minutes we are behind to -

guess what? - a set piece goal. Stoke defender Ryan Shawcross rises unmarked to head a Liam Lawrence free kick into the net and give the home side the lead.

Just 14 minutes later and we are undone again from a long throw, with Jordan getting his head to the ball and diverting it past his own keeper. Just over half an hour gone and two down. Not the start we wanted, and with the home crowd sensing blood we hang on to half time, thankfully without further damage.

I consider a change of tactic, thinking I may switch wrists with the lucky wristband, but am loathe to as it served us so well on the right wrist last season. Better stay as I am.

By now the rain has started so I desert my post in the garden for the warmer climes of the conservatory and, too nervous to listen to more Radio Lancashire commentary, switch to Sky Sports on the telly. Matt Le Tissier is the match summariser and he feels we have started the second half much brighter so after 15 minutes I put the earplugs back in to Radio Lancashire and switch the sound off Sky Sports.

I am relieved to hear arch rivals Rovers still trail to big spending Manchester City, and am surprised to see Aston Villa trailing at home to Wigan.

We seem to be having plenty of possession now whilst not exactly threatening and appear to be coming in for some bruising treatment from the Stoke defenders, particularly Amdy Faye who whilst picking up a yellow card is fortunate to stay on the pitch.

With about 20 minutes to go, Eagles and Guerrero replace Blake and Paterson, and immediately the young Ecuadorian starts to make things happen and looks a very exciting prospect. Thompson replaces Alexander with 10 minutes to go as we go in search of goals but unfortunately we can't find any and the game finishes with a 2-0 defeat.

How do I feel? Slightly disappointed but also not too despondent as in the second half we seem to have found our feet if not our teeth.

Given our defensive frailties and having to go into this game with only Carlisle as a recognised centre back, the result was not unexpected, and should serve as a valuable lesson. In this league, mistakes and lack of concentration costs goals, and we need to learn this lesson quickly.

The Mail on Sunday headline is: "Burnley's return to big time is thrown off course by deadly Delap" and I guess that about sums it up.

Owen Coyle is disappointed but says: "I thought we contributed a lot to the game, passed and moved well, but there's no getting away from the goals we conceded.

"We knew exactly what Stoke can do from set-pieces and we shot ourselves in the foot. We've got three centre halves missing but I'm not making excuses. That's the sort of thing you need to deal with if you want to do well in a league, and we didn't."

On this opening weekend of the season the two other promoted clubs both lost, Birmingham unsurprisingly at Manchester United and Wolves at home to West Ham. Other losers were Villa, Blackburn, Bolton, Hull, Portsmouth and much fancied Liverpool.

However bad I felt at 5pm on Saturday night can't be half as bad as the poor fans of Everton who saw their side go down 6-1 at home to Arsenal, with the solitary Everton effort coming in the last minute. So the first game back ended in defeat but we were not alone and were in good company.

Result: Stoke City (Shawcross 19, Jordan og 33) 2, Burnley 0.

Team: Jensen; Mears, Carlisle, Jordan, Kalvenes; Paterson (Eagles 72), Alexander (Thompson 82), Elliott, McCann, Blake (Guerrero 72); Fletcher.

Subs (not used): Penny, McDonald K, Gudjonsson, Eckersley.

Attendance: 27,385.

Position in Table after 1st game: 18.

Season Record: Played 1, Won 0, Drawn 0, Lost 1, Goals for 0, Goals against 2, Points 0.

As the dust settles on the opening day defeat, and the media collectively congratulate themselves on telling us that this would be our fate, a dawning realisation that this may happen a lot this season comes over me.

I read Dave Thomas's feature on Clarets Mad, where he propounds the theory that nobody wanted the pre-season to end, and I find myself in total agreement. The last season was so unbelievable and the end so glorious that we didn't want the dream to end, but Saturday at Stoke marked that end. Now we are no longer the invincibles but more likely the whipping boys and that's a prospect I'm not sure I'm relishing.

Still, not too worry. It's only the current champions and beaten Champions League finalists up next.

Tuesday sees the signing of Andre Bikey for an undisclosed sum and my mood lifts immediately. At a stroke the defence which seemed decidedly dodgy now looks greatly improved by this single addition of a player who I have rarely seen play.

I think this is typical of most football fans as their mood swings from sublime optimism to dire pessimism and vice versa on the strength of a transfer in or out, or a one off victory or defeat. OK, so we lost on Saturday but on a freak weekend for the Premier League, so did nine other teams as there was not one draw in the opening programme of games.

I am further encouraged by United's reported crop of injuries affecting their keeper and defence, and their inability to overwhelm Birmingham in their opening fixture in which they triumphed by a solitary goal. If only we can take something from this game against the champions it will give us a massive lift.

Caldwell and Duff will again be unfit but we now have Bikey and Edgar available for selection, both having completed their suspensions. Bikey is reportedly keen to return to the Premiership to push his claims for a place in the Cameroon national squad for the 2010 World Cup finals. There can be no better game than this for him to start to stake that claim.

Game 2 – Wednesday, August 19, 7.45pm – Manchester United - Home

AS I get ready for the game on Wednesday, August 19, I decide on a change of tactics. The wristband, which worked so well on the right wrist last season but failed at Stoke, is transferred to my left wrist and worn the other way up. As an additional precaution I find the nearest pair of underpants to claret I possess and don these.

It's a lovely evening with no sign of the predicted rain and a temperature of about 20 degrees as I start to walk to the ground having been dropped off a couple of miles away by my wife. I decide to walk as I fear parking will be a nightmare and having secured a lift home with an early afternoon text to a neighbour, make good progress along with many fellow Clarets.

As a result I arrive in good time at the stadium about 45 minutes before kick off. Time for a beer I think. After downing a solitary Carlsberg I go up to my seat to have a look at the changes to the ground and renew acquaintances with my fellow Claret colleagues, most of whom I haven't seen since last season.

The first thing that strikes me as I look down at the pitch is the number of players we have out there warming up. Two seasons ago we wouldn't have had that many on the books. That's a sharp illustration of our changed circumstances as we now have established first teamers who can't make an 18 man squad when everyone is fit.

I have a look at the opposition warming up and there are some awesome reputations out there with the likes of Wayne Rooney, Ryan Giggs, Paul Scholes, and Dimitar Berbatov, but no Nemanja Vidic or Rio Ferdinand, the rocks of their defence being both out injured.

The ground is packed by kick off time and the decision to split the Cricket Field Stand between home and away support means that for the first time in many years, we have fans on all four sides of the ground.

This is a tremendous assist as it not only limits the number of opposition fans but gives us a vocal presence over the players' dressing rooms situated under that stand.

As the game gets under way it feels just like Wembley has been transported back to Turf Moor and even the warm temperature is reminiscent of that glorious day. Predictably the game starts with United pushing us back and there are one or two close calls in the first 10 minutes.

Then gradually we begin to grow in confidence and start to knock the ball about and get some forward momentum going.

After a good 10 minute spell and some concerted Clarets pressure the unbelievable happens. A cross from the left is headed out by full back Patrice Evra to the edge of the box, and who is waiting there with the trigger cocked? None other than 'Bad Beat Bob' Robbie Blake.

As the ball drops he hits a volley of such awesome power that the ball is in the net before anyone can move. Silence for a split second, then a nuclear explosion of sound as the best part of 20,000 Clarets erupt. Bloody unbelievable.

One up with 19 minutes gone, dazed and almost lost for words I dash off a text to my daughter holidaying in Wales. How could she miss this?

United try to battle their way back but we are relatively untroubled until the stroke of half time when a rash challenge by Robbie on the advancing Evra sees us concede a penalty. Oh well. A 1-1 scoreline at half time would be better than we hoped for.

Up steps Michael Carrick and hits a rather leisurely strike to the right of Jensen. Unfortunately he had not reckoned with the superpowers of the Beast who throws himself in the right direction and beats out the effort which is hastily cleared into the stand. Again a wall of sound erupts, which is heard by my wife returning from her keep fit class three miles distant.

Half time and we have the lead. Can we do it? United are good but without Cristiano Ronaldo they don't seem to have their usual cutting edge despite the unstinting efforts of Rooney to coax them to life.

The second half continues in similar vein with United having much more possession but finding it difficult to breach a magnificent Burnley defence ably assisted by the midfield. Our forwards continue to pose sufficient threat on the break to deter an all out assault by the Red Devils and the game edges closer to its conclusion.

A word here for Andre Bikey who has stepped straight in after only two days with his new team-mates and is a colossus at the heart of the defence.

The magnificent back four are breached on a few occasions but each time the Beast comes to the rescue and the clock ticks down. On 90 minutes, predictably the fourth official produces the extra time board showing four minutes and we are left to sweat, chew our nails, and shout our heads off for a few more minutes of purgatory.

Then with one blast on the whistle it's all over. We have achieved what many would tell us was the impossible. Victory over United. How sweet is this?

The fans, who have contributed hugely all night to this famous victory, collectively wear grins like Cheshire Cats and breathe a sigh of relief that could blow a man over. It's impossible to put feelings into words at this point. Better to wait till tomorrow and then I'm sure it will all come out.

I head for home with my neighbour who can barely speak, and promise myself the largest whisky in the world. He prescribes the same nerve tonic for himself as 20,000 Clarets here and many more around the town, the country, and the world go to bed walking on air.

Thursday's press doesn't disappoint. I open my copy of the Daily Mail to see in huge print the headline: *"FERGIE TAMED BY BEAST."*

Chief Football Correspondent Matt Lawton's article then goes on: "What an incredible night. What an incredible goal. What an incredible sensation when Robbie Blake's stunning volley flew beyond the reach of Ben Foster and into the back of the Manchester United's net in the 19th minute. The James Hargreaves stand shook so violently it was actually a little unnerving. They just don't build stadiums like this anymore."

He continued: "As collector's items go, Blake's goal will take some beating. It was a peach of a strike, the kind of finish Wayne Rooney would have been proud of and one Michael Owen, watched by Fabio Capello last night, only wishes he could buy".

Of the victory: "It will succeed only in enhancing the reputation of Coyle, and deliver a warning to the rest of this division that this fantastic little ground could prove a difficult place to visit this season.

Inside a stadium that boasts the most stunning view in the English top flight, the sense of excitement was terrific. The noise generated by the 20,000 spectators was remarkable, a deafening roar accompanying not just the first whistle but the sight of Owen so nearly connecting with a teasing cross from Patrice Evra."

In the Times, Oliver Kay is equally thrilled, citing fate as the explanation of what happened then adding: "But fate alone cannot explain the manner in which United were beaten in every department: from the pitch, where they were outfought and just occasionally outclassed, to the dugout, where the impressive Owen Coyle out-thought Ferguson, and most certainly to the stands, where 33 years of frustration gave way to an ear-splitting roar at the final whistle. It was a brilliant night, the type that affirms your faith in everything that is good about Premier League football."

His conclusion: "This could be a long season for United, but not every opponent will play them as brilliantly as Burnley."

As I arrive at work I find emails stacking up from well wishers including a Woking fan with whom I used to do business. This fellow is an absolute star, and has a real passion for horse racing and gives me occasional tips.

Today's is a horse called Eagles Nebula and he recommends an each way bet next time out. Now with a name like that how can I resist? Is this the hand of fate again?

Also in my inbox is the following: "On behalf of everyone connected with Leeds United Football Club we would like to thank Burnley FC from the bottom of our hearts for beating the red side of

78

Manchester. The only people more excited about this result are Burnley fans and I'm sure you must have enjoyed the night like no other (with the exception of Wembley '09 possibly). Anyhow couldn't let this one go by without sending our congratulations and thanks, I'm sure there's already a song made up to sing at Elland Road this Saturday to celebrate your win or should I say to celebrate the Reds' defeat!" Perhaps I have misjudged Leeds fans after all .

Result: Burnley (Blake 19) 1, Manchester United 0.

Team: Jensen; Mears, Carlisle, Bikey, Jordan; Elliott, McCann, Alexander (Gudjonsson 73), Blake, Fletcher (Thompson 81); Paterson (Eagles 73).

Subs (not used): Penny, McDonald K, Guerrero, Kalvenes.

Attendance: 20,872.

Position in table after 2ⁿᵈ game: 12.

Season Record: Played 2, Won 1, Drawn 0, Lost 1, Goals for 1, Goals against 2, Points 3.

After that fantastic experience it's time to draw a line and move on. Mission impossible achieved, and the first win under our belts. Time now to switch our attention to the next opponents Everton, who started disastrously at home, losing 1-6 to Arsenal. The game is switched to Sunday as they have played a Europa Cup game on Thursday night in which they restored some pride with a 4-0 home leg win against a side from the Czech Republic.

Game 3 – Sunday, August 23, 3pm – Everton – Home.

SUNDAY games are not my favourite as they tend to disrupt the whole weekend.

Saturday is the normal day for football for Stephanie and myself, Sunday being the day for family walks in the country or at the coast with my wife Julie. This week we reverse the days and on Saturday have a lovely walk at Malham, taking in Janet's Foss, Gordale Scar, Malham Tarn and finally the Cove in perfect weather.

Stephanie is back from her short break in Wales and is looking forward to her first sight of the Clarets since Wembley. Anticipating parking problems again we set off in plenty of time and park the car a good mile from the Turf.

Not being able to do anything at a leisurely pace, Stephanie strides out and we are at the ground by about 2.10pm.

Here I learn another valuable lesson about Premier League football ie the price of a cup of tea reflects our new found status. It's £1.60 for a tea bag in a cardboard cup. Premier League, premier prices. The only positive thing I can say was that it was wet, and duly refreshed at a cost of £3.20, we prepare for the action.

At 3pm, the game kicks off and this time we are quickly into our stride as in what seems like no time at all Martin Paterson connects with a cross from the left. His header smacks the Everton bar with the keeper beaten, but Fletcher is unable to turn in the rebound.

Shortly after, Pato is presented with an easier opening after a cross from the right but contrives to put his effort wide from six yards out. Everton are clearly rocking from an impressive start and again the fans are at full throttle.

Gradually our opponents start to settle and begin to come into the game as an attacking force without creating too much of a stir in what is once again a solid looking Burnley defence.

Then after 34 minutes Wembley goal hero Wade Elliott produces another piece of magic with a curling left foot effort which takes a slight deflection but puts us in the lead.

It's the cue for the fans to once again break the sound barrier with what is now becoming a familiar wall of sound. What a transformation from the almost silent atmosphere in the ground of recent years and how heartfelt the passion of these long suffering fans.

Half time and for the second time in a few days we lead against one of the Premier League big boys. Wake me up, I must be dreaming.

But I'm not dreaming and as we get deep into the second half despite an improved performance by the visitors, we still look comfortable and are creating the better chances. Tim Howard in the Everton goal is at full stretch to tip over a Chris McCann overhead kick and Clarke Carlisle is close to making the game safe.

Then on 75 minutes, disaster strikes as Everton's Tony Hibbert gets a fortunate break on the ball and hurtles into the box. Sensing the danger McCann and Blake pull out of a challenge but to no avail as Hibbert throws himself to the ground. Well and truly conned, referee Phil Dowd points to the spot and for the second time in days we are facing the fact that a penalty may spoil our dreams.

Can the Beast do it again? No need, Louis Saha makes a complete hash of it and misses the target. Justice done.

From here on in we survive without too many traumas and even give the young Ecuadorian Guerrero 10 minutes to sample the atmosphere. Only 19 and looking about 12, he must wonder how he has found himself caught up in this fairytale. Until he can learn some English I guess we will never know what he is making of the crazy world of Burnley FC.

McCann picks up a ball in midfield and pursued by a posse of defenders is implored by 18,000 Clarets to "give him it." Receiving the ball wide left he heads at speed for the box and at this point everybody is waiting for the stepovers.

But no, spotting the keeper out of position he improvises a cheeky lob, narrowly missing the target. That one bit of unconventionality convinces me that we may have a real find on our hands if we can get the boy settled, and I look forward to seeing more.

After the customary four minutes added time, Dowd blows up and we have done it again. A magnificent team effort with effective contributions from each and every player and the second memorable game at Turf Moor in a week..

Bikey is voted Man of the Match, but it could have been anyone. Chris McCann had perhaps his best display yet for the Clarets and showed a developing confidence and maturity that will make him a top player in the top league.

Result: Burnley (Elliott 34) 1, Everton 0.

Team: Jensen; Mears, Carlisle, Bikey, Jordan; Blake (Guerrero 83), McCann, Alexander, Elliott, Fletcher (Thompson 85); Paterson (Eagles 78).

Subs (not used): Penny, Gudjonsson, McDonald K, Kalvenes.

Attendance: 19,983.

Position in table after 3rd game: 7.

Season Record: Played 3, Won 2, drawn 0, Lost 1, Goals for 2, Goals against 2, Points 6.

After an incredible first week, the lows after the loss at Stoke and then the highs of the morale boosting wins against two of the top five teams from last season, I am exhausted.

My first week of Premier League football has been all and more than I hoped for. The tremendous support for the team manifested itself in the loudest vocal backing I can remember, and the optimism surrounding the club is truly a breath of fresh air. It's early days yet and it can all still go horribly wrong but who would have thought after the first week we would be sitting with six points from two major scalps?

Premier League history tells me that the poorest team so far was Derby County, who in 2007/8 amassed only 11 points all season from one win and eight draws. We are already more than halfway there, and have more wins than they managed all season.

News of a reported interest in signing ex-Manchester United and England midfielder Nicky Butt has me a bit surprised. At 34 years of age and with a wealth of experience at the top level, he is a great player but I'm not sure he fits our profile. We already have good professionals who can't make the bench and the signing of an ageing player will only push them further down the line.

The whole of our success is built around superb team spirit and we must be careful we don't do anything to jeopardise this. However OC has got us here and I'm sure he will do what he feels is best without my advice.

Carling Cup Round 2 – Tuesday, August 25, 7.45pm – Hartlepool United – Away.

THE wheel has turned full circle and we find ourselves back to where, after a faltering start, our season 2008/9 season started to come together, ie the Carling Cup.

Last year, early wins against lower league opposition in Bury and Oldham then led on to the inspiring triumphs against Fulham, Chelsea, Arsenal and almost Spurs.

Our elevated league status means this time we don't come into the competition till Round 2, where we face League One Hartlepool away, and they are in confident mood after an extra time winner away to Coventry in the previous round.

Ahead of the game Owen Coyle declares his intent to having a long cup run but announces he will make changes to give some of the squad who haven't played yet some pitch time. True to his word he makes 10 changes, the only player keeping his shirt being Andre Bikey and this is probably due to injuries to Caldwell and Duff, the latter of whom turns out for a very young and inexperienced reserve team in a 3-0 defeat to Everton on the same day.

In goal is Diego Penny, making his first appearance since the opening game of 2008/9, and the four man defence has no less than three players making their Burnley debuts in a competitive game, namely the three Es, Eckersley, Edgar and Easton.

The midfield four are Eagles, Kevin McDonald, Joey Gudjonsson and Guerrero, with Rodriguez and Thompson the strikers in an attacking line up. There are no replays in this competition, drawn games at 90 minutes going to extra time and then penalties, so the emphasis is on putting out a side to win.

I miss the start on Radio Lancashire but get in about 15 minutes into the game to hear the score is still 0-0 in an entertaining game. I switch off and go for a bath but by the time I switch on again, horror of horrors, we are one down and it's half time.

No need to panic. We will surely step it up a gear in the second half and the goals will flow. Not so, and with about 20 minutes to go, I'm getting nervous.

Around the hour mark, OC had introduced the big guns Fletcher and Paterson for the misfiring Rodriguez and Thompson, and five minutes later Blake for Eagles. The introduction of the subs seemed to turn the game back our way and on 84 minutes we are level with a well taken first competitive goal for Steven Fletcher, who must be relieved to get his goal tally under way.

Despite more good chances in the last six minutes we are unable to wrap it up and it's extra time, at the start of which we revert to our bad old ways and are lucky to stay level as the hosts hit the woodwork. Worse is to come as 'Issy' Eckersley is sent off, Radio Lancashire reporting it as a straight red card for swearing at the referee.

But in the second half of extra time Fletcher heads a second after a good cross from a tight spot by Paterson and we ride our luck to go through somewhat fortuitously to Round 3.

How ironic it would have been if last season's all conquering giant killers, now turned giants, had been slain at the first attempt. But we survived, and as is the hallmark of OC's teams, never knew when we were beaten and kept going till it came right.

I now look forward to the third round draw on Saturday, and with the big guns to come in and most of our Lancashire rivals in the hat, there is a real prospect of a cracking tie. I feel a little sorry for our old pal Jeff Stelling, who gave us such encouragement on Sky Sports ahead of the season, and his Hartlepool team who played by all accounts very well, and wish them well in the rest of their season.

Result: Hartlepool Utd (Boyd 39) 1, Burnley 2 (Fletcher 84, 108) - After extra time.

Team: Penny; Eckersley, Bikey, Edgar, Easton; Eagles (Blake 65), McDonald K, Gudjonsson, Guerrero; Rodriguez (Fletcher 61), Thompson (Paterson 61).

Subs not used: Jensen, Alexander, Jordan, Elliott.

Attendance: 3,501.

For us next, a complete contrast. From Hartlepool to Chelsea in the space of five days as we resume our quest for league points.

I bet our old friend Didier Drogba can't wait to see his Claret and Blue mates and I wonder if he will bring lots of coins to disperse amongst our fans as he did in our last meeting.

Chelsea at the Bridge, scene of probably last season's greatest triumph and the catalyst for our successful campaign, and we are ready for them. Chelsea have started the season well and sit with maximum points after three games. Can we stop the run? Watch this space.

Ahead of the game at Chelsea and while we eat lunch, we decide to tune in to Sky Sports News to see if we can pick up any news of the Carling Cup Third Round draw. We are just in time as the draw is being made live as we watch, eagerly awaiting a home tie against a 'biggy.'

I mean it with no disrespect, but Barnsley away? The Championship strugglers who took six points off us in our promotion season? It couldn't have been much worse. Oh well, that's the luck of the draw.

We just have to get focused and get on with it, and there are more pressing matters to attend to at Stamford Bridge.

Game 4 – Saturday, August 29, 12.45pm – Chelsea – Away.
WELL, what can I say about the game?

I think all, TV pundits, media journalists, Owen Coyle, the team, and the fans, agreed that we took a bit of a battering.

It might, but only might, have been a different story had we taken the early chance that fell to Paterson after Tyrone Mears dispossessed Frank Lampard. Unfortunately Martin missed the target and from then on we were on the back foot.

We almost made it to half time with our goal intact but then conceded in time added on. Two early goals in the second half and we were starting to fear a rout.

Today as opposed to last November we met the opposition at full strength and in this form unstoppable. Wave after wave of attacks saw gallant defending from us and heroics from the Beast, but we still attempted to play passing football as per Owen's philosophy.

In games like this we need to try and stem the relentless pressure caused by the opposition pouring forward. To this end we need to be able to hold the ball better when it is played out to give the defence a bit of a breather and time to reorganise. We also need to be giving the opposition defenders something to think about in order to deter them from rampaging forward.

Having said that, we managed to come out of the game with our dignity intact, and for sure better teams than us will come away from Chelsea with heavier beatings this season. With maximum points from their first four fixtures and currently firing on all cylinders, they are a team packed with power and pace, and are certainly serious contenders for the Premier League title.

The Daily Mail thought the good news for Burnley was that they don't have to play Chelsea every week, but next up is Liverpool.

OC's view was: "We'll need to defend better because there's no doubt Liverpool have similar qualities to Chelsea, with world class finishers at their disposal. But we'll look to take the positives from the start we've had, move on and be ready to give our best. If we do that, we've a fighting chance of staying in what I believe is the best league in the world."

Result: Chelsea (Anelka 45, Ballack 47, Cole 52) 3, Burnley 0.

Team: Jensen; Mears, Carlisle, Bikey, Jordan; Blake (Guerrero 78), Alexander (McDonald K 74), Elliott, McCann, Fletcher; Paterson (Gudjonsson 59).

Subs not used: Penny, Kalvenes, Eagles, Thompson.

Attendance: 40,906.

Position in table after 4th game: 10.

Season record: Played 4, Won 2, Drawn 0, Lost 2, Goals for 2, Goals against 5, Points 6.

How can we be disappointed? We have six points from the first 12, and that after playing three of last season's top five. If anybody had said this would be the case before the season started I doubt I would have believed them.

August has seen a magnificent start to our adventure and we leave the month exactly half way in the table in 10th position. A bit of a rest now for most of the squad as next weekend it's international games and World Cup qualifiers, and then another big ask at Liverpool.

A quick Sunday evening check of the gossip is in order with the transfer window to close at 5pm on September 1.

I see we are linked with a season-long loan bid for Daniel Cousin from Hull City. The French striker, now 32, has played most of his career in France but was signed by Hull for £1.5 million from Glasgow giants Rangers.

He appears to have fallen out with Tigers boss Phil Brown, who is a friend of OC, and with Hull currently signing strikers for fun seems surplus to requirements. He is rumoured to be a player with questionable work rate and temperament so he may not be the ideal guy we are looking for, although an experienced top flight striker would certainly add to our options.

SEPTEMBER

A New Striker

TRANSFER deadline day seems to be going very slowly. I check all the websites frequently during the day but nothing seems to be doing.

Our rumoured move for Daniel Cousin seems to have some substance as even the local press are reporting that OC has his sights set on him. However with no further developments during the course of the day it seems this may be a dead deal.

As I drive home, Radio Lancashire's five o'clock news reports a very quiet day for the local clubs with only Blackpool making signings. Now that makes a change. For some time our seaside friends, known affectionately as the 'Donkey Lashers,' have been regarded as the poor relations of the major Lancashire clubs. But this time round under new manager Ian Holloway they have made a promising start to the season and are looking to build on it.

As I sit down to eat my tea, my daughter informs me that she thinks we have signed the ex-Preston striker David Nugent from Portsmouth on loan. I tell her this cannot be as none other than Radio Lancashire itself has denied any incomings, and in fact the rumour had been that he was rejoining North End on loan.

But five minutes later I am eating humble pie for tea as national radio confirm his signing for the Clarets as per my daughter's revelation. Nugent was reported to have been a target for Burnley in his early days after an impressive performance against us for Bury in the Carling Cup, but he later signed for Preston.

He continued his rapid progress, signing a big money deal taking him to Premier League Portsmouth and winning full England recognition. However, things don't seem to have worked out for him on the South Coast and he has had very limited opportunities.

Portsmouth are currently a club in turmoil with a new foreign owner and I guess the player is delighted to secure a move back to his native North West and a chance to resurrect his career. He is someone who has always had the unfortunate knack of scoring against us. Let's see if he can now redirect this talent onto the proper path.

With the signing of Nugent, the transfer window closes and barring emergencies, we go with what we've got, at least till the next window. The ex-Preston man signed just before the deadline on loan till January with the option to extend or make the move permanent. With the constraints of our limited budget this seems a sensible move as we get the opportunity to see if he can recapture the form that won him an England cap before we commit to a contract.

The striker apparently had the option to join us or Hull and his decision to opt for the Clarets is a good sign. Obviously being a North West boy he favours a move back to his home territory and this will hopefully enable him to settle in quickly.

It will be interesting to see how the fans react to him as a former Preston player, and one that they perceived as having chosen North End before Burnley previously. In games against us he was not popular and often a target for the fans. This ill feeling continued after his move to

Portsmouth and particularly following his exuberant goal celebrations after scoring against us in a Carling Cup tie.

The Clarets Mad messageboard jury seems to be split on the signing, but fans are nothing if not fickle and a goal at Anfield in the next game will soon endear him to the unconvinced.

The unprecedented number of summer signings and loanees now gives us a squad size that 12 months ago was unimaginable. Yet with the increased numbers comes the problem of keeping everybody happy. Each position now has at least two credible contenders and some even more.

Squad rotation is a totally alien concept for the players and fans at Turf Moor and indeed previously the squad had on occasions been too thin to even fill the subs' bench. However the demands of a Premier League season allied hopefully with a couple of successful cup runs will require a contribution from all of them.

Many fans, myself included, are a little concerned that some of the younger home grown talent will now find opportunities very limited, and this will hamper their development. It's not an easy problem for the manager to solve as he looks towards experience to establish a foothold in the division.

In addition, with five strikers at our disposal, competition for forward places is intense. Similarly, with at least five recognised centre backs vying for two positions, somebody is inevitably going to be disappointed. This is a clearly a time for OC to demonstrate his man management skills. It may be that come the January window we will be looking to loan out some of our fringe players to get them some first team action.

On Thursday, September 3, FIFA announce a ban on incoming transfers at Chelsea until 2011. Our recent conquerors will not be able to sign players during the next two transfer windows as punishment for inciting a young French winger to breach a contract with his club Lens in order to join them.

This is not the first time that they have been implicated in this type of activity with several recent high profile cases, but they immediately announce their intention to appeal.

No surprise there then, and I and many others will not be surprised to see the authorities 'chicken out' and probably commute to a suspended sentence. The big clubs seem to be able to flaunt the laws at will whilst the smaller clubs feel the full weight of any penalties for financial misdoings.

A club of Chelsea's stature should be able to ride out such a short term ban with the player resources they already possess but interestingly this time they are set to lose probably four key players due to African Cup of Nations commitments in January.

Come on FIFA. Stick to your guns, reject the appeal and strike a blow for the little guys.

Speaking of little guys, our near neighbours and the butt of many soccer jokes, Accrington Stanley, are faced with a winding up order if they are unable to repay a £308,000 tax bill to HM Revenue and Customs in the next eight weeks.

Stanley folded due to debt in 1962 and lost their place in the Football League, only to reform and slog their way back up the leagues to reclaim League status in 2006. Yet as they are geographically in an almost hopeless position, trapped midway between Premier League Burnley and Blackburn Rovers and suffering poor gates as a result, it is an almost impossible task for them to survive.

In a magnificent gesture by the Clarets, we immediately announce a friendly game is to take place between the two clubs at Turf Moor on Tuesday, September 8, all proceeds to go towards Accrington's survival fund.

The game was proposed by OC who said: "Burnley have had hard times in the past so we want to do what we can to keep Accrington going."

He added: "I will be putting out a strong team. It will be a chance for the fans to see 90 minutes of Fernando Guerrero, and also first team players like Chris Eagles and David Nugent. The more Burnley fans that come the better because it's a fantastic cause, and that's why we've priced it reasonably."

The club plan to charge £10 for adults and £5 for concessions. Let's hope it's a reasonable night for weather and we get a few thousand down to boost the Stanley coffers. Obviously buoyed by our gesture, Accy go to Bury on September 5 and come away with a 2-0 victory to give them their first away points of the season.

True to form, as I drive home from work on the night of the friendly it is wet and grey, more like November than September. I am faced with a simple choice, down the gym with wife and daughter or

Turf Moor in the rain. No contest, tea down quick, in the bath and off to the match.

The fans seem to be split. On one side there's the 'holier than thou' crowd, who feel they have to boycott the game. Their argument goes along the lines that they cannot give money to Stanley because they should have made sure they paid their tax bill instead of spending the money elsewhere. Then there are the more forgiving souls who think: "There but for the grace of God go I."

However, I think a large majority of the crowd are there because they are feeling relatively starved of soccer, with only two home games having taken place by September 8 and no chance so far to see the likes of Nugent and Guerrero.

So despite the inclement weather, a crowd of 5,301 turn out for the game. Given the short notice and the rain I think this as good as could be expected and should make a significant contribution to the fighting fund.

The game, billed on the admission ticket as an SOS Cup game, that is 'Save our Stanley,' turns out to be a very entertaining affair particularly if you are a Claret. Fielding a very strong and attacking line up in a 4-4-2 formation we run out 4-0 winners in a one-sided contest that should have seen more goals.

Impressive wing play by Eagles and Guerrero, the latter of whom seems destined to become a big crowd favourite, is topped only - in my opinion - by Kevin McDonald in midfield. Looking more like the player we saw in flashes last season, he looked a class act with great strength and vision allied to determination. We also saw a very encouraging performance from Jay Rodriguez who for much of the game played in an unaccustomed midfield role.

The goals came from Guerrero from a threaded through ball from McDonald, a neatly worked free kick on the edge of the box 'passed' in by Eagles, and two from Rodriguez, the first beautifully flighted past the keeper into the roof of the net. The atmosphere was excellent with the Stanley fans chanting for Burnley and Owen Coyle in gratitude for their efforts in staging the game and helping the cause.

A good night for all I think. Accy got the money, the Clarets got a good run out with several individuals doing their first team prospects no harm at all, and there was some great attacking play for the fans to enjoy.

I suppose the only disappointment was no goals for debutant Nugent. He worked hard, made some good runs and took up good positions but couldn't hit the net. A bit more sharpness in the finishing department would have given him a hat trick but it was a decent effort all the same.

Near the end, four of the young professionals, Alex-Ray Harvey, Chris Anderson, Ben Hoskin, and Wes Fletcher got on for a feel of the atmosphere and all could be pleased with their contribution.

I'm glad I went and hope that in years to come, when Stanley step out in a Champions League game at the Crown Ground, I can say I did my bit to help them survive.

What a disrupted start to this Premier League season. We play four then a blank weekend, back for four then a blank, and in November after a further four matches, there's another no gamer. Of course, this is all caused by the need to fit in the World Cup qualifiers ahead of the finals in South Africa 2010.

And on Wednesday, September 9, this all becomes worthwhile as England brush aside Croatia 5-1 at Wembley to clinch their place in the finals with two qualifiers still to play. An impressive eight wins from eight so far in qualifying make Fabio Capello's England unstoppable and the manner of the performance against high ranked opposition gives us real cause for optimism that we will see an end to what in 2010 will be 44 years of hurt.

The Clarets have four players called up for World Cup duty, but only Northern Ireland's Martin Paterson gets a game. Both the Scots and the Northern Irish lose at home leaving England as the only Home Nation likely to qualify.

Two of our probable opponents at Liverpool on Saturday have eventful evenings for England with good displays from Steven Gerrard, who scores twice with headers, and Glen Johnson who has another forceful game at right back.

Johnson seems to be making the position in the national team his own now with eight consecutive appearances, and his attacking play is proving a lethal weapon. His defensive capabilities, however, seem to be coming in for some criticism and the Croatian goal comes as a result of a cross from his flank. Let's hope that's something we can exploit on Saturday.

Once again the secret of success at Anfield I'm sure will be our ability to stem the wave of anticipated attacks and a key part of this will be keeping the full backs occupied and trying to get them going backwards. Owen please take note.

Belated apologies to Andre Bikey. He was also called up on World Cup duty for Cameroon, but was an unused substitute.

Game 5 – Saturday, September 12, 3pm – Liverpool – Away.

CONSIDERING the magnitude of the task, it's strange that on the eve of this game I am not so nervous as I usually am about meeting one of the big four.

Liverpool have had a mixed start to the season and sit three places above us on the same points but with a much better goal difference, courtesy of a big home win over Stoke. Their last home game resulted in a defeat to Aston Villa as the Villains defended resolutely and caught them on the counter attack to run out 3-1 winners.

The Reds have after four games lost as many matches as they did in the whole of last season, and had to come from behind with a late winner from Gerrard for their victory at Bolton in the last game. On paper then, not such a daunting prospect as Chelsea in full flight. However as I have said before, games aren't played on paper.

OC is well aware of the danger and his pre match message is: "We are under no illusions about the enormity of the task but we are looking forward to it and excited about the prospect of going to Anfield. It's a measure of how far we have come that we are talking about Burnley going to Liverpool and hoping to achieve something positive from the game."

Just under 3,000 Clarets will make the 55 mile trip, but not me. I shall make the same trip around the same time but one day later as I take Stephanie back to start her second year at Liverpool John Moores University.

It is a road I have got to know well over the last year, and I have to confess that after some apprehension about my daughter going there, both my wife and I are very impressed with the city, which of course was 2009 European Capital of Culture. It has a mix of fine old buildings and new constructions, not all of which are everybody's cup of tea, but the friendliness and cheerfulness of the natives is never in doubt.

Our last victory at Anfield was 35 years ago in September 1974, when a fine goal from Ian Brennan and a magnificent goalkeeping display from Alan Stevenson gave us a 1-0 victory in a game I was fortunate to witness. That was 35 years ago, a long time, and today seems a good day to settle some more old scores.

Crash, Wallop, Thump, Thud! Me and my ill founded confidence about this match are shattered as the Reds hit us for four. Ouch.

I hate to be a know-all but I did warn OC that we needed to stem the incessant attacks that destroyed us at Chelsea. But no, we perish in the same manner.

The game starts for me in a beautiful sun-filled back garden on one of the best days of the summer, to the nerve wracking Radio Lancashire commentary where even a throw in sounds like a goalscoring opportunity. There can be no worse way for a committed fan to follow a game than by radio commentary, as the reporters in their attempts to describe the action have an uncanny knack of making every half chance sound like a certain goal. Because we are unable to see the action we wait for the net to bulge only to be then informed it went a yard wide of the goal.

In time honoured fashion, this game starts just like the others and within the first minute I am punching the air to celebrate a Martin Paterson goal only to be informed he has put it a yard wide. Oh dear. This sounds like a rerun of Chelsea, with an early chance missed then backs to the wall.

The clock ticks on and we almost reach the half hour in one piece, then on 27 minutes we are breached by Yossi Benayoun. I sit back on the sun lounger and fear the worst as the red tide starts to overwhelm us.

Getting towards half time and after enjoying a decent spell of possession, we go two down, this time as Dirk Kuyt taps in after the Beast fails to hold a shot from 20 yards.

Realistically that's game over at half time but we have to play the second half and try to preserve our dignity. Against one way traffic and the magnificent skills of Steven Gerrard it is a desperate effort, and we concede twice but it could have been many more. Benayoun ends the game with a hat trick and probably should have had more, Pepe Reina in the Liverpool goal is practically untested and we come away soundly beaten for the second consecutive away game.

The match stats show 27 attempts at goal by Liverpool to our six, and if anybody gets that many attempts, goals are bound to follow in significant numbers.

There is a strong argument that Burnley's season will not be decided by adverse results at the likes of Chelsea and Liverpool, but rather by their ability to take points from the clubs who are likely to be in the relegation mix with us.

This is all well and good, and we are I believe sitting on bonus points acquired from the United and Everton games, but we need to look at the statistics from the three away games from which we are goalless and pointless. Even at Stoke City in the opener we had little goal threat and were effectively beaten after conceding the first goal.

We need to develop a bit more punch up front or even the weaker teams are going to attack us at will as they realise we are toothless tigers. There is now sufficient quality in the squad to make some changes both tactically and in terms of personnel and I am sure that is already uppermost in the manager's thoughts.

Result: Liverpool (Benayoun 27, 61, 82, Kuyt 41) 4, Burnley 0.

Team: Jensen; Mears, Carlisle, Bikey, Jordan; Fletcher, Elliott, Alexander (Gudjonsson 75), McCann, Blake (Eagles 58); Paterson (Nugent 70).

Subs not used: Penny, McDonald K, Guerrero, Thompson.

Attendance: 43,817.

Position in table after 5th game: 12.

Season Record: Played 5, Won 2, Drawn 0, Lost 3, Goals for 2, Goals against 9, Points 6.

The week commencing Monday, September 14 is, I guess, what you would call a real slow news week around Turf Moor. Apart from the reserves notching their first points of the season with a 1-0 away win to Sunderland, thanks to a Jay Rodriguez goal, there's nothing else to report.

My daughter is back in Liverpool, albeit for five nights only before she heads home on Friday for her 20th birthday celebrations and the home game with Sunderland on Saturday.

I can't believe my ears when I speak to her by phone on the Thursday evening and she is actually complaining that she will have to go out partying again for a fourth consecutive night. What a hardship. The chance of four nights out in a month would be a novelty for me.

Work is getting both my wife and myself down as we strive to do the impossible for the ungrateful, and this seems to be the norm in any manufacturing environment. On top of that, summer is rapidly drawing to a close, the nights are shorter and I am starting to have to burn gas again.

I need some soccer therapy, and being starved of meaningful match action at home since Sunday, August 23, a much needed home victory this weekend will lighten the mood enormously. Let's hope the lads can deliver, especially in front of the Sky TV cameras as we go out as the early Saturday game to the usual vast worldwide audience.

Game 6 - Saturday , September 19, 12.45pm – Sunderland – Home.
AFTER the opening 'baptism of fire' games, from which we emerge with a creditable six points, Sunderland present a different test.

Before the season started, many fans and pundits predicted this would be the first game where we had a realistic chance of taking points. This match and the four which follow next week's away clash at Tottenham are all against what could be regarded as weaker sides in the division.

These games are seen as key to our survival chances, and with that comes a different type of pressure. After coming through games where we were serious underdogs with no expectations, now we have to step up to the plate and claim the points against the teams that are perceived as our rivals for survival.

Having said that, Sunderland have started the season well and currently sit sixth in the table with three wins and nine points from their first five games. I expect this match to be as hard fought as any other this season and anything we get from it will be hard earned.

"A New Striker" was the chapter heading for September. Perhaps more accurately it should have been a reborn striker.

David Nugent, in what is becoming Clarets fairytale world, steps off the bench and wins the game with two spectacular strikes. It's the sort of thing I was brought up on with Roy Race of Melchester Rovers and his antics in the Tiger comic of my youth.

On a warmish September day, my daughter's birthday, we make our way to the ground for the early kick off and arrive in good time and bump into my mates, the two Johns, knocking back a pre-match Carlsberg under the stand. After the usual pleasantries, schoolteacher John asks for my honest opinion of how I think the game will go. He tries to influence me by telling me that everybody he has asked so far today has been pessimistic about our chances and he would like some positivity. I have to tell him that my gut feeling is for a 1-1 draw.

The game gets underway and Sunderland, fielding an expensive selection of strikers, soon have us on the back foot. Worse still, we look extremely jittery in defence and are giving away possession far too easily, and the first 10 minutes are uncomfortable to say the least.

Then on 13 minutes as Wade Elliott breaks into the box, a rash challenge from Anton Ferdinand sees him concede a needless but certain penalty. Up steps the king of spot kicks, Graham Alexander, and just at this point my pal in the next seat decides to wonder if this is when he will start to miss them. Not very helpful that and I silently decide to throttle him if he does.

Not this time though. It's not the best penalty he has ever taken as it goes straight down the middle, but it's hard and low enough to hit the back of the net. More Turf Moor mayhem as we thankfully grab an undeserved lead.

The goal temporarily knocks our opponents out of their stride but gradually they start to regain their dominance and not unexpectedly they level approaching half time. We appeal in vain for offside and Darren Bent, one on one with the Beast, makes no mistake.

We are in at half time level and with my pre-match score prediction on track, although I express my view that the first half was not good enough and more of the same will result in defeat.

Thankfully we come out for the second half a bit more positively, and whilst not making scoring opportunities, are taking the game to the opposition a bit more. Then the masterstroke, as on 57 minutes Nugent is on for Martin Paterson followed shortly on 64 by Chris Eagles for Steven Fletcher.

Almost immediately the game is transformed as an excellent move down the right involving Eagles, Tyrone Mears and Elliott results in a lovely cross into the box. The build up is equalled by the finish as Nugent thumps a rocket header into the net and the Clarets are back in front.

Suddenly the game has become much easier and the opposition are much less effective despite the introduction of the highly rated Kenwyne Jones. What a difference substitutions can make, with ours key to turning the game and theirs, in my opinion, weakening their threat.

Nugent, now with a huge weight lifted from his shoulders and playing with a smile, is clearly in the mood. Entering the final stages, he receives the ball just inside the box, surrounded by defenders and with his back to goal. He makes a yard, turns and deftly curls a left footer high into the net.

It's all over, we've won our ninth consecutive league game at the Turf and our third in the Premier League, and in front of the TV cameras. There's a sea of smiling claret and blue faces and the world is a better place than it was only two hours ago. That's made my weekend and my beer will taste so good as I relive the highlights on Match of the Day tonight.

I'm delighted for Nugent, as are all the crowd except the Sunderland fans, and we hope these goals can be the first of many to keep our dream alive. It's a real battling performance from the team to come back from a shaky start and win in the end with some style. Fortress Turf Moor is still intact.

Result: Burnley (Alexander 13 pen, Nugent 67, 86) 3, Sunderland (Bent 39) 1,

Team: Jensen; Mears, Carlisle, Bikey, Jordan; Fletcher (Eagles 64), Elliott, Alexander, McCann (Gudjonsson 28), Blake; Paterson (Nugent 57).

Subs not used: Penny, McDonald K, Guerrero, Thompson.

Attendance: 20,196.

Position in table after 6th Game: 9.

Season record: Played 6, Won 3, Drawn 0, Lost 3, Goals for 5, Goals against 10, Points 9.

Monday brings bad news ahead of the game at Barnsley. Chris McCann, who limped out of the match on Saturday after a crunching tackle, is facing a possible long lay off with what may be a serious knee injury. Chris is very much a first choice midfielder and although still very young seems to have been around the first team for years.

Results of tests later in the day confirm medial ligament damage to the knee and this will probably sideline him till Christmas. That's a bad blow for us but a reminder of the need for a sizeable squad if we are to stay in the Premier League.

OC says he will make changes for the game at Barnsley but not quite as drastic as in the last round at Hartlepool where there were 10 alterations from the previous line up.

Carling Cup Round 3 – Tuesday, September 22, 7.45pm – Barnsley – Away.

TRUE to his word, OC rings the changes with six this time, but surprisingly keeps the Beast in goal when it seems an ideal opportunity to rest him ahead of a likely hard game at Tottenham on Saturday.

The other four who play are Clarke Carlisle and Andre Bikey, presumably to try to continue building an understanding, and the forwards Fletcher and Paterson. Barnsley field a strong line up and are obviously intent on taking our scalp. We have an attacking 4-4-2 formation featuring both wide men, Eagles and Guerrero.

The game starts brightly for us and we are in lively form up front with the wingers prominent. All is going well until after 15 minutes Paterson collapses without any contact and is stretchered off to be replaced by Rodriguez. It never bodes well when a player goes down without any challenge and we must wait to learn the full extent of the injury.

We continue to force the pace and go ahead on 21 minutes with a goal from Steven Fletcher, but our joy is short lived as the Tykes equalise within 90 seconds. Worse is to come as the Beast and the man mountain that is Darren Moore collide, resulting in the Beast also being stretchered off.

Incredible. No serious injuries all season except that to skipper Steven Caldwell playing for Scotland, and now three in the space of two games.

Diego Penny takes over in goal but suddenly we seem very short of keeper cover, and Diego has very limited experience in England.

In the period leading up to half time Eckersley follows his red card at Hartlepool in the last round with a yellow here and his reckless and ill-disciplined approach threatens further retribution from the referee.

Just before half time we concede a second, so we go in a goal down and with two of our main players injured. Oakwell is indeed a very unlucky stadium for the Clarets. It's 77 years since we last won there, and no, I didn't see that one.

At the break, OC is clearly worried about Eckersley seeing red and removes him from the action.

In the second half, we are not great with the exception of Eagles and the outstanding Guerrero, and the two combine on 52 minutes with excellent work from Fernando teeing up Eagles to level the score.

As the game progresses towards likely extra time and penalties we continue to press but the final goal comes to our opponents with 15 minutes to play. Despite the usual huffing and puffing we are unable to score again and the Carling Cup is over early for us this time round.

Tonight has been expensive in terms of injuries and we have also the bitter disappointment of defeat to swallow. Now we can only wait and hope for good news on our injured players, both of whom would have been likely starters at Spurs.

Result: Barnsley (Macken 22, Anderson da Silva 45, Colace 75) 3, Burnley 2 (Fletcher 21, Eagles 52).

Team: Jensen (Penny 34); Eckersley (Duff 46), Carlisle, Bikey, Kalvenes; Eagles, McDonald K, Gudjonsson, Guerrero; Fletcher, Paterson (Rodriguez 15).

Subs not used: Edgar, Easton, Elliott, Blake.

Attendance: 6,270.

Wednesday, and I check the media during the day for reports on Jensen and Paterson. Early indications are that the Beast may not be too bad, but Paterson is more of a concern. By early evening it emerges Jensen may be fit for Saturday with his injury thought to be a 'dead leg,' but Paterson faces surgery to determine the extent of a cartilage injury.

Wednesday evening and my mate from the office, Ed the PNE fan, is going reluctantly to Deepdale to watch their Carling Cup tie against Spurs.

Although a North Ender by birthright Ed, I have to say of late, has lapsed and his enthusiasm for them and life in general has taken a knock. It was quite a shock for him then when his mate rang and pronounced that he had got him a ticket for the game.

With heavy heart and considerable moaning, off he goes and promises to text me the score. By half time nothing, so I check the Internet, and find them 2-0 down. I decide to cheer him up and text him to tell him there is still all to play for and to kick a few of the 'fancy dans' for us ahead of Saturday.

Nothing through the second half and then at the end a one word text: "Gutted." Not knowing the final score I text back to ask. Again no response and I go to bed none the wiser.

But on Thursday morning as I switch my phone on, the message is there. "Close do. They nicked it 5-1 in the end!" I should imagine that will finish his Deepdale appearances for the season.

Our discussion later that morning at work confirms my own feelings about the difference between Premier League and Championship teams. Ed reports that North End had many chances but took only one whereas Spurs put away five of theirs. Despite lots of possession they could not produce the killer ball or finish whilst their opponents could absorb the pressure and pick them off at will.

His conclusion was that the Spurs forwards were excellent but their defence poor, and this is borne out by the evidence of their recent games when they have been free scoring but have conceded too many goals.

Tottenham look destined again to be one of the sides stuck in the middle of the league, not good enough to push for honours but too good for the relegation battle. PNE could have done us a favour by denting their confidence but unfortunately they seem to have done exactly the opposite. Typical.

Thursday evening brings more bad news with the revelation that Martin Paterson's injury is confirmed as a torn cartilage and this will rule him out for three months. That almost certainly means a start at Tottenham for Saturday's goal hero David Nugent, and it will be interesting to see if it is a straight player swap or if OC is going to try a different system.

There's no doubt we need to arrest what is becoming a disturbing trend away from home in the league with 2, 3, and 4-0 defeats

111

in the last three games. With Tottenham's free scoring attack and our at times woeful defending, what odds a 5 this weekend?

The Beast's prospects of playing are being kept a closely guarded secret and should he miss, it will surely be a game that will make or break Diego Penny.

I have to confess feeling a little sorry for Diego who was brought in from Peru and expected to challenge Brian Jensen for the goalkeeper's shirt. After playing the first game last season which ended in a heavy defeat, he was left out and the magnificent form of the Beast has kept him sidelined ever since. If he plays it will be a massive test of both his ability and his confidence and hopefully he will produce a match winning performance.

With Chris McCann's place also up for grabs, it will be a different starting line up for the Clarets in the league this time. Points please tomorrow boys to cement a very reasonable start to our campaign.

Game 7 – Saturday, September 26, 3pm – Tottenham Hotspur – Away.

I DON'T know what the odds were for a five, but bloody hell, they got it.

I find it unbelievable that we take pretty much the same players to away games as we field in home games but the travelling results are so horrendous. The stats show away from home we have lost all four, conceded 14 goals, and scored zero.

How can this be? What happens to our guys outside Turf Moor? Do they shrink, age prematurely, and suffer amnesia to the point where they forget what they've gone for? How does this malady cure itself on our return to the cosy little homestead that is the Turf?

My daughter is studying sports psychology. I think I'll get her to enlighten Owen and myself on this one. We really have to stop this escalating away day madness or we are truly sunk.

The Beast is pronounced fit and plays, and as the game starts fairly quietly, despite the odd scare we seem to be giving as good as we are getting. Then after 18 minutes a moment of rashness from Andre Bikey sees him concede a penalty, which is duly put away by Robbie Keane. Keane is a player I have rated highly for many years, but little do I know the havoc he is about to wreak.

Now we enter a crucial period. Can we come back from a goal down which has proved impossible so far away from home, or do we cave in?

Two decisive moments provide the answer.

Firstly Steven Fletcher finds the home net, only for the goal to be chalked off for offside. Subsequent TV replays suggest this is a wrong decision by the assistant referee but this is no consolation.

Then on 33 minutes, Spurs double the lead with a shot which deflects off Stephen Jordan giving the Beast no chance. Again there is a strong suggestion of a foul on Jordan before Jermaine Jenas strikes the shot but again we are on the wrong side of the decision. Isn't that typical? The home side, particularly the bigger names, always seem to be favoured by the decisions.

Once again two down and facing a mountain to climb, we make it to half time with no further damage.

But with our recent history we appear to have little prospect of getting back into it in the second half, and this is how it pans out.

Despite having good spells in the game and Carlo Cudicini saving from Blake before the same player hits the post after a mistake by the keeper, we concede three more times, all to Robbie Keane.

I wasn't there but from what I can glean from those who were, it's a similar story to Preston on Wednesday ie lots of effort from our lads but no incisiveness, and then cruelly picked off by pace and power.

Watching the TV screen at the end of the game I see OC looking a little glum, which is unlike him. He, like us, knows this away form can't continue but how to arrest it is his problem.

The next away game is the arch enemy Blackburn Rovers, and God couldn't be so cruel as to inflict a heavy defeat on us there could he? Following them is another potential 'tonking' at mega-rich Manchester City. It certainly doesn't get any easier.

The other problem with the abysmal away form is the pressure it creates to win the home games, particularly against fellow strugglers. Next week sees Birmingham City at the Turf and once more we need points, preferably all three.

A look at the league table doesn't look to drastic yet, and we sit after seven games in 11th position, five points clear of the relegation places. Bottom are Portsmouth who have reeled off seven consecutive defeats to remain pointless, while above them on four points are Hull City who were defeated 6-1 at Liverpool, which makes our result at Anfield look almost respectable. Making up the bottom three are West Ham United but they have so far only played five games.

Result: Tottenham Hotspur (Keane 18 pen, 74, 77, 87, Jenas 33) 5, Burnley 0.

Team: Jensen; Mears, Carlisle, Bikey, Jordan; Fletcher (Thompson 72), Elliott, Alexander, Gudjonsson, Blake (Guerrero 81); Nugent (Eagles 63).

Subs not used: Penny, Caldwell, Duff, McDonald K.

Attendance: 35,462.

Position in table after 7th game: 11.

Season Record: Played 7, Won 3, Drawn 0, Lost 4, Goals for 5, Goals against 15, Points 9.

West Ham play the Monday evening game at Manchester City and lose 3-1. No surprise there then, and they remain in the drop places at this early stage.

Even though it's early in the season, the table has an almost inevitable look about it, with three of the so-called big four, Manchester United, Chelsea, and Liverpool, occupying the top three positions and the other, Arsenal in sixth, having played a game less.

At the bottom, the only surprises are possibly the lowly placings of West Ham and Fulham, 18th and 17th respectively. Of the newly promoted clubs we are faring best in 11th, with Birmingham and Wolves 14th and 16th respectively, both two points worse off than ourselves.

Our fans continue to debate the poor away form on the messageboards, some blaming tactics whilst to others it is down to team selection. Many argue that with the strength of opposition we have met

115

away so far the results are as good as we could have reasonably expected, whilst others fear the effect of consistent defeats on confidence.

It's true that having met three of the current top four away from home already, we have had a tough opening to the campaign, and we hope that there will be points from the so-called easier games to come.

Saturday sees a return to the Turf for the game against Birmingham and then we are into the international break again. A repeat of the Sunderland score will do nicely and give us a relaxing couple of weeks before the trip to 'Deadwood Park' and our 'high noon.'

Wednesday, September 30 sees the Clarets play their first ever 'home' Premier Reserve League game at the Crown Ground, Accrington. The team run out deserved 2-1 winners but at a considerable cost with injuries to Rodriguez, Kevin McDonald and Guerrero. The latter is again in electric form but has to go off near half time with a hamstring injury.

Thursday brings more bad news as the seriousness of the injuries are assessed and it's Rodriguez who comes off worst with a broken ankle and another three month lay off. Guerrero and McDonald's problems are less serious, being a tweaked hamstring and a bang on the knee respectively.

But with only one victory, three defeats, and now three serious injuries, I have to conclude that September was not a great month for the Clarets. From a position of having five 'out and out' strikers two weeks ago, we are now down to three.

However, Steven Thompson, who scored twice for the reserves, one an absolute beauty, fortunately seems to be running into form at the moment when his services might most be needed.

Roll on October.

OCTOBER

You Win Some, You Lose Some

Game 8 – Saturday, October 3, 3pm – Birmingham City – Home.
AWAY from home we might perform like frightened rabbits, but at Turf Moor we are TIGERS.

I'm really looking forward to this match as it's a civilised kick off time, and with that goes the opportunity for a pre-match trip to the pub. These will be my first Premier League game pub pints and will taste all the better for that.

The morning weather is awful with heavy showers and strong winds, and it's difficult to know what to wear in these conditions. After I position the lucky wristband on the correct wrist, Stephanie and I leave the house with a selection of clothing.

We are in good time and even make a spot on the traditional car park, so the omens are good. By now the rain has stopped and it seems to be brightening a bit so I decide to chance not taking a waterproof and opt for a fleece.

As we reach the White Hart I witness a new phenomenon, a bouncer on the door and 'Home Fans Only' notices. Never saw that in the Championship.

The pub is fairly full of Clarets in good humour and I opt for a pint of Lytham Amber and catch a bit of Preston v West Brom on the big screen. The crowd looks pretty sparse for two teams well in contention at the top of the Championship and with the score at 0-0, I thank my lucky stars that hopefully I have something better than that to come later.

After the second very satisfying pint of Amber it's time to be off to make the Turf for kick off time. As we arrive and take our seats a quick look at the team shows a recall for fit again skipper Steven Caldwell. So who is left out from the centre backs? The answer is nobody as Joey Gudjonsson drops back to the bench and Andre Bikey is given a central midfield role with Graham Alexander and Wade Elliott.

It looks like OC feels we need a strong physical presence in the midfield against Brum and it may also be that he wants to try Bikey there ahead of the away clash with the Rovers which is coming up next.

For my own part I'm not too convinced about two defensive midfielders in a home game that we have a realistic chance of victory in. I think this will mean a lot of running for both full backs to bolster our attacking options.

We start the game brightly and are taking it to the opposition but there is no early breakthrough and the game loses its way for a patch. Birmingham's Lee Bowyer muffs a chance from in front of goal, but that is our only real scare.

I try to follow Bikey's contribution but whilst he is his usual determined self in the tackle and presents a substantial physical presence, I'm unconvinced by his positioning and distribution as he struggles to get to grips with the role. Still, there are plenty of options on the bench if things don't improve.

Generally we are playing good football and Elliott catches the eye with his ability to turn away from opponents and mount driving runs at their defence. Perhaps the more solid defensive base afforded by Bikey and Alexander is giving him more freedom in this respect.

Half time comes and we go in level at 0-0, looking good and relatively untroubled. A goal or two in the second half will see us home and dry, and I set off through the massed Clarets to relieve myself of those two pints of Lytham Amber.

The second half starts in similar fashion to the first but it's not long before we are ahead, a clever ball from the breaking Mears finding Fletcher racing through the inside left channel. I half expect him to square it to Nugent who is also heading for goal on his right. But not so, as he shoots and curiously the ball goes in off keeper Joe Hart's legs.

It is later claimed Hart expected Fletcher to shoot across him and when he didn't, it threw him. But who cares? It's 1-0 to the Clarets and thoroughly deserved.

I am delighted for Fletcher who carries the burden of being the record signing at £3 million, and his first Premier League goal will be a great relief. Football is all about confidence and that's what the goal brings as within minutes, Fletcher controls a ball brilliantly on his chest and brings it down. His shot beats the keeper but rolls agonisingly on to the base of the post and out. Another chance for the fired up Scot is then saved, and the lad could have been celebrating a hat trick.

It's all us now and on 62 minutes comes a monster of a goal to get the crowd on their feet. Bikey wins the ball in a challenge just inside the Birmingham half. He heads straight for goal with considerable power and pace before exchanging an exquisite one-two with Nugent on the edge of the box. That puts him clear in the area and he makes no mistake, firing home superbly.

Bikey's rampaging run and convincing finish has won the hearts of the Clarets and to a man they stand to chant his name. Magnificent stuff, and we continue to almost the end of the game in majestic style. Bikey is now clearly enjoying himself and playing with real enthusiasm, I can't think of one player in the team who is playing below par, and the game is won comfortably.

The four minutes of added time is just about up as Bikey concedes a free kick about 30 yards from our goal to the left side, and Sebastian Larsson steps up to hit an unstoppable shot that the Beast could only admire as it passed him. To be fair he was probably asleep as he had so little to do all afternoon.

The goal took a little of the shine off our win, but it was so little you wouldn't notice. What a great day again at the Turf.

Result: Burnley (Fletcher 53, Bikey 62) 2, Birmingham City (Larsson 90) 1.

Team: Jensen; Mears, Carlisle, Caldwell, Jordan; Fletcher (Eagles 72), Alexander, Elliott, Bikey, Blake (Kalvenes 90); Nugent (Thompson 86).

Subs not used: Penny, McDonald K, Duff, Gudjonsson.

Attendance: 20,102.

Position in Table: 9.

Season Record: Played 8, Won 4, Drawn 0, Lost 4, Goals for 7, Goals against 16, Points 12.

With that result we have become Premier League record holders, being the first newly promoted team to win their first four home games, beating the record set by Blackburn Rovers in 1992. So much for the pundits who said we would be the worst Premier League side ever. We have already amassed more points from eight games than Derby County managed in their whole 38.

That win was also the 10th consecutive home victory at fortress Turf Moor and that's no mean achievement. The atmosphere at the ground is now so positive that I'm sure this conveys itself to the players and gives them the confidence to go out and play their normal attacking game.

Defeats will come at home, and by the law of averages the first can't be far off, but I think we will win more than we will lose and hopefully this will provide the solid base for our survival battle.

So we now approach the second international break of this stop-start season, the second batch of four games bringing exactly the same six point reward as the first batch of four.

The first of the next batch of four games will bring us up against the Rovers, a game which for most fans is the most eagerly awaited match of the season, with the possible exception of the reverse fixture at the Turf.

I have to confess that for me, this is not the case. Being a veteran of many derby games with the enemy going back to the years when the two sides met regularly in the same division, I am now rather sickened by the over-hyped so-called hatred between the two clubs.

For many Burnley and Rovers fans who have barely seen any competitive games between the clubs, what used to be a healthy rivalry has been transformed into some sort of contrived hatred. To the more moronic elements of fans at both clubs, the event now provides the opportunity to indulge in violence or, failing that, criminal damage.

The result is that the clubs, under strict police supervision, have to change the kick off times in an attempt to avoid excess alcohol consumption. They then have to ensure that the only way away supporters can buy match tickets is by also purchasing coach travel, and they will then only be allowed to travel to the game via this method under police escort.

This leads to some ludicrous situations whereby Burnley fans who live in Preston have to come in their cars up the M65 past Blackburn to Burnley, park and get the coach back to Blackburn, and then repeat the trip in the opposite direction at the end of the game. Even with these arrangements, the lunatic element will still subject each other, ordinary fans and players to a torrent of foul language and abuse for 90 minutes before going home no doubt proud of their afternoon's work.

Having endured this atmosphere several times and each time finding it more and more incomprehensible as I get older, I have no intention of subjecting myself or my daughter to it at Ewood Park. So for myself and many others I know, what should be one of the most anticipated games of the season is now a fixture that we will be glad to see pass, hopefully peacefully.

In the Daily Mail of Wednesday, October 7, they run an article entitled *"7 Reasons Why The Season Has Started With A Bang."* At number 4, we find: "TRAVEL SICK, Burnley great at home, rotten on the road."

Writer Ian Ladyman then goes on: "It's not just the richer clubs shaking up the traditional hierarchy. In Lancashire's industrial heartland, little Burnley are writing a story all of their own. With a weekly wage ceiling of £15,000 a man, Burnley hardly have any right to sit alongside Chelsea and Manchester City. But in contrast to an away record that makes Britain's Davis Cup tennis team's look passable, Owen Coyle's claret and blue titans are four from four at home.

"They have already sent Manchester United, Everton, Sunderland, and Birmingham back to Turf Moor's tiny dressing room wondering what had hit them. With a game against Blackburn looming large, Burnley will also be involved in a new Premier League phenomenon – the North Lancashire derby. These are fierce games, as tribal as any in the British Isles. I can tell you're not convinced, but just wait and see what happens at Ewood Park a week on Sunday. Coyle, of course, will love it. He is already a candidate for manager of the year and turned down Celtic to stay at Burnley in the summer. Sometimes – just sometimes – the good guys get what they deserve."

Well, Ian Ladyman certainly seems to have some idea of the importance of this game, but I have to question his geographical knowledge as the game will obviously be known in these parts as the East Lancashire derby.

In the week ahead of the game, my wife and I take a well earned break from work and spend a few days in the South visiting places like Bath and Marlborough, which are about as unlike Burnley and

Blackburn as you can get. This not only relaxes us both but gets us away from the pre-match hype which I guess is being stoked nicely by the local press.

On my return on Friday, I find the Burnley Express has the now customary pull out feature on the game, and the Saturday papers all carry build up stories likening the event to World War Three.

Sunday morning's Mail on Sunday sets the scene with: "When you hear the air attack warning, you and your family must take cover. The moment the final whistle signalled Burnley's play-off win at Wembley on May 25, both sets of fans started the countdown to East Lancashire Armageddon and we are now at Defcon 1. It's freedom loving Owen Coyle against totalitarian Sam Allardyce and when two tribes go to war, a point is all that you can score".

No wonder the local headcases get carried away. Let's hope the players don't believe it all.

Game 9 – Sunday, October 18, 1pm – Blackburn Rovers – Away.
KICK off time, and I take up a position on the right flank of the lounge, earphones in and tuned to Radio Lancashire.

The atmosphere in the stadium sounds great and within minutes I am out of the chair punching the air as a super strike from Robbie Blake gives the Clarets a vital early lead.

Oh, what joy. After all those years, can the Clarets humble the old enemy?

Oh, how short lived that joy. Within minutes David Dunn fires the Rovers level and the game has started explosively.

For the rest of the first half, it's the familiar downhill slide. Rovers take the lead after a terrible defensive effort, as the Beast goes down tamely from a collision with his own team mate. Alexander compounds the error by inexplicably heading the loose ball back across goal to give Franco di Santo his first ever Premier League goal and surely the easiest he will ever get.

It's Sunday afternoon and the in-laws are coming soon for lunch. I pray we can get to half time at 2-1 and regroup. But no, the killer third goal arrives shortly before the break from Pascal Chimbonda. Suddenly, roast beef with all the trimmings has lost its appeal as my appetite for lunch, and the game, drains away.

As we eat I switch off the radio and play the second half blind, except for sneaky glances at Sky Sports News to check the score.

Nearing the end and still 3-1 down, I assume that's it, but now back in the lounge I get a text from the North Ender Ed. He informs me Eagles has grabbed a second, but it is too little too late.

An improved second half showing aided by a lack of ambition from the Rovers helps us make the score more respectable. However, most fans and reporters seem to agree that we got just about what we deserved ie nothing.

Away from home we really are a soft touch and that's now 17 goals conceded in five matches. When we needed a big performance from the Beast, he seemed on this occasion to freeze, yet the blame is not with an individual but with the whole team. An occasion much looked forward to by the fans once again turned into one of disappointment and the hurt goes on.

On the positive side, we managed our first away goals, and two quality efforts they were. However, if we are to pick up anything away from home we must stop conceding more than three goals per game, which is now the average. It was tragic to lose again to our most bitter rivals but we are definitely getting closer to them in terms of quality.

The result still leaves us two points better off than them, and they now face two difficult away fixtures at Chelsea and Manchester United. For us it is two at home with Wigan and Hull the visitors, and we must look to take points from these teams who may well be involved in the relegation dogfight.

Despite a massive police operation at Ewood, there are 55 arrests, many of them in a pre-arranged pub brawl with bottles and glasses hurled at police horses. I can't wait for the return at the Turf in March.

Result: Blackburn Rovers (Dunn 9, di Santo 21, Chimbonda 43) 3, Burnley (Blake 5, Eagles 90) 2.

Team: Jensen; Mears, Carlisle, Caldwell, Jordan; Fletcher (Eagles 60), Elliott, Alexander, Bikey (McDonald K 78), Blake; Nugent (Thompson 72).

Subs not used: Penney, Kalvenes, Duff, Gudjonsson.

Attendance: 26,689.

Position in Table: 10.

Season Record: Played 9, Won 4, Drawn 0, Lost 5, Goals for 9, Goals against 19, Points 12.

Nine games in and no draws yet. Am I tempting fate ahead of Saturday's game against Wigan? Having seen a little of their home draw against Manchester City and their recent win over Chelsea, they don't look a bad side and we may have to settle for a point this coming weekend.

Game 10 – Saturday, October 24, 3pm – Wigan Athletic – Home.
WELL, it had to happen sooner or later, but I would have preferred later. Our magnificent home run of victories has come to an end.

As I make my way to the ground and the pre-match pints at the White Hart, all seems to be well. I meet up with the two Johns at the pub and despite one John about to be made redundant at Christmas and the other John regaling me with his tightfisted money saving schemes, everybody seems in good humour and the Black Sheep ale is good.

Even the weather, which had been foul, wet and blustery, suddenly takes a turn for the better with the sun coming out to leave nearly 20,000 people completely overdressed.

Hardly has the game kicked off than we are treated to the beautiful sight of Robbie Blake leaving his opposing full back for dead before delivering an inch perfect cross with his left foot for Steven Fletcher to steer home from close range. What a start and what a boost for Fletcher, today returned to his more natural position leading the attack rather than stuck out on one of the flanks.

The only change from the defeat at Blackburn had seen Chris Eagles in for his first start of the season following his good showing as a sub last time out, with Nugent dropped to the bench. So an early lead, sun shining, all set fair for another three points, but then...

A harmless looking cross from the right is misjudged by the Beast, at which point he attempts to turn and crumples to the ground. The ball runs on to Hugo Rodallega who can't miss an open goal from a few yards out.

All square but the Beast is still down and it looks serious. After protracted treatment he manages to stand but is clearly hobbling and in this condition is undoubtedly a liability. Fortunately, before any damage can be done we manage to get Diego Penny on and the Beast leaves the field to a resounding ovation. He may have looked dodgy at Blackburn and cost us a goal here but the crowd know that over the last 12 months he has been our saviour on many occasions and that we owe him a big debt of gratitude.

Diego is now on for his Premier League debut and as previously noted is well short of big match practice, but now is the time for him to make his mark. Fortunately his last game was a man of the match performance in a 2-1 victory for the reserves at Manchester City in midweek, where he managed to twice save a penalty.

For the rest of the first half he is well protected by the defence and is virtually a spectator, as is the opposition keeper as the game hits a rather scrappy patch.

Our opponents from Wigan look more like a basketball team than a football team but having said that, they have a good shape and possess some more than decent players.

Up front Fletcher is having his best game yet for the Clarets, revelling in his favoured role. Against a huge defence he is winning more than his share of ball in the air and has good touch and mobility on the ground. Unfortunately nobody seems to be able to read or want to gamble on his headed flicks and they come to nothing.

The main problem seems to be the midfield with Elliott unable to make any impression and the two holding midfielders Alexander and Bikey giving away too much ball.

The start of the second half sees a great chance for the Clarets with Eagles bursting into the box on the right, but with players available square he goes for goal and puts it wide.

It's a great chance gone begging and how costly this turns out to be as after a quick break the ball is cut back to Rodallega on the left hand edge of the penalty area. He hits a fine shot which goes in low off the far post and gives Penny no chance.

Up against it now and we need a change to liven things up. This comes in the form of Nugent for Blake, and almost immediately we start to look menacing.

For a short spell we look like we can get level with Nugent causing all sorts of havoc and the Wigan defence holding on grimly, but from a set piece we concede again and it's all over. A left wing corner is flicked across goal to an unmarked Emmerson Boyce who sticks out his left foot to steer it past Penny, the keeper again having no chance.

A bit more huffing and puffing and Big Kev on for Bikey, a header from Carlisle hitting the top of the bar, but the result stays as it is.

Once again my tea is spoilt, and it will be a quiet night till the beer drowns the memory. It was a game we thought we could have won, but it just wasn't our day. Again we didn't take the few chances that came our way and were punished by a side that did.

I was quite impressed by Wigan although they did have a penchant for gamesmanship that we could have done without. I think they may surprise a team or two before the season is out and, having already beaten Chelsea, they could add more big name scalps.

Result: Burnley (Fletcher 4) 1, Wigan Athletic (Rodallega 11, 51, Boyce 76) 3.

Team: Jensen (Penny 15); Mears, Carlisle, Caldwell, Jordan; Eagles, Alexander, Elliott, Bikey (McDonald K 82), Blake (Nugent 67); Fletcher.

Subs not used: Duff, Gudjonsson, Guerrero, Thompson.

Attendance: 19,430.

Position in Table: 11.

Season Record: Played 10, Won 4, Drawn 0, Lost 6, Goals for 10, Goals against 22, Points 12.

My Saturday night is partially rescued by the news that Blackburn have lost 5-0 at Chelsea to remain two points behind us, albeit with a game in hand.

However, as I look at the results I am starting to get that sinking feeling as the clubs below us seem to be a lot nearer now than they were a week or two ago. A draw between Hull and Portsmouth does neither of them any favours, but wins for Birmingham and Bolton and draws for Wolves and West Ham are making me increasingly anxious.

Leafing through the papers, I come across an article that suggests Chelsea are to attempt to bypass the imposed transfer ban on incoming players during the January window. As previously noted, they stand to lose a significant number of players to the African Nations Cup in January, and this will seriously compromise their Premier League and Champions League ambitions.

They plan to use a tactic currently being employed by a Swiss side that are in a similar position. The ploy is to appeal against the original ruling and to be allowed to continue transfer activity pending the result of the appeal. Due to the protracted nature of the appeal process this would then allow them to bring in players during the window and their scouts are currently being instructed to monitor potential targets.

It's this sort of action that makes a mockery of the whole punishment in the first place. If they are allowed to get away with this it is another blow to the credibility of the football authorities' ability to control the 'super clubs.' Such actions are undermining the love and respect for the beautiful game and promoting a growing cynicism amongst the fans.

On a lighter note, I mentioned my mate's discussion of money saving tactics during the pre-match warm up at the pub. The whole discussion centred around redundancy and retirement possibilities as the three of us are now in our late fifties.

His advice was to take early retirement and basically cut our cloth to suit our purse. Now this sounded plausible until he outlined his plan, which included going to bed at 9.30pm to save on heating and lighting expenses and watching television with a blanket wrapped around him and his wife to avoid heating costs. Finally, having identified alcohol as a major expense, he said he planned to drastically reduce his intake. Now wouldn't you just want to slit your throat and get it over with?

He then went on to inform us that at our age, it was highly likely that in the next 10 years one of us would have 'popped our clogs.' Oh happy days! Needless to say I won't be following any of his advice, and I doubt very much will he.

It's Friday night, the eve of the last game in October, and a month that started so promisingly with the win against Birmingham has now turned a bit sour with two defeats following that victory.

Tomorrow it's the turn of serious strugglers Hull City to visit the Turf and it's a real six pointer. If we can take maximum points we pull seven points ahead of them, a not inconsiderable gap in this league, but if they take the points they close to within one of us.

This week has been a difficult one for Hull, as they have had to deny rumours that they have sacked manager Phil Brown, there have been revelations of serious financial problems and their chairman has resigned.

Brown, a pal of Owen Coyle, looks a condemned man and defeat at Burnley tomorrow will probably seal his fate, but I'm sure Owen knows there is no room for sentiment here.

With two difficult fixtures coming next, away at free spending Manchester City then home to high flying Aston Villa, points are a must tomorrow.

We need to get back to the high tempo we set in the early games when the novelty of the Premier League experience and the excitement of the crowd carried us to unexpected victories. The fans have a big part to play again tomorrow, let's hope they are up for it and can create that intimidating atmosphere once again.

Game 11 – Saturday, October 31, 3pm – Hull City – Home.
SATURDAY morning and the weather looks set fair, contrary to the forecast which predicted heavy rain in the morning improving in the afternoon.

After the usual family Saturday morning fitness room session followed by lunch, Stephanie and I head for the pub.

On arrival we are met with the two Johns, neither exactly looking at their best. One is recovering from what he terms "Horse Flu" and a week off work, while the other has been suffering from vomiting and hot flushes, which he puts down to Southend beer which he consumed during last week's visit to his mother-in-law, who resides there.

The game on the big screen is Arsenal v Spurs and as we get to the bar Robin van Persie puts Arsenal three up and ends it as a contest. We are impressed by Arsenal's speed and fluency for a few minutes but then they take their foot of the gas and the game becomes boring. We comment that both teams seem to move the ball much quicker than ourselves, as our build up often seems quite laboured. Perhaps it just looks that way on the telly.

A couple of pints of Black Sheep for me and we're off to the ground. On the way I express the opinion that there are not many games in this division where we start favourites but that this is probably one where we are slightly so.

We have the same starting eleven as last week with the Beast recovered from his ankle injury, whilst Hull are without their first choice keeper Boaz Myhill who has damaged knee ligaments.

The game starts fairly quietly with not much goalmouth action but we seem to be passing the ball well and Eagles is looking a threat down our right.

On 19 minutes, a good move down the right flank sees Mears racing into the box with players waiting in the middle for the cross. Suddenly he is sprawling on the deck with the referee pointing to the penalty spot. It all seemed to happen so quickly but I feel he must have had his legs whipped away as he was well set to make a telling cross and had no reason to go down.

Up steps Mr Reliable Graham Alexander and as usual makes no mistake from the spot. Great, just what we needed and probably just about deserved. We play out the rest of the half on the front foot, knocking the ball about well but unable to add to our tally.

The under fire Phil Brown obviously has strong words for his team at half time and they come out for the second half looking determined, forcing us backwards.

Then comes the deciding point of the game. We concede a soft free kick just outside the box. Hull's Brazilian playmaker Geovanni steps up to put the ball over our 10 man wall and despite getting his hands to it, Jensen fails to keep it out.

Cue celebrations from Geovanni and the Tigers which are quickly halted as they realise the referee has disallowed the goal and awarded a free kick to Burnley for pushing in the wall. A very harsh decision I think, and just the sort of thing that goes against you when you are struggling.

Geovanni also thinks it's a harsh decision but unlike me, decides to tell the referee something along those lines, which earns him a booking. Clearly still wound up by the decision a few minutes later he upends Fletcher and it's a second yellow and an early bath for the influential midfielder.

With the extra man it should now be game over, and shortly after it is as substitute Kevin McDonald sets up the marauding Alexander in acres of space to fire low past the keeper. The rest of the game is largely a one way procession towards the Hull goal but over-elaboration and poor finishing by us sees the game end 2-0 when it should have been more.

That result was just what we needed and re-establishes a bit of a cushion between us and the other strugglers. I have to say that although we probably merited the victory there is no doubt we got the benefit of the crucial refereeing decisions.

I couldn't help feeling slightly sorry for Phil Brown whom the crowd taunted with the chant: "You're getting sacked in the morning."

It was once again an illustration of how cruel the game can be when luck turns against you. Brown achieved an almost Owen Coyle-sized miracle in getting Hull to the Premier League and then managing to keep them there, but it seems he will soon be cast to the wolves.

Result: Burnley (Alexander 20 pen, 77) 2, Hull City 0.

Team: Jensen; Mears, Carlisle, Caldwell, Jordan; Eagles (Guerrero 85), Alexander, Elliott, Bikey, Blake (McDonald K 72); Fletcher (Nugent 78).

Subs not used: Penny, Duff, Gudjonsson, Thompson.

Attendance: 20,219.

Position in table: 10.

Season Record: Played 11, Won 5. Drawn 0, Lost 6, Goals for 12, Goals against 22, Points 15.

The month ends with two wins and two losses which is a reasonable return despite the disappointment of defeat to the Rovers. Good form at the start of the month, then a dip in the middle but finishing on a high gives us a points total as good if not better than we could have hoped for.

NOVEMBER

Off The Mark

UNUSUALLY for Owen Coyle, following the victory over Hull City he has a bit of a go at a section of the fans who have been critical of team selection and certain players in particular.

Defending our two goal hero he said: "Graham Alexander, at 38...it was an outstanding performance, not only because he got two goals. I was a little bit disappointed with some of the stuff I heard during the week. We lost a home game for the first time in nine months and all of a sudden everybody that knows how to pick a team was clamouring for changes.

"Graham Alexander doesn't get afforded a bad game. If Graham Alexander has a bad game it's because he's too old; it's not because he's just had a bad game like someone of 19 or 20. I showed loyalty to that group last week, and they've come up trumps again. I think the so-called experts should stick to what they're doing and let the guys in charge get on with picking the teams and trying to get the best for this football club."

He went on to stress the importance of the win. "This was a massive game for us because it puts seven points between yourselves and Hull. We'll not be kidded, we know that's a group of teams we're going to be in and about. We have to make sure we do our utmost to make sure in those types of games – similar to the Birmingham game – we come out on top.

"We did that, and some of the play, some of the movement side-to-side is everything I'm after. Now, having earned 15 points at home, we have to go on our travels and start picking up points. We've got a nice wee one at Manchester City! But we'll be ready."

Thursday, November 5, and a good day as my season ticket refund of £396, courtesy of chairman Barry Kilby's "Premiership Pledge," lands on my doormat. As a reward for purchasing my season ticket in the discount periods during the dark days of the Championship, the chairman has honoured his promise to give me my "Season in the Sun" in the shape of a free campaign of Premier League action.

In a lovely letter, he refers to me as "Dear Fellow Claret" and hopes I enjoy my season in the Prem. I almost feel like one of his mates now. No need to worry on that score, I would have enjoyed it with or without the refund.

I immediately text my work colleagues, both current and ex, who are of different persuasions, notably, Rovers, Bolton and North End, so they can share my good fortune, in spirit only of course. Quickest response comes from North End Ed, with some cheap shot. I point out to him that Preston could adopt the same scheme and it would cost them nothing as they would never have to pay out.

Coming up on Saturday is another difficult away fixture at Manchester City, the mega-rich millionaires bankrolled by 'loadsamoney' Arab investors.

139

This game would be worrying enough in view of our lamentable away record this season, but our concern is further aggravated by our abysmal record against them in recent history. In the last 20 seasons, the sides have met on seven occasions, resulting in one draw and six defeats, with five goals for and 24 against. Hardly the opponents you would choose to end a terrible away record against.

Game 12 – Saturday, November 7, 3pm - Manchester City – Away.
PERHAPS a good omen for this game is that we will be playing at a new ground for us, namely the City of Manchester Stadium at Eastlands, so maybe our fortunes will change here.

As the teams are announced, the uninitiated would believe this is a total mismatch, the total value of the Clarets on display reported as £7 million whilst their opponents weigh in at £160 million. However, we Clarets have learnt from the teachings of Owen Coyle that money guarantees nothing and on the field it will be eleven against eleven.

The day is a typical foul, wet November day in Manchester, ideally suited to our band of Brits, and not generally to the liking of the opposition's hotch potch of citizens of the world.

I find myself missing the kick off on the radio as I battle with the crowds in Tesco who fill the car park to overflowing and make leaving it like rush hour in Istanbul. By the time I make it home I am already receiving texts from Ed the North Ender. He has managed to get some live coverage, presumably through some dodgy foreign TV channel, and he reports a near miss early on by Blake.

Shortly after, as I am preparing to put my headphones on and clean the windows - I certainly know how to enjoy a Saturday afternoon - I get an abbreviated one word text saying simply "Pen."

Bloody brilliant. WHO FOR?

I am struggling to get the radio on and also attempting Sky Sports News when from somewhere I hear the name Graham Alexander. It can only be for us.

Can the penalty king do it again? He certainly can and unbelievably we have the lead in a game the bookmakers have given us odds of 12/1 to win. I learn the penalty is for handball by Joleon Lescott from a Mears cross.

With the radio commentary now being delivered direct to my head, I am stunned as Eagles sets up Fletcher and its 2-0. Cue nervous bookmakers in the Burnley area as the unthinkable is unfolding.

We continue to play magnificent attacking football until almost half time with no sign of the customary defensive collapse which we usually produce away from home.

But just as I am about to enjoy a 15 minute respite, City pull one back as a shot from Shaun Wright-Phillips takes a deflection off ex-City man Stephen Jordan which takes it past the Beast and into the corner of the net. How bloody cruel. Radio Lancashire commentator Scott Read and his ex-Claret summariser David Eyres can't believe it either.

I text Ed at half time with my thoughts that we are in for a second half battering, and my worst fears soon prove well founded. After 55 minutes, Kolo Toure levels the scores after a dubiously awarded free kick, and within three minutes we are behind to a Craig Bellamy goal.

Three goals conceded away again and in the space of 15 minutes either side of half time.

My half time text prediction has quickly come true and now we are really on the rack. The free flowing attacking football of the first half has disappeared and our opponents seem likely to score with every attack.

Shortly after we go behind, OC replaces Bikey, who has been yellow carded, and Blake with Gudjonsson and Kevin McDonald, and not long after Eagles gives way to Nugent. The game edges towards the close and on the radio I detect the stadium going quiet and almost a feel City think the game is won.

But there's a big shock coming up, as with three minutes to play Nugent picks out the head of Fletcher who cushions a header back across goal straight into the path of the onrushing Big Kev. I hold my breath as the commentators seem to take an age to confirm that Kev has in fact hit the net, but hit it he has and I am over the moon.

We play out the remaining time, plus the customary four minutes of added time, and we have it, our first elusive away point. We are indeed off the mark, and what a relief. A game we looked to have won, and then lost, is saved at the death and the minnows have once again shocked the big boys.

Writing in the Mail on Sunday, Joe Bernstein says: "The unpredictable nature of the Premier League was displayed in all its glory yesterday when the richest club in the world were held 3-3 by Burnley, the smallest team to play in the top flight since the league was founded in 1992."

He continues: "City have now drawn their last five matches and stand outside the Champions League places. Embarrassingly, their starting line up yesterday cost £160 million even without record £32 million signing Robinho, who is sidelined through injury. In contrast, Burnley spent just £7 million on their entire team.

Manager Owen Coyle, relishing his side's underdog status, said after collecting a first away point of the season: "We are the smallest town ever to have Premier League football. Getting promoted last season, given our limited resources, was a massive achievement but staying in this league would surpass that by far. Our fans were brilliant again and we will try to carry on playing football. At the end I was prepared to lose 4-2 to give us a chance of getting the equaliser."

In his match report Bernstein went on to say: "And as City fans howled their protests at the end, the truth is that Burnley could have returned home with all three points."

In conclusion he said: "As for Burnley – with four free transfers in their team and only three players costing more than £1 million – the have nots around the world will salute you."

Result: Manchester City (Wright-Phillips 43, Toure 55, Bellamy 58) 3, Burnley (Alexander 19 Pen, Fletcher 32, McDonald 87) 3.
Team: Jensen; Mears, Carlisle, Caldwell, Jordan; Eagles (Nugent 71), Alexander, Elliott, Bikey (McDonald 62), Blake (Gudjonsson 62); Fletcher
Subs not used: Penny, Duff, Thompson, Guerrero
Attendance: 47,205.

Position in Table: 10.

Season Record: Played 12, Won 5, Drawn 1, Lost 6, Goals for 15, Goals against 25, Points 16.

It's Sunday, November 8, and on a sad note I learnt today of the death of an old friend and Claret folk hero, Billy Ingham, the 'Ginger Pele.'

Billy was just about the most modest man I have ever met, and liked nothing more that a pint, a fag and a bet. He never craved the limelight and I believe was as happy driving buses in Burnley and Pendle as he was playing football, most of which was at a high level. Who can forget his brilliant solo goal in the 1-0 win against Chelsea when he completely bamboozled the giant Mickey Droy before volleying home?

Although in recent years we had lost touch apart from when we met at rare family occasions, my wife and I will always remember happy times with Billy and his first wife Susan as we celebrated Saturday nights, which usually culminated in the pair of us propping up the bar at the Angels nightclub whilst the girls danced.

Billy was an honest trier, a really likeable guy and a sad loss at the age of only 57.

The City game completes another block of four games ahead of another blank weekend dedicated to internationals. This block of four saw us starting badly with two defeats but ending better with a home win and then the first away point.

Four points from a possible 12 was not the greatest return but it kept things ticking along and gave us 16 points in total after almost a third of the season. If we could average this sort of return over the remaining two thirds, we will be comfortably home and dry, but there's a long way to go yet and no doubt lots of twists and turns.

Morale in the camp seems as good as ever and despite the three serious injuries, there is still plenty of competition for places. We've had some heavy defeats but OC has managed to keep the players' heads up and the home form, apart from the Wigan blip, has been unbelievable. For my own part I am still finding myself rubbing my eyes and wondering if it's all a dream, but the league table tells me it's not.

Another weekend break coming up then to rest my shattered nerves, and after a pretty crap week at work, I think I will be ready for it.

I was hopeful of a big windfall on Saturday morning when I heard that there were two UK winning tickets sharing a total of £90 million in the Euro Millions lottery, particularly as I had just paid my share of the syndicate to 'Rover Nige' or the 'T-Man' as he has taken to calling himself after getting a job with Ringtons.

But this was a forlorn hope as the bloody berk failed to get the numbers on in time. He then told us not too worry as we hadn't lost and he had credited our accounts with £1.50 each. I promptly texted him to tell him he was a dead man walking and to never show his face in Harle Syke again.

On Monday, November 16, Scottish national team manager George Burley is relieved of his duties after a hopeless 3-0 defeat to Wales in Cardiff. His reign yielded only three wins in 14 games and his dismissal was inevitable following failure to qualify for the World Cup final tournament.

Immediately, and by now quite understandably, Owen Coyle's name emerges as a possible candidate. Cue anxious moments for Clarets fans.

However, hopefully these fears are groundless as on Tuesday the 17th, the great man himself says: "I love it at Burnley. My job is here and that's what I will look to continue to do. I have a job here to do what we are doing in the Premier League and I don't want any distraction ahead of the game against Aston Villa on Saturday.

"I am the Burnley manager. I have been in the position before when there's been advances from other clubs. I have always said I am loving everything I am doing at the football club and that remains the case, so I think that would tell everybody my feelings."

Well I think we get the picture from that OC. Let's hope the Scottish FA do.

Wednesday, November 18 and it's the day of Billy Ingham's funeral, and what a horrible day it is too. It's the sort of seeping, wet, miserable, cold day on which you want to be playing the likes of Arsenal, with a packed Turf Moor baying for blood, but that will have to wait a couple of weeks yet.

The turn out for 'Ginger Pele' by his ex-colleagues would I'm sure have brought a smile to this most unassuming man's face, and to have ex-international footballers carry the coffin is a testimony to the esteem he was held in by his peers. Leighton James, his old mate from their days lodging together, gave a lovely speech and described him as a legend in the town. It was a very moving tribute to the popularity of Billy.

This type of occasion, which saw the mixing of former big name players like Leighton, Frank Casper, Martin Dobson, Paul Fletcher and many more, along with us mere mortals who knew Billy as friends and neighbours, is I believe unique to towns like Burnley and reflects the tight bond between the people of the town and its adopted sporting sons.

The Plumbe Street Miners Club might not be the swankiest place in town, but it is just the place that Billy would choose to go for a pint and a game of cards or dominoes, and was a fitting place for his family, relatives and old colleagues to raise a glass to him.

Back to the action, and after what seems an age without football, it's the Villa up on Saturday at the Turf, and all set for another cracker. The Villains are sure to pose a major threat with the attacking pace of Gabriel Agbonlahor and Ashley Young and the physical presence of John Carew, but our confidence following the City game should be sky high.

Let's hope we can maintain our recent impressive scoring form of five goals in the last two games, and give Villa something to think about at the back to curb their attacking threat.

Game 13 – Saturday, November 21, 3pm – Aston Villa – Home.
SATURDAY at last and a foul, wet one at that.

Stephanie and I make it to the pub without too much of a soaking, although she is complaining that one of her boots is letting in water. It's incredible that somebody with as many pairs of shoes as Imelda Marcos has none that are waterproof.

As I approach the pub door, I find that mine too have suffered the ravages of time and I am condemned to an afternoon with a soggy right foot.

A good crowd at the White Hart and it's jam-packed at the bar, but my pint arrives and we watch a bit of the lunchtime kick off, Liverpool v Manchester City, on the pub's big screen. Liverpool are leading 1-0 but City are pressing and deservedly level as Emmanuel Adebayor has a free header in the box.

In the space of the next seven minutes both sides score again with defending that can best be described as chaotic. As I watch I come to the conclusion that for all the money spent by both these teams, there is really little difference between them and us.

We arrive at the Turf in showery, blustery conditions and kick off attacking the Cricket Field End with the wind behind us.

Villa have a full strength line up with the feared attacking three who I previously mentioned all starting, and for good measure, £12 million signing Stewart Downing and England forward Emile Heskey are on the bench.

However, it's the Clarets who are making the early running, and on nine minutes we are in front. Robbie Blake sends in a curling free kick, aided by the wind, from the left flank and skipper Steven Caldwell rises between the defence and keeper to head the Clarets in front. The home crowd, already in good spirits despite the bad weather, are lifted even higher and the sizeable Villa contingent is silenced.

The atmosphere is again electric and the noise levels awesome as we continue to dominate the first half with only rare forays from our much fancied opposition.

Andre Bikey goes close from a Fletcher set up as the striker continues his run of good form since his switch to a central role. The team is functioning well in all departments and it's difficult to see a weakness.

The Mail on Sunday's reporter Leo Spall commented: "The home side over-ran Villa in the first half and while the second period was more even, it was hard to tell which team held credible top four aspirations."

Despite our dominance we go in at half time with just the one goal lead but well pleased with the manner of the performance.

The second half sees the weather deteriorating as the rain comes down harder and the wind, now against us, seems to strengthen.

Villa, with the wind at their backs and no doubt subject to a half time rocket from manager Martin O'Neill, start to take the game to us. We are looking to catch them on the counter and are giving them sufficient concern to prevent them going all out for it.

As the game edges towards the close and legs start to tire, the substitutions start to appear, Villa putting on the aforementioned Downing and Heskey, whilst we replace Eagles, Fletcher, and Blake with McDonald K, Nugent and Gudjonsson respectively.

Entering the last five minutes, we are coming under increasingly frantic pressure and unfortunately concede. We fail to clear a corner sufficiently and the ball is recycled into the box for Heskey to nod in.

What a tragedy we couldn't hold out for the maximum points, but we'll take the one and reflect on how close we were to beating a side currently in the top four.

I think the most satisfying thing about the game was that we didn't look out of place against a top side. There was no desperate chasing of shadows and we were able to compete in all departments as equals.

There's no doubt that we are developing into a solid Premier League team and the quality of football we are playing is worthy of the top league. It's a measure of how far we have come in a short period of time that we made our way homewards slightly disappointed that we had not beaten our illustrious opponents.

It was Owen Coyle's second anniversary as Burnley manager and who would have believed two years ago what we would achieve? It is truly fantasy football at Turf Moor these days and 2009 will go down in our history as a year of 'vintage claret.'

Result: Burnley (Caldwell, 9) 1, Aston Villa (Heskey, 86) 1.

Team: Jensen; Mears, Carlisle, Caldwell, Jordan; Eagles (McDonald K, 69), Alexander, Elliott, Bikey, Blake (Gudjonsson, 81); Fletcher (Nugent, 74).

Subs not used: Penny, Duff, Thompson, Guerrero.

Attendance: 21,178.

Position in Table: 10.

Season Record: Played 13, Won 5, Drawn 2, Lost 6, Goals for 16, Goals against 26, Points 17.

Monday, November 23 and the televised game on Sky is Preston North End v Newcastle United.

PNE are currently enjoying a poor run of form with only one win in the last seven games, and have dropped out of the Championship play off places. It's a game guaranteed to make my mate Ed miserable.

I text him in the early evening to see if he is feeling edgy and twitchy like Harry Redknapp, and does he think Preston can win? No, no, and no is the response, so I text again to tell him to keep me informed as I have no Sky.

After 15 minutes we have the following text exchange:

Ed – North End look like the away team. Looks ominous.

Me – Perhaps they are lulling them into a false sense of security.

Ed – No.

Me – Perhaps they are adopting an Italian style 'catenaccio' defensive strategy before unleashing a brand of 'total football' as favoured by the Dutch in the 70's.

Ed – Bollox.

Me – Perhaps they should revert to thumping it at Parkin's head and hoping for the best.

Ed – God, we are shite.

There's no cheering some folk up is there? I can remember when we were shite, but only just. He was right though. They lost 0-1.

Tuesday's Burnley Express runs a story headlined: "Board remains upbeat despite record losses."

The story says Burnley Football Club have recorded record pre-tax losses of £11.7 million for the last financial year ending June 30th,

2009. However chairman Barry Kilby is confident that promotion to the Premier League should more than compensate for the alarming deficit. Apparently the figure has been aggravated by bonuses paid to staff on achieving promotion.

The post-tax operating loss was £8.9 million, while interesting figures in the accounts were an uplift in the wage bill from £9.76 million to £13.42 million in the year, and an increase in turnover from £8.57 million to £11.192 million.

Mr Kilby said in his statement: "The increase in turnover from being in the Premier League should more than compensate for the losses incurred over the past few years and I expect to report a significant profit for the financial year to bring our balance sheet back into a healthy position.

"Immense credit must go to Owen Coyle and his team. Appointing Owen as manager in November 2007 was probably one of the best management decisions the board of directors have ever made. That decision had already been vindicated had we not achieved promotion, but to do so showed the leadership skills Owen clearly possesses in abundance. Now we are here it is the intention of the directors to do all we can to stay in the elevated company in which we find ourselves."

Major contributions to the growth in turnover came from match income and television rights which rose from just under £5 million to £7.3 million, figures largely related to the great runs in the Carling and FA Cup and the play off games. Club shop sales also rose from £824,000 to £1.12 million.

The report went on to say: "The directors feel that this debt is manageable in the context of the considerable increase in revenues as a result of the achievement of Premier League status for the 2009/10 season. These losses are being funded in a number of ways. Once again we are indebted to certain directors who have increased their loans to the company, and to our season ticket holders.

"However there is no doubt that we will need to manage the finances of the club with great care in the coming 12 months while still striving to maximise the resources available to Owen Coyle in order to preserve the hard-won prize of a place among English football's elite clubs."

Thursday morning and we've slipped into the bottom half of the Premier League after Wednesday's evening games, in which we don't feature. A 3-0 home win for Fulham over Blackburn Rovers prevents the enemy from going above us, but the downside is that Fulham leapfrog us. In the other game, Hull edge out underperforming Everton 3-2 to get within two points of us, albeit having played one game more.

No need to panic yet but with two away games coming up next against strugglers West Ham and Portsmouth, away points would be very much appreciated.

A quick glance at the morning paper before I leave for work suggests Burnley have beaten Celtic, Charlton and some other lot to the signature of the young Cork City centre back Kevin Long. Clarets Mad later report that the player is flying over to Burnley today to complete the move. They say we have beaten off competition from Celtic and Everton with interest also being shown by Preston.

The player is just 19 years old and has already been called up for the Republic of Ireland under 21 side. Hopefully this deal will be completed and follows the signing the previous day of 16-year-old Neil Yadolahi, another centre back from the Republic of Ireland, on apprentice terms.

OC certainly seems to be continuing the policy of recruiting promising young talent and developing it, and this augurs well for the future. Driving home, I hear 2BR Radio announce the signing of Long for a six figure fee.

Game 14 – Saturday, November 28, 3pm – West Ham United – Away.

SATURDAY sees us back in the capital for an away game at West Ham United.

Last season we were so successful against the London clubs in the Carling Cup that we celebrated by bringing out a DVD entitled "Capital Punishment." This time round, our trips so far have not proved so fruitful with a 4-0 reverse at Chelsea topped by a 5-0 loss at Tottenham.

Still, the Hammers are not in the same class as those two and have only managed two wins so far this season. On the back of our improved away form of late, we have to be optimistic of some return here.

The game starts as it inevitably does these days with us taking the play to our opponents and looking positive. A narrow escape for the home side as a Clarke Carlisle effort is cleared off the line maintains my optimistic outlook. The Radio Lancashire commentators seem delighted with both teams' desire to play the ball on the ground and think we are in for a footballing treat.

But then in predictable fashion, the wheels fall off. First from a quickly taken free kick by Scott Parker, we are caught napping and its 1-0 on 18 minutes. I listen fearfully as I try to busy myself with domestic chores almost expecting the next blow, which duly arrives on 33 minutes.

The next goal is going to be crucial. One for us and we are back in it, another for them and it's curtains. Before we can reach the sanctuary of half time, it's curtains, and a penalty to add insult to injury.

I switch off Radio Lancashire as I can't take any more, and opt for Jeff Stelling and Sky Sports, hoping against hope that this will change things for the team. How ridiculous.

Not long into the second half and number four arrives, to be followed shortly after by another penalty and 5-0.

Why, oh why, do we defend so bloody hopelessly away from home when at home we seem to be able to contain even the best teams? Five goals against a struggling side make me once again fear for our survival chances despite our magnificent home form.

Substitute David Nugent, on for Blake, then contrives to miss two good chances but realistically they would have only been consolations. Nugent's arrival prompts a change of formation with Eagles switching to the left flank and Elliott to the right and we go 4-4-2.

Eagles, clearly enjoying himself, sets up Fletcher on 68 minutes, and with almost a replica, we get a second on 74 minutes. All of a sudden our hosts look a little twitchy and another now will really have them rattled. That almost happens as Eagles hits the outside of a post.

In injury time Steven Caldwell is sent off for a professional foul, but there is still time for Eagles to add a third and suddenly the score looks almost respectable.

That though is the problem. The three late goals, although very welcome, have papered over the cracks. The fact is the game was well and truly lost by half time and five down early in the second half could have seen us buried as badly as Wigan in their recent 9-1 drubbing at Spurs.

From not being able to score away from home in the first four games, the next three have yielded EIGHT goals, but unfortunately only one point. We have to stop the unending flow of goals against.

It may be time to look at the formation. Matt Le Tissier suggests in his report on Sky that strangely we looked more solid as a 4-4-2 than we did at 4-5-1. This situation however may have been influenced by the state of the game and an easing off by the opposition with the match already won.

However, it has to be said that the scoring of the three goals was vital to our goal difference and managed to keep us above Blackburn and Wigan. By the end of the weekend we have dropped to 12th but it could have been worse.

Result: West Ham United (Collison 18, Stanislas 33, Cole 43 pen, Franco 51, Jimenez 64 pen) 5, Burnley (Fletcher 68, 74, Eagles 90) 3.

Team: Jensen; Mears, Carlisle, Caldwell, Jordan (Kalvenes 55); Eagles, Alexander (McDonald K 70), Elliott, Bikey, Blake (Nugent 55); Fletcher.

Subs not used: Penny, Duff, Gudjonsson, Thompson.

Attendance: 34,003.

Position in Table: 12.

Season Record: Played 14, Won 5, Drawn 2, Lost 7, Goals for 19, Goals against 31, Points 17.

On Sunday I am in Liverpool visiting Stephanie and eagerly awaiting the FA Cup third round draw. Surely we must be due a home tie now?

Nobody texts me to let me know we've drawn a 'biggie' and on arrival home I find we are away at League One MK Dons, a potential banana skin. It's difficult to imagine a more unappetising draw but that's what it is and we'll just have to make the best of it.

DECEMBER

Festive Cheer?

ALREADY it's December and the season of good cheer is almost upon us, or is it? For us Clarets fans, 2008/09 was certainly a season of good cheer and we fervently hope that 2009/10 continues to be so.

After a relatively sparse month of action, with only three games in November, December sees us much busier with six fixtures which will take us into the second half of the season. It's a month that could be very influential in whether our season ends in mid-table glory or valiant failure.

On paper, it does not look the most difficult sequence with three away games and three at home, and only one of these against a top four outfit, that being Arsenal at the Turf on Wednesday, December 16. The other home games are Fulham on the Saturday before that Arsenal clash and the Boxing Day fixture with Bolton Wanderers. Away, we face bottom of the table Portsmouth this coming Saturday, with Wolverhampton and Everton making up the three.

With our good home form, we would hope to take some points at the Turf, and if we are to survive in this league, a point at least at Pompey and Wolves should be a target. Everton too are underperforming badly this season and if we could get something there on Monday, December 28, it would end the year nicely.

However, while not wanting to repeat myself but doing just that, I have to say again matches aren't played on paper and if I could predict results with any accuracy I wouldn't be stuck in an office all day long.

Come to think of it, I may not be soon, as today being the first of the month is Premium Bond draw day and ERNIE may just be set to make me a millionaire. I will be up early tomorrow awaiting the knock on the door from Agent Million, and the start of my new life as a jetsetting playboy. Needless to say, the knock on the door never came and it's back to bloody work again on Monday.

Friday, December 4 is draw day for the 2010 World Cup final stages, and I'm so excited that I forget all about it until I receive a text whilst pushing the trolley on the weekly shop in Tesco in the early evening. It's from one of the Johns and he is inquiring as to who we got in the draw and why nobody has mentioned Scotland, from where he claims to come.

I make a mental note to check the draw on Teletext when I get home and reply to him that you have to win some games to qualify and then you can be a part of the draw. It's so long since they got there that he can't remember how it works.

On arrival home I am delighted to find England's opponents in the group stages will be Algeria, Slovenia and the USA. Whilst not wishing to belittle anybody or count chickens before they have hatched, we should certainly be good enough to dispose of that lot.

In usual over the top fashion, Saturday's newspapers have us as good as in the final, and incredibly have produced pull out guides to the finals with wall charts to map the team's progress. Now I might be wrong but I don't think the games start till June. Who the hell is going to keep a blank wallchart for the next six months, and where would you put it? I think I'll bin mine and wait till they inevitably produce another one in June.

Game 15 – Saturday, December 5, 12.45pm – Portsmouth – Away.

WHAT can I say about this one? Not much I'm afraid, as the unending succession of away defeats continues, albeit broken by the draw at Manchester City, where we contrived to throw away a two goal lead and then snatch a late equaliser.

I don't know about the players, but it's getting demoralising for us fans. Here was a game, even more so than last week, where we looked to have a real chance of getting an away win. Our hosts are a team in turmoil, rooted firmly at the bottom with a new, sinister looking manager in the shape of Avram Grant, and players who last month had, not for the first time this season, not been paid.

But conversely, if you were in their position, who would you most look forward to playing at home? Yes, Burnley, they of the colander defensive formation.

Before the game, which is moved to the early kick off spot and featured live on Sky, I ask Stephanie, who has now returned from her studies in Liverpool for a five week holiday, how many she thinks we will concede today and we are both optimistic and go for three.

The defence is forced into a change at centre back due to Caldwell's suspension and Bikey drops back, with Big Kev McDonald coming in to midfield.

Under the impression the game kicks off at 1pm I sit down to eat lunch and switch the radio on to hear the unmistakeable sound of live commentary at 12.52. I am delighted and surprised to learn that we are seven minutes into the game and still not behind.

I listen and eat, content in the knowledge that we are playing well and as usual taking the game to our opponents, who sound pretty woeful. I am now so confident that I leave the lounge and head upstairs to fit a digibox on the bedroom television to resurrect its function following the digital switchover.

But I am soon brought crashing back to earth with my wife's shouts indicating a penalty to Portsmouth, and head back to the lounge. The Radio Lancashire commentators are incredulous and outraged by the decision and believe it to be a case of blatant cheating.

Why, oh why, do we continually seem to be on the receiving end of these crap decisions? I bet at the end of the season when the number of penalties against each team is quoted in some obscure anorak's statistics, we will easily top it.

But God has decided to intervene on this occasion in the shape of Brian 'The Beast' Jensen, and he saves the pathetically taken kick. So on we go to half time, making and missing chances as only we can do.

Into the second half and I am informed I am going out. My wife Julie wants new Christmas tree lights and I am the means of transport to get her to them.

Before we leave the house, the Sky Sports News reporter says if this game was being played at Burnley we would be 3-0 up by now, and confirms that Pompey are the worst team he has seen.

Looking good then, but don't you believe it. Before I can get through the door, on 65 minutes Hermann Hreidarsson puts the basket cases ahead.

I optimistically shout upstairs to Stephanie to text me if we equalise but make the short journey to Homebase anxiously awaiting news on the car radio. No joy on arrival so it's into the store and down to Stephanie now.

It must be getting desperately close to the end as I examine the twinkling lights and fake Christmas trees. I'll settle for a point now. Then there it goes, the unmistakeable buzz and vibration in my trouser pocket. A text! Not even words, just 2-0, and the finality of it sinks in and my spirits drain. Not in the mood now so the lights stay on the shelf.

Eight away games played, lost seven, drawn one, the last two defeats to teams at or near the bottom. I'm lost for words and crestfallen. We made chances but we missed them. It's the same old story with the same old result.

Manchester United have played the same last two fixtures as us in reverse. Last week they were at Pompey and won 4-1, while today they have been at West Ham and won 4-0. Given that, how the hell did we manage to beat them?

Manchester City, where we have managed our only away point, beat Chelsea 2-1 at Eastlands. What can I say?

Result: Portsmouth (Hreidarsson 65, Dindane 84) 2, Burnley 0.

Team: Jensen; Mears, Carlisle, Bikey, Jordan; Eagles (Guerrero 73), Alexander, Elliott, McDonald K, Blake (Thompson 68), Fletcher.

Subs not used: Penny, Duff, Kalvenes, Gudjonsson, Easton.

Attendance: 17,822.

Position in Table: 13.

Season Record: Played 15, Won 5, Drawn 2, Lost 8, Goals for 19, Goals against 33, Points 17.

In The Sun newspaper of December 8 is the staggering revelation that none other than Prince Charles is a secret fan of the Clarets.

The article, entitled "Princely support for Burnley FC" goes on to say: "The heir to the throne has taken a keen interest in the Lancashire town since a visit in 2005. His charity the Prince's Trust has an office in Burnley, and he has called the "remarkable town" his number one priority."

"It has now emerged that the Prince keeps an eye out for the Clarets' results and would like to visit their ground Turf Moor for a game. He made the admission in a private conversation with the club's director John Sullivan at a gathering in Holyrood Palace in Edinburgh.

"Mr Sullivan said: "The Prince was delighted at the progress made by the club and has expressed a desire to visit us and see the good work we do in the community for himself, should his diary allow." This is Burnley's first ever season in the Premiership. They stunned

163

champions Manchester United in August with a 1-0 victory at Turf Moor, their first home game in the top division for 33 years. A Clarence House spokesman said any conversation between the Prince and Mr Sullivan was private, but added that Charles's links with the town were well known."

Well, well. They don't come much higher profile as a celebrity fan than Prince Charles. It certainly puts Alastair Campbell and John Kettley down the pecking order.

Perhaps we could turn this to our advantage by getting him to imprison anybody who dares to score against us on the grounds of treason. I hope he does get the chance to come and sample the fantastic atmosphere of a full Turf Moor and I'm sure he would get a tremendous reception. Perhaps he should pick a game when it is Ladies Day so that Camilla can enjoy the occasion too, and join the other 'Ladies' on a right royal Clarets girls' booze up. Now that would be an eye opener for her.

Wednesday, December 9 and I'm mentally reviewing the season to date. The thought crosses my mind that after a dream start we are falling away a bit in terms of points won. The record shows just two points from the last four games, coming from the draws with Manchester City and Aston Villa.

However, a quick look at the results doesn't bear out this theory of diminishing points return. After 15 games, if we split the season so far into three blocks of five matches, there is a close correlation between them. The first five yielded six points, then six and five respectively.

If this form were to be repeated over the full season it would give a total of 43 points, which should be sufficient for the all-important

164

preservation of our elevated status. Interestingly enough, that number of points last season would have put us exactly in the position we currently occupy, ie 13th.

I think what is making me increasingly edgy is the fact, or perception, that the teams below are closing the gap, and indeed it is true we are slipping down the table.

However, what is certainly happening is that with the odd exception the top teams are regularly beating the bottom teams home and away. Now this may seem obvious and indeed it is, but what it can do is skew the table at any one time, depending on recent fixtures. For example, a month of games against the 'big four' can see a near zero points return and a catastrophic slide.

This confirms the belief that we have to pick up as many points as we can against the teams around us and below us and hope that the title contenders then do the business on them as well.

This seems to be working out for us in terms of home results but the recent away defeats at West Ham and Portsmouth are exactly what we don't need. Even a point each from these games would have been important in maintaining a healthier points differential.

Currently the bottom five are Portsmouth, Bolton, Wolves, West Ham and Hull and with games against two of these this month, results will be crucial. We also have games against Fulham and Everton who are similarly placed to ourselves and from whom we should look to profit. A real bonus would be points from Arsenal next Wednesday at the Turf, but let's take all three from Fulham first.

I'm sure OC will be telling the players to take it one game at a time, learn from the losses and enjoy the victories.

Game 16 – Saturday, December 12, 3pm – Fulham – Home.

SATURDAY at last and as I enjoy the pre-match pints, Theakston's Black Sheep today, I take in a bit of the lunchtime kick off game, Stoke City v Wigan. The score at present is 1-1, which is probably the best result for us as it keeps Wigan below us and Stoke within reaching distance three points ahead.

Suddenly and from completely nowhere I see probably the best goal ever scored in a Premier League game.

A foul by Stoke in the Wigan half sees Latics' Honduran full back Maynor Figueroa spot the Stoke keeper off his line as he takes a quick direct free kick. From a distance of 61 yards and with a velocity of 49 mph, the shot arcs over the despairing Thomas Sorensen's outstretched arms and flies into the net. It is a moment of pure magic that stuns the whole of the stadium.

How tragic that Wigan can only keep the lead for two minutes before they concede a soft goal from a corner as parity is restored much to the delight of the crowd of Clarets in the pub. In almost predictable fashion Wigan then contrive to miss a last minute penalty and have to share the points. What a cruel game football can be.

Pints finished it's off quickly to the Turf and hopefully a demolition of Fulham, who are currently enjoying a good run of form putting them in the top half of the table, but who haven't won at Burnley since 1951, the year of my birth.

166

We have one change to the starting line up from last week with Steven Caldwell returning from suspension, ironically at the expense of last week's man of the match Kevin McDonald.

We start the game in dodgy fashion and Fulham make the early running, giving the Beast some early saves to make which he does with some style. They are knocking the ball about well and I feel somewhat uneasy.

However, as the first half continues we settle down and start to play a bit ourselves with Chris Eagles looking particularly effective.

I know what is making me feel uneasy. The visitors won the toss and set us to attack the Jimmy McIlroy Stand end first, which is never a good omen. We seem to be doing OK, but are a bit physically mismatched against tall but athletic opposition.

However, half time duly arrives with the scores level at 0-0, and I head down for a bit of 'relief' and to get Stephanie a cup of what is, at £1.60, probably the most expensive tea in Europe.

Half time texts from PNE Ed inform me that the Sky reporter at the game thinks it's a poor one. I reply that it's not poor but fairly even, but I still feel uneasy.

The second half starts as the first finished with both sides trading blows, but nothing looking too threatening. After about five minutes an opportunity opens up for Wade Elliott but he fails to trouble the keeper and almost instantly I feel more uneasy.

From a quickly taken free kick around the half way line, we are as usual half asleep at a set piece. Bobby Zamora, who has been a handful all afternoon, is left one on one with Caldwell, easily beats him for pace and shoots past the Beast from a tight angle.

The goal was very similar to the one created by Scott Parker at West Ham, when his quickly taken free kick allowed Jack Collison to score. We need to be much more alert at dead ball situations, they are costing us dearly.

The goal is the cue for a change of tactics by us as we bring on Nugent as the second striker and go 4-4-2, with Elliott going wide right and Eagles wide left as Robbie Blake is sacrificed.

Almost immediately we seem a more potent force with Nugent's thoughtful and powerful burrowing runs at the defence, and on 60 minutes we are level as Jordan's cross finds its way to Elliott in the box and his arcing volley is in as soon as I see it leave his foot.

The Mail on Sunday reporter described it as follows: "From the left, Stephen Jordan hoisted the ball high into the Fulham area. It fell to the unmarked Wade Elliott and he calmly lofted it past Mark Schwarzer and suddenly the stands were ablaze with passion. You could feel the tension, see the effort, marvel at the running as both sides went for the winner, with Burnley underlining their commitment with a second striker, David Nugent, sent on to partner Steven Fletcher.

"While Burnley responded with fire, Fulham continued to play their interesting triangles with Zoltan Gera sent on to add strength to midfield. Fire often looked like winning as Schwarzer found himself being put under pressure. Chris Eagles should have done better with a free kick from the left but he drove it high and wide with players lining up. He was replaced but as Burnley continued to press in the closing minutes the 'final ball' malaise continued to afflict them."

Towards the end of the game, Kev McDonald came on to replace Bikey and his willingness to involve himself at the hub of all the plays was instrumental in driving the Clarets on. I think it can only be a matter of time before he claims a regular starting position in the midfield engine room.

It finished 1-1, but was it a point gained or two dropped? I think taking the game as a whole, a draw was a fair result, but on a weekend when results at the bottom didn't really go our way, how we could have used those extra two. Fulham, not a bad side, still haven't won at the Turf since 1951, and long may it continue.

Next up is Arsenal at home on Wednesday and today they have just won at Liverpool, so they're going to be pretty confident. Let's hope for a cold night and a hostile, noisy crowd, and then we'll see.

Result: Burnley (Elliott, 60) 1, Fulham (Zamora, 50) 1.

Team: Jensen; Mears, Carlisle, Caldwell, Jordan; Eagles (Guerrero 86), Alexander, Elliott, Bikey (McDonald K 77), Blake (Nugent 56); Fletcher.

Subs not used: Penny, Kalvenes, Gudjonsson, Thompson.

Attendance: 18,397.

Position in Table: 13.

Season Record: Played 16, Won 5, Drawn 3, Lost 8, Goals for 20, Goals against 34, Points 18.

Not for the first time this season, the Clarets Mad messageboard has rumblings of discontent among some of the fans regarding tactics and team selection following the second successive home draw and the disappointing recent away defeats. No doubt this is fuelled by the tightening up of the bottom half of the division and the narrowing of the points gap between us and the relegation strugglers.

Everybody, including myself, is an expert of course, despite never having played the game outside of school football, and many of these 'experts' are now beginning to openly criticise aspects of OC's judgement. This is heresy and who amongst us can have the temerity to question a manager who only six short months ago had achieved a God-like status among the fans?

It's another illustration of how fickle the supporters can be, but also of how the tension is beginning to get to them. Let's hope this tension does not start to spread to the players on the pitch who are still managing to produce a standard of football not seen at Turf Moor in many years.

Much of the dissent appears to revolve around the centre back pairings and the playing of Andre Bikey in a midfield role. However, also coming in for some keyboard criticism are previous 'untouchables' such as Robbie Blake and Wade Elliott.

Arsenal is another extremely tough ask, but a win against all the odds would no doubt do wonders to dispel the nervousness that is starting to descend as we approach the season's halfway point.

News is filtering through on the BBC website that Arsenal have serious injury concerns ahead of the game whilst there are rumours that we may soon have long term injury victims Martin Paterson and Jay Rodriguez available.

Wolverhampton Wanderers, fresh from a much needed and unexpected 1-0 victory at Tottenham on the previous Saturday, have an even harder away fixture at Manchester United on Tuesday, December 15. Controversially, Wolves manager Mick McCarthy decides to rest 10 of the players who achieved that victory and effectively fields a reserve team at United.

The reasoning behind this strange decision is that this is a game they are unlikely to get anything from so he wants to keep his players fresh for a match on the coming Sunday which he feels they have a realistic chance of winning. And their opponents in that Sunday clash? None other than good old Burnley.

Now this raises a number of interesting points, not least the effect this decision has on other clubs involved in the race for the title, as it effectively gifts three points to one of the challengers. Will Wolves make this even all round by taking the same course of action at Chelsea, Arsenal and Liverpool?

Secondly, what does this say to the poor old suckers who have forked out mega-bucks for a ticket and travelled on a winter's evening up and back down a crowded M6? "You shouldn't have bothered," sounds like the answer to me.

Thirdly, how do the players who achieved the victory against all odds at Spurs feel knowing the club has likely now surrendered three points without giving them the opportunity to fight for them? I would think they will be feeling pretty disappointed by this decision.

171

It's impossible to imagine OC ever making this particular move, his philosophy being that he tries to win every match, and surely this has to be the right approach.

Predictably and deservedly Wolves lose at Old Trafford 3-0. That surely heaps the pressure on them to beat us now or the whole thing will put Mick McCarthy in a very difficult position.

Game 17 – Wednesday, December 16, 7.45pm – Arsenal – Home.

WE set off for the game dressed fit for a Polar expedition following forecasts of dire cold weather conditions. This is just what we want against our Southern foes, who have a team packed with players from sunnier climes, with the exception of the dangerous cold-blooded Russian assassin Andrey Arshavin.

All the predicted Arsenal injuries have magically healed overnight and they send out a pretty much full strength side against us. OC, recognising the need to counteract the speed of the Gunners down the flanks, makes one change in personnel, Kevin McDonald in for Robbie Blake, and also a tactical switch to 4-3-3, allowing the pacy Chris Eagles and Wade Elliott to nullify the threat on the wings and pose their own problems.

The omens are better this time as we start the game attacking the favoured Cricket Field End in front of an almost capacity crowd which includes a good following of Arsenal fans. There's something a bit special about night games with a full house, especially against the top sides. The crowd are invariably 'up for it' and tonight is no exception.

Minutes from the start, we are almost ahead as a goalbound Clarke Carlisle header comes off the head of an Arsenal defender and beats keeper Manuel Almunia but hits the bar. We have our tails up and the crowd is roaring encouragement.

Then inexplicably but all too familiarly we self-destruct. Bikey, on the edge of his own box, decides to dilly and dally while 20,000 fans are urging him to clear the ball. Facing his own goal he looks like he is about to embark on a mazy dribble round the Beast before circumnavigating the whole defence and then launching a defence splitting long ball. Not so. What he is actually doing is freezing on the spot to allow one of the best midfielders in the country, Cesc Fabregas, to pick his pocket and slide the ball home.

Stunned by this setback, the defence then goes into a period of calamitous schoolboy defending which should see us three down in the first 15 minutes, only for Arshavin to be denied by the post and Fabregas to fire wide. We seem to have granted good old Cesc the freedom of Turf Moor as he imperiously strolls around without sight of a marker, wreaking havoc at will.

But Arsenal fail to capitalise on their superiority and the Clarets slowly start to play their way into the game, encouraged by a vociferous crowd.

Bikey continues to have one of those games where he seems to be in a different time zone to everybody else on the pitch and is regularly caught in possession. Fortunately Big Kev has taken up where he left off at Portsmouth and Eagles is proving a real handful.

Suddenly, Andre comes to life as a ball into the box sees him head it on and as he goes on to 'pull the trigger,' he is downed by the Arsenal defender Thomas Vermaelen. Penalty it is, and there is little protest as the referee points to the spot.

Up steps Graham Alexander, the penalty king, who has never missed one yet for the Clarets, and I immediately start to think will this be the first. No need to worry as Graham, cool as a cucumber, bangs it straight in and we are level with the mighty Arsenal.

For the remainder of the first half we continue to have the bulk of the possession and are giving as good as we get. The half time text from North End Ed suggests we will go on to win it, but having seen our defending, I reply that we will need to score five to do so.

The second half continues in similar vein and Eagles almost breaks the deadlock with a delightful run taking him into the box on the right hand side, his powerful shot cannoning off the post.

Arsenal seem to be getting a lot of possession but our previously sieve-like defence has now become a ring of steel protecting the Beast and they can find no way through.

We continue to hit them on the break although we now have a trigger-happy linesman to contend with. For some reason this guy, who couldn't spot an offside for love nor money in the first half, can now see them everywhere in glorious Technicolor. What a prat.

The crowd rise as a man as McDonald lays on a pass into the box for Fletcher to hit the net, only to be silenced by our flag-waving friend. TV replays subsequently show the goal to be good and we are once again robbed by an incompetent official.

The game ends all square, the third consecutive 1-1 draw at the Turf, but there is no disappointment for the home fans who are delighted by the performance.

This was truly Burnley, driven on by fantastic support, back at their battling best and on their day as good as anybody in this division. If the draw against Fulham was two points lost, this was definitely a point won after overcoming a horror start.

Result: Burnley (Alexander 28, pen) 1, Arsenal (Fabregas 7) 1.

Team: Jensen; Mears, Carlisle, Caldwell, Jordan; Alexander, McDonald K, Bikey (Gudjonsson 70); Elliott, Fletcher (Blake 83), Eagles (Nugent 83).

Subs not used: Penny, Kalvenes, Thompson, Guerrero.

Attendance: 21,309.

Position in Table: 13.

Season Record: Played 17, Won 5, Drawn 4, Lost 8, Goals for 21, Goals against 35, Points 19.

Next day, the national press and media are full of praise for the Clarets and the BBC sports website carries a very good blog by Phil McNulty in which he reviews the different approach taken to this week's games by OC and Mick McCarthy.

The report is entitled "No white flag for Burnley's Coyle" and goes on: "Owen Coyle is not in the business of hoisting the white flag as Burnley's response to facing the Premier League's biggest names. As a result of this approach, some might even call it unorthodox in the light of recent events, Coyle found himself facing a searching inquisition on the subject of Wolverhampton Wanderers after his side took a deserved point off Arsenal.

"Wolves boss Mick McCarthy's decision to effectively concede defeat when he wrote out his team sheet at Manchester United was still a hot topic at Turf Moor after another meeting between the top flight's haves and have-nots. Burnley's stand of taking on Arsenal – "standing toe-to toe" in the words of Owen Coyle – could not have been further removed from the surrender that so angered the Wolves fans who shelled out to watch their reserves meet an inevitable end at Old Trafford.

"Ironically, the bold manner in which Burnley set about Arsenal, even after gifting Cesc Fabregas an early goal, offered support for both sides of McCarthy's argument. There is a new vulnerability about the Premier League's top teams this season, an opportunity to claim points that were not on offer in previous seasons.

"So the route forward has to be the way outlined by Coyle after this thrilling draw when he said: "I always feel we can win any game and that's the way we go about it."

"On the other side of the debate, Burnley played with such vibrant freedom and desire that you almost saw the logic in McCarthy saving his best for the meeting of the two teams at Molineux on Sunday – until you came to your senses that is. How did the Wolves players who sweated to win at Spurs feel about being left out at Old Trafford? What has happened to the momentum built up by that outstanding victory at White Hart Lane?

We're not worried: John and Judy W smile for the camera as the Blades fans fail to get into the party mood.

Glamour Girls at Wembley: left to right, Stephanie, Julie and Judy W get ready to grace our national stadium.

Smiling through: The author, third from the right, mouth open, attempts to disguise his pre-Wembley nerves in a bar on the stadium concourse.

The dream begins: Captain Steve Caldwell lifts the Play Off trophy at Wembley.

Where did all their fans go?: The view from the author's seat at Wembley shows the difference between winning and losing as 36,000 Clarets celebrate while approximately 36 Blades supporters remain in the stadium.

Party on, guys: The town of Burnley is delirious as the victorious team tour the town in an open top bus on their return from Wembley.

You're staying, right?: Has Martin Paterson had a premonition of things to come as he wags a finger at Owen Coyle during the open top bus parade?

One is a Claret: Burnley chairman Barry Kilby, left, presents a personalised club shirt to slightly uncertain Prince Charles, watched by the club's operational director Brendan Flood, second right, and chief executive Paul Fletcher.

"Yes, the hectic fixture list can be questioned, but Burnley also played at the weekend and where is the concrete evidence that they put less effort into a draw against Fulham than Wolves did in winning at Spurs? The judgement on McCarthy's actions will start when Burnley come to town and the final reckoning will follow when Wolves either stay up or go down at the end of the season.

"One thing is for sure. If Wolves do not beat Burnley, he will have some explaining to do.

"As a general principle, though, give me the manager who thinks he can win every game rather than the one who limply accepts there are times when his team have no chance. In other words, Owen Coyle.

"Burnley's record once the team coach gets 30 yards away from Turf Moor is atrocious, but do not expect their fans to be making vocal demands for their cash back because Coyle has sent out a team designed to get what he regards as an inevitable defeat out of the way. It is not in the Scot's psyche."

Reviewing the game, McNulty went on: "If fortune favours the brave, then Burnley and Coyle's approach will be rewarded and they showed what they are all about on another fevered night at Turf Moor. The one and only Stuart Hall, in between revealing in the match programme that he was once banned from Burnley's press box for making fun of the chairman's wife's hat - "an upturned chamber pot decorated with outsized floribunda" - waxed typically lyrical about Coyle's approach. "To feet, to space, to attack. Football is tribal. To most teams it's win at all costs. To Owen Coyle and his superb team its win in style." Coyle's team drew in style against Arsenal and provided a resounding answer to those who may be tempted to copy the McCarthy theory that states, in football terms, that there are days when you might as well just hand over your pocket money to the biggest boys in the playground."

Summing up his review, McNulty concluded: "This was an uncomfortable night for Arsenal, who failed to build on a win at Liverpool that had Wenger announcing they were "mentally and mathematically" back in the title race. And the reason for their discomfort was that Burnley's first choice team, inspired by their manager's example, had the guts, heart and belief to take on opponents even they would admit are superior in most aspects of the game. Burnley got the reward of a point that could prove vital at the end of the season. There might just be a lesson there."

On Friday, December 18, news is circulating on the local radio stations that Burnley have made an inquiry about taking young Arsenal and England Under 21 starlet Jack Wilshere on loan till the end of the season. Interviewed on Sky Sports News, OC confirms that he would indeed be interested in taking the player, as he would any other good young player.

There seems to be real substance to this rumour though as Arsenal manager Arsene Wenger goes on to confirm that he would allow the player to go to Burnley.

"I said it is possible, as long as he plays," said Wenger. "Burnley is a very good club and they play good football. We need to ask Jack if he wants to go there and we need some assurances from them that he will play. I like the idea, but we are a bit short at the moment. Jack has been in nearly every squad this year."

On Saturday night, after Manchester City edge out Sunderland in a 4-3 thriller to go sixth in the table, manager Mark Hughes is sacked. Not only do they sit in a healthy position in the table but they are also Carling Cup semi finalists. Clearly this is not good enough for their obscenely rich owners and Sparky has to go. What a disgrace.

Game 18 – Sunday, December 20, 1.30pm – Wolverhampton Wanderers – Away.

WELL, after all the furore surrounding Mick McCarthy's 'resting' of his first team during the week, it's time to see if indeed it was justified. Or will the Clarets, fresh from their morale boosting effort against Arsenal, take the points and heap the pressure on Mick?

Once again it's a peculiar kick off time and day, done for the benefit of Sky TV of course, and I opt to go for radio coverage rather than the box.

I have been studying the league table at lunch and the ramifications of a likely defeat. Things will not look good if it happens but we can't yet hit the bottom three.

Interestingly enough we actually moved above the enemy Blackburn Rovers yesterday without kicking a ball, following their defeat at home to Spurs and the damage inflicted on their goal difference. However a win for recovering Pompey over hapless Liverpool again closes up the points differential.

I reckon that the top nine in the table are probably safe, and the dogfight will be between 11 clubs for the three relegation places.

Unsurprisingly, we go with the same team that started against Arsenal, and equally unsurprisingly Wolves make nine changes, restoring the first team for the challenge of mighty Burnley.

The game starts in unspectacular fashion although Radio Lancashire's commentator doesn't sound too impressed by our early efforts.

On 15 minutes the inevitable happens as from a Wolves attack Matt Jarvis fires in a shot that Jensen saves, but none of our defence gets to the loose ball before Nenad Milijas who puts the home side ahead.

The commentators continue to bemoan our lack of belief and determination as the game drones on. On 34 minutes we lose Clarke Carlisle, presumably injured, to be replaced by Michael Duff for his first outing of the season. Nothing much seems to happen and after what seems like an age the first half ends with us 1-0 down.

In the second half, we start more brightly but after a brief spell of pressure, we concede the second as Caldwell is outmuscled by the puny Kevin Doyle to fire the hosts into what should be an unassailable lead.

We then bring on David Nugent for Andre Bikey in an attempt to get back in the game and our hosts sit back to hold their lead. On 68 minutes we lose the second centre back Caldwell and, having already replaced the natural stand-in Bikey, we are forced to go with a makeshift pairing of Alexander and Duff in central defence. Joey Gudjonsson replaces Caldwell, who I again presume is injured.

I sort of half listen to the rest of the game as I am somewhat distracted by a phone call from my wife who informs me that she has got stuck in snow and had to abandon her car about a mile from home. While I wait for her to walk home I listen on in the vain hope of a West Ham-style revival, but it's not to be today.

We have plenty of attacks but no real guile to carve out clear cut opportunities and our hosts have their third win in four games, shooting them up the table to 12th, the position we occupied at the start of the day.

So nine away games played, eight lost and today never a chance of it being anything else. Now we are only five points ahead of the bottom club and three ahead of third bottom Bolton who have two games in hand.

The next match marks the season's halfway point and guess who it is? Yes, Bolton for a Boxing Day derby at the Turf that should have the fur flying.

Result: Wolverhampton Wanderers (Milijas 15, Doyle 50) 2, Burnley 0.

Team: Jensen; Mears, Carlisle (Duff 34), Caldwell (Gudjonsson 68), Jordan; Alexander, McDonald K, Bikey (Nugent 53); Elliott, Fletcher, Eagles.

Subs not used: Penny, Blake, Thompson, Guerrero.

Attendance: 27,410.

Position in Table: 14.

Season record: Played 18, Won 5, Drawn 4, Lost 9, Goals for 21, Goals against 37, Points 19.

Not for the first or the last time following an away defeat, there are rumblings of discontent among some of the fans. Again these revolve primarily around team selection and tactics, some feeling that OC is too loyal to some players and not giving others their chance, and that tactically he is naïve.

Obviously the defence and goalkeeper are most often named as the culprits but going largely unnoticed is the fact that in the last four games we have scored only twice, one of those being a penalty.

Of course everybody has their own ideas on the team's problems and this is one of the joys of being a fan, but significantly most fans that voice their opinions have different perceptions of the problems and correspondingly different solutions.

These opinions and ideas are rapidly multiplying as we approach the January transfer window and the increasing sense of nervousness kicks in.

Recently we have seen some change in the starting line up and almost certainly we are about to see more as the defence appears to be in for major patching up due to both Carlisle and Caldwell being considered major injury doubts following the Wolves game.

To add to the problem Andre Bikey will shortly be leaving to join Cameroon for their Africa Cup of Nations tournament, which could see us severely challenged in central defence.

It remains to be seen if there are funds available for team strengthening in the window, but for sure the clamour for new faces is intensifying daily, as I'm sure it is at all 20 Premier League clubs.

Game 19 – Saturday, December 26, 2pm – Bolton Wanderers – Home.

I LIKE Boxing Day home games. After the excesses of Christmas Eve and the big day it's nice to get out in the cold fresh air and get some male company again.

Unfortunately, Burnley don't seem to like Boxing Day games and I can't remember the last time we won one. Last season Christmas coincided with our worst run of the season with five consecutive league defeats, something we definitely don't want this time.

Our opponents today are Bolton who are having a fairly miserable season and languish in the bottom three, although they have games in hand.

I hit the pub a little earlier than usual due to the police deciding they want to start the game an hour early, presumably so they can get home in time for some festivities.

I am met by John G who informs me he has shook the hand of a celebrity in the pub, none other than departing Radio Lancashire presenter and celebrity Clarets fan Tony Livesey. Tony is about to leave his very successful Radio Lancashire early morning show for Radio Five Live. Good luck to him.

Unfortunately, he is being replaced by the returning Graham Liver, a notorious Rovers Fan who has also been stadium announcer at Deadwood Park. Looks like I will have to change my radio station for the drive to work.

There's a good crowd in the Turf and they are already generating a lively atmosphere as the game kicks off. The early exchanges don't bring about any real scares at either end as we struggle for fluency and Bolton, looking every inch a bottom three outfit, attempt to test the Beast from distance, leaving him largely untroubled.

We have been forced into changes at the centre of the defence due to the injuries to Carlisle and Caldwell, and this gives us a pairing of Bikey and Duff. David Nugent is the other beneficiary, getting a rare starting opportunity. I am glad to see Bikey restored to defence and I think he is too as he dominates in the air and generally looks much more comfortable than in midfield.

On 25 minutes, Bolton's towering defender Zat Knight is caught dithering in his own penalty area a la Bikey versus Arsenal. Elliott whips the ball off him and delivers the perfect low cross to the waiting Fletcher who has only Jussi Jaaskelainen to beat. It's surely a certain goal, but horror of horrors, he pokes it wide.

What usually happens when we miss a sitter? Yes, you've got it. From a free kick on our left side about 25 yards out, Bolton's Matt Taylor strikes it "exquisitely," as Owen Coyle later described it, over the wall and into the corner of the net.

Trailing to the worst side we have seen at the Turf all season and it should all have been so different. We play in fits and starts to half time without really threatening an equaliser and we need a big improvement in the second half.

Thankfully, that's just what we get and from the off we are making and missing chances in all too familiar fashion. We have certainly stepped up a gear and the football is flowing down both flanks through Eagles and Elliott. Big Kev McDonald almost levels it with a magnificent left footer that crashes down and out from the underside of the bar.

Is it going to be one of those days? No! On 56 minutes Eagles switches the attack with a ball from left to right finding Mears. Tyrone's push forward to Elliott is then rewarded by a measured cross which finds Nugent rising magnificently to head home unstoppably.

We then proceed to batter Bolton mercilessly, missing chances as we go and being foiled by some magnificent goalkeeping from Jaaskelainen. Bolton make substitutions that are greeted with cries of derision from their fans, and poor old Gary Megson must be the most unpopular manager in the Premier League.

Try as we may, and driven on by the now fanatical support, we can't find the winner and for the fourth consecutive home game have to settle for a 1-1 draw. We go home knowing it's two points dropped but still happy with the magnificent flowing football being served up.

This game marks the halfway point in the season, and in 10 home games we have lost only once. The standard of fare being served up at home is fantastic and if only we can reproduce some of this away from the Turf we will be safe.

Result: Burnley (Nugent, 56) 1, Bolton Wanderers (Taylor, 29) 1.

Team: Jensen; Mears, Duff, Bikey, Jordan; Elliott, Alexander, McDonald K, Eagles: Nugent, Fletcher (Blake 80).

Subs not used: Penny, Kalvenes, Edgar, Gudjonsson, Guerrero, Thompson.

Attendance: 21,761.

Position in Table: 13.

Season Record: Played 19, Won 5, Drawn 5, Lost 9, Goals for 22, Goals against 38, Points 20.

Game 20 – Monday 28th December, 15.00 – Everton – Away.

GAMES come thick and fast at Christmas and no sooner has one been put to bed then the next one is up.

And so we head to Merseyside for a Monday afternoon game at Everton. Our hosts are not enjoying the greatest of seasons with injuries being a major factor and currently sit just below us in the table. However, victory today would reverse the positions.

This is going to be a difficult game for me to follow as, in accordance with time honoured tradition, today is 'potato pie day,' which is one of our annual feast days at this time of year. This consists of the visit by friends to partake in family games and drinking, with the main event being large helpings of home made 'tater pie and mushy peas.' The day is topped off by a visit to the pub to ensure the pie is thoroughly swilled through the system.

Clearly it would be rude to subject our guests to a radio commentary of our anticipated struggles with the Scousers.

About five minutes before kick off I am sat at my computer writing the report of our almost glorious effort against Bolton when I receive a text from North End Ed. He has managed to pick up the game on some computer channel with what he claims to be a good signal and says he is looking forward to it. I text him back to let him know we are having guests and for him to keep me informed.

186

The guests are not expected till four so I should get good coverage of the first half at least and usually by half time the game is out of sight anyway. I sit at the computer with my mobile phone and I have so much technology to hand it's almost like Mission Control at Houston.

First text in after 10 minutes reports all Blues so far. Nothing for a while then I get "Everton all over you then you create three chances and miss them all." Bloody typical.

I decide this is not a good way to follow the game and put on my earphones and tune the mobile's radio to Radio Lancashire for the usual away day torture. At the same time I try to find a computer link and after a minute or two I get a magnificent picture of the Beast looming large on the screen and settle for this.

How strange. My radio commentary is ahead of the action on the screen so I am actually watching soccer history. It's all a bit frustrating especially as after about five minutes, the picture freezes with only the Beast in view. I decide to opt for the low tech option so switch off the computer and go with the radio.

Surprisingly, time has ticked on and we have made the sanctuary of the half time dressing rooms without conceding.

In his own unfailing way, the commentator immediately then condemns us with the kiss of death. He informs us that this is only the second time this season in an away game that we have made it to half time with no goals against, the other being at Portsmouth where we went on to lose 2-0.

How could he? If he had thought about it, he could have kept his trap shut but no, he had to blurt it out and seal our fate.

Guests are arriving so I have to head downstairs and switch off the radio. I am in Ed's hands now.

I am getting roundly thrashed on the Nintendo Wii bowling game when the text comes: "Jordan sent off." Bloody marvellous.

I look at my watch. I reckon about 15 minutes to go. Can we hold out for a point?

The answer, as I always secretly knew it would be, is no, as inside the last 10 minutes we go one down. This is inevitably followed at the death by a second and incredibly our away record now stands at played 10, lost 9, drawn 1, and we have one point from a possible 30.

Thankfully this is the last away game of 2009. Surely 2010 must bring us some success away from Turf Moor.

I later learn both Mears and Jordan picked up bookings so both regular full backs will miss the away FA Cup tie at MK Dons. Perhaps this is not a bad thing as they will serve their suspensions in a game that whilst important is not as crucial as the pursuit of league points.

Result: Everton (Vaughan 83, Pienaar 90) 2, Burnley 0.

Team: Jensen; Mears, Duff, Bikey, Jordan; Elliott (Blake 85), Alexander, McDonald K, Eagles; Nugent (Kalvenes 63), Fletcher (Thompson 81).

Subs not used: Penny, Gudjonsson, Edgar, Guerrero.

Attendance: 39,419.

Position in Table: 14.

Season Record: Played 20, Won 5, Drawn 5, Lost 10, Goals for 22, Goals against 40, Points 20.

So December saw six games played and only three points from a possible 18. Hardly festive cheer.

However the performances in most cases were better than the results and we have to hope that our luck is about to change. Nobody thought that it was going to be easy and they were right, but we have more points than most people imagined possible and we still have a fighting chance.

Now is no time for faint hearts. We have to keep our belief and go for it. January sees the opening of the transfer window and already we are linked with a host of new faces. Let's hope some arrive to bolster the cause.

Today, December 29, Ed tells me Preston have sacked their manager Alan Irvine. He is another victim of the vicious circle that is soccer management.

All the clubs in the Championship are searching for what we have got, an Owen Coyle. Thank God we got him first.

JANUARY 2010

Treachery. We Are Undone!

FIRSTLY, may I wish all my readers a Happy New Year, nay a Happy New Decade.

Who could have predicted at the start of 2009 what was to happen during that fantastic year? But this time round, the events of the last day in December leave me wondering what is about to unfold in 2010.

I am strolling round Harrogate on a pre-New Year outing with wife and daughter, who have money burning holes in their purses, when I am drawn to looking through the window of a brightly lit pub. On the screen is the not so shocking revelation that Bolton Wanderers have sacked their manager Gary Megson.

No surprise there, but soon comes the realisation that once again Owen Coyle's name would be appearing on the bookmakers' list of favourites for the vacant post.

OC, as a past player and good friend of their chairman Phil Gartside, is an obvious candidate. Indeed it was Gartside who recommended Coyle to Burnley chairman Barry Kilby, thereby initiating the trail of events that subsequently led us to the Premier League.

Not too concerned about this. I expect to hear Owen rule himself out of the running and to a large extent he seems to do so. However, as with previous rumours he doesn't categorically end the speculation. Hmm.

It then transpires that we are unlikely to sign David Nugent in the January window. His club Portsmouth, once again in dire financial straits and facing a winding up petition over unpaid tax and VAT payments to HMRC, are so desperate for cash that they need to sell any asset they can. But we are unwilling or unable to meet the fee and the player's likely wage demands so unless we can extend the loan he is on his way back.

FA Cup third round – Saturday, January 2, 3pm – MK Dons – Away.

ONCE again we face an away cup tie, this time at League One MK Dons, who were formed from the original Wimbledon FC. Due to our abysmal away record, we are viewed by the media as the Premier League team most at risk of a shock early exit.

I am out and about around kick off time and can't get to a radio, and by the time I do the game is already a few minutes old.

I learn that Nugent is not in the squad as presumably Portsmouth do not want him cup-tied. Mears and Jordan both miss out as they are suspended and are replaced by Richard Eckersley and Christian Kalvenes. Caldwell and Carlisle are still injured so Duff and Bikey make up the centre of defence.

Robbie Blake comes in for Nugent and despite our strange defensive line up we have gone for a fairly strong side. Surely today, against inferior opposition, we can break the away day jinx in what is the first game of a new decade.

No early scares and after an early tactical switch, bringing Blake back slightly and going 4-5-1 from the opening 4-4-2, we start to establish some dominance over our hosts.

The radio commentary hints at a lack of passion and atmosphere in the ground and this can only work in our favour. Normally in an away tie against lower league opposition, we would expect an 'up and at 'em' early barrage, particularly as we are now 'big time Charlies.' But this just doesn't seem to materialise and by midway through the first half we are in control and going forward.

An error from the Dons full back sees possession conceded to Fletcher who makes his way into the box from the right hand side. He is confronted by another defender and cleverly pushes the ball past him as he goes down over his protruding leg.

Penalty! A rather soft one it seems but we've had our share given against us. Up steps Mr Dependable Graham Alexander and as usual it's no contest as he finds the corner and we are ahead.

Then 10 minutes later, we have the comfort of a two goal cushion as Eagles and Fletcher link cleverly for the latter to fire home.

We coast to half time at 2-0 and suddenly we don't look so much to be the most at risk big boys. Our radio friends think we should be four up but I am quite relaxed about the 45 minutes to come and can enjoy a half time cup of tea.

The second half continues in the same vein with Elliott hitting the bar and Fletcher the post before a belated barrage about 15 minutes from time from our hosts.

It appears too little too late until MK score what can best be described as an 'agricultural effort.' In usual style we fail to adequately clear a route one long throw by some giant recently introduced into the fray, and the recycled loose ball is turned in to give the Dons something to shout about at last.

Despite the customary four minutes of added time, there are no real scares and we are on our way to Wembley again.

We've broken the away duck and we are unbeaten in 2010. Could this be our year?

Result: MK Dons (Morgan 89) 1, Burnley (Alexander 25 pen, Fletcher 35) 2.

Team: Jensen; Eckersley, Duff, Bikey, Kalvenes; Elliott, Alexander, McDonald K (Gudjonsson 71), Eagles; Fletcher (Thompson 88), Blake.

Subs not used: Penny, Edgar, Easton, Guerrero, Harvey.

Attendance: 11,816.

As I watch the highlights later on Saturday night TV, I see assistant manager Sandy Stewart sent out to do the press conference, which is unlike OC. Immediately the media sense a possible story of OC's imminent departure for Bolton and probe Sandy as to why he is taking the post-match interview.

193

Sandy fields it nicely if not totally convincingly by stating that OC has had to leave the stadium quickly to make a flight to Scotland to spend some New Year time with his parents.

However, the Sunday papers are reporting that he was seen in the tunnel 45 minutes after the game ended. Hmm! The Mail on Sunday are convinced he is as good as gone and once again we are left wondering what the hell is going on.

I have to say that I am a bit puzzled by the speculation. Sure OC has close ties with Bolton but a move there would only be a sideways step, not an upward one. Of course money may be a strong consideration, but I guess we are already paying him fairly well to keep the bigger fish at bay.

What concerns me more than anything is the timing of this unwanted diversion, with the month long transfer window now open and the Clarets desperately in need of a new face or two. Please, please, let's not have total disruption now at this crucial time of the season.

For the moment we are left to sit and stew but on this occasion I don't think for long.

Anyway, guess who is the most at risk Premier League side? Yes, the champions Manchester United who go out 1-0 at home to League One Leeds.

And as for our next opponents on the road to Wembley, well it's away again to the winner of the Liverpool v Reading replay. God wants us to do it the hard way!

By Monday, the national and even the local media are convinced that OC is going. How the hell could he? We are at the most crucial part of our season with just under half the games to play, the window open and deals presumably in the pipeline, and he is contemplating jumping ship.

People react differently in these situations and I check the messageboards to gauge the fans' feelings. Of course, there is the whole spectrum, from those who think we should thank him for what he has done for us and wish him well, to the practical types who say it was only a matter of time anyway, and finally those, like myself, whose initial reaction is one of anger and disbelief.

The focus of this anger is the whole bloody timing of this episode. If he had given it a full season and we were relegated he could have gone and everybody would have thanked him for 'an incredible journey.' If we had stayed up he could have gone on to better things and again everybody would have thanked him and looked forward to the next battle against the odds.

But this is unbelievable. We are in a relegation dogfight and he is going to a club that is in it with us and is perceived by our fans as no bigger or better than ourselves.

On Monday afternoon, the media report that Coyle has met with Bolton chairman Phil Gartside during his visit to his family in Scotland and he is returning to discuss the situation with Burnley chairman Barry Kilby on Monday evening. Burnley FC say they will not be making any further statements until after this meeting.

Around 10pm, news emerges that both sides have agreed to consider their position overnight and no statements will be forthcoming before Tuesday afternoon at the earliest. It looks like Barry has made a good shot at persuading OC to stay but we all fear the worst and it is like waiting for the axe to fall.

Personally I feel Barry should have sat him down and played him the Phil Collins song, "No Son of Mine" with the chorus:

"He sat me down to talk to me
He looked me straight in the eyes
He said:
You're no son, no son of mine
You're no son, no son of mine
You walked out, you left us behind
And you're no son, no son of mine."

I think that would have reflected what most of those wonderful fans Owen often liked to praise would now be thinking.

Just after 1.30pm on Tuesday, January 5 comes the official announcement from the club that Owen Coyle wished to leave Burnley FC to take up a position with Bolton Wanderers.

How do I feel? Gutted, stabbed through the heart by someone we thought was a friend and an adopted son of Burnley. Owen could have become a legend in Burnley and enjoyed the status of icons like Harry Potts and Jimmy McIlroy, but he has tainted the glorious episode he wrote in our history. He has gone from God to Judas, and hero to zero in less than one week.

All Coyle's fine words about building something at Burnley and football not being all about money have been shown to be hollow.

That's the worst thing at the end of the day. A guy we thought was genuine turned out to be just as shallow and self-centred as all the rest, and some of the magic surrounding Burnley FC has died.

I am sure that at some point in the next few days or weeks I will be able to write a more reasoned piece about this tragic event, but at the moment I am just too bloody angry to see it any other way.

So what now? We do the only thing we can do and move on. The king is dead, long live the king, whoever he may be.

Who do we want to replace him? Perhaps another 'chosen one,' such as Jose Mourinho. I think he may still be a bit out of our price bracket.

Early bookmakers favourites are Darren Ferguson, son of Sir Alex, and ex-Claret Michael Phelan, currently with Sir Alex at Manchester United.

Not Darren for me. He has no top flight experience. Phelan? Perhaps. He has ties with the club and aided by ex-Clarets already here such as Steve Davis and Martin Dobson he might be able to do something.

My preference would be for a short term appointment of somebody with Premier League experience to get us through the 18 games that will decide our future. My choice would be ex-Reading boss Steve Coppell, who would fit the bill in terms of experience and managing on a tight budget. He also has the pedigree of having played at the top level, which would command the respect of the players.

Also in this category and of the right age for a challenge is Gareth Southgate, the ex-Middlesbrough boss. I'm sure over the next

197

few days a whole host of possibles will be linked but we can only hope that an appointment is made sooner rather than later to give us a chance in the January window.

I have to confess to having some sympathy with the players who bought into OC's dream and followed him to Burnley only to be left high and dry mid-season. Let's hope whoever comes in will see them as part of his plans.

One thing is for sure, life at Burnley FC is never dull. Anything can and does happen here.

Friday, January 8, and we have now had approaching a week of the whole sorry saga of Owen Coyle. The manager, having stated his wish to leave for Bolton, is sidelined on 'gardening leave' as the chairmen squabble over the compensation figure. Meanwhile Steve Davis is given the role of caretaker manager for the home game against Stoke City.

What will be the reaction of the players to these events? Who knows? But it is vital that we get something from the game.

The reaction of the fans is easier to predict as they are backing the club 100 per cent and castigating the now despised Coyle. I can't help but feel Coyle has shot himself in the foot with his part in this sordid affair, but only time will tell.

For sure, the reaction in the national media is one of disbelief and condemnation of his actions.

Meanwhile, the bookies are having a field day with a range of candidates for the new manager. At its peak at least 40 names are being quoted, from realistic to the wildest flights of fantasy. I really can't imagine Kevin Keegan or Sven Goran Eriksson being interested, nor for that matter the Burnley board pursuing them.

Early favourites seem to be Phelan, Coppell and Peter Reid, but by later in the week Paul Lambert of Norwich City and Paolo Sousa of Swansea are emerging as front runners.

This is of course very distressing for the fans of their respective clubs, and we are in danger here of damaging our reputation by pursuing the same tactics as Bolton. However, it could justifiably be argued that we are in a 'dog eat dog' situation, the gloves are off, and anything goes. Watch this space.

By Friday lunchtime, the snow and ice and expected sub zero overnight temperatures lead to the postponement of the Stoke game and, as later becomes clear, Steve Davis's last chance to lead the side is lost.

Compensation is agreed between the clubs at an as yet undisclosed figure and Coyle is free to join Bolton. Good riddance.

Paul Lambert rules himself out of consideration for the manager's post, but now Simon Grayson of Leeds United is being strongly rumoured as a front runner along with Lee Clark of Huddersfield Town.

The Premier League programme on the Saturday is decimated by the weather and only two games go ahead. These are mostly irrelevant to the relegation battle, with only Everton from the bottom half of the table involved. The Toffees earn themselves a very creditable draw at Arsenal, and look to be easing themselves into mid-table safety.

On Sunday it is revealed that caretaker manager Steve Davis and goalkeeping coach Phil Hughes have also left the club, presumably to join Coyle at Bolton, and also chief scout Cliff Roberts.

Youth team manager Martin Dobson and coach Terry Pashley are put in temporary charge pending the appointment of the new manager. This is all getting slightly worrying and I can see myself having to both pick the team and play if things continue in this vein.

On Monday, January 11, Coyle holds his first press conference at the Reebok Stadium, at which he tries to explain away his defection from the Clarets.

He cites the lack of available transfer funding at Burnley as the reason for his departure, claiming that even if he could have got us survival this time, he didn't feel there would have been sufficient funds in place in the summer to avoid a struggle next time. He feels that in a transition stage he was trying to push the club on faster than the finances would allow.

So no mention here of his 'old chestnut' that he would only have left us for Celtic or Bolton. If this is the real reason for his treachery then surely he would have left us for any other Premier League club and at least 75 per cent of the Championship clubs.

No. The truth is that Owen has got too big for his boots and has started to believe the hype that has built up around him.

What has happened to all the rhetoric of how he loves the place and what we are trying to build? What has happened to the vision of building the phoenix from the ashes? All gone and with it all our coaching staff. The heart has been ripped out of the club and bang in the middle of the season.

Coyle knew what the budgets were before the season started and before he signed his four year contract with the Clarets, but that was before an apparently better offer appeared. Those magnificent fans who enjoyed every minute of the ride to promotion and beyond, who sang his name fervently as the messiah, are now ditched with barely a mention.

All we hear now is what he can do for Bolton. Well, good luck to them, and let's hope for their sake the next offer from Celtic is not coming soon.

He was a hero in Burnley but now most people would cross over the street if they saw him coming.

They would have wrote a book about him in Burnley, but now his treatment of a fine club and exemplary employers will merit only a couple of pages in the history of this great and famous club. He has damaged us, but I fear he may have damaged himself more.

We may only be a small town, but that engenders a fervent loyalty, and when you kick one Claret you kick us all. We are feeling well and truly kicked now, but we will recover and led by the quiet dignity of the finest chairman in the Premier League, Barry Kilby, we will have our revenge.

On Wednesday, January 13, and after a week of torment and misinformation by the press, the Clarets appoint their second manager in Premier League history, Brian Laws.

Now, I have to say that for many fans Brian is not the number one, or for that matter second or third choice, and his appointment is not greeted with dancing in the streets.

Brian started his career with the Clarets as a young right back and left the club 26 years ago, a victim of the John Bond era. He went on to have a very successful playing career, earning top honours at Nottingham Forest during Brian Clough's wonderful reign.

His managerial career has covered Grimsby Town, Scunthorpe United and most recently Sheffield Wednesday, where he was recently relieved of his post after a run of poor results. How could he have imagined when sacked by the Owls, who were near the bottom of the Championship, that one month later he would be managing a Premier League team? As they say, it's a funny old game.

It doesn't seem so long ago that he was fighting off the attentions of the Clarets over Wednesday striker Marcus Tudgay after our promotion, and very determinedly he did so. How ironic it would be if Tudgay now turns out to be one of his targets from the cash-strapped Owls.

Those same fighting qualities may soon be put to the test again as predators come circling our young starlets. The general feeling is that Brian did a good job at Sheffield Wednesday but was unable to push a big club upwards because of the massive debts and tight budgets he was working with.

Tight budgets are certainly something that he will have to be able to manage on at Burnley, but there may just be a little left in the coffers to afford him a transfer window flutter.

Coming with Laws in the role of assistant manager will be Russ Wilcox, with whom he has an association going back many years.

Whatever the fans think about the appointment of Brian Laws, we now have to get behind him to a man, and show the team we still have belief. He has a mountain to climb, but faith can move mountains as has already been shown at Turf Moor, and we can do it again.

One of the really good things to come out of the Coyle affair is that as a result of the loss of the coaching staff, there are suddenly vacancies. And on the same day as Laws' appointment is announced, Graham Alexander is named player/coach under the new regime. What a great reward for Grezza as he comes towards the end of his playing career, and just reward for his outstanding efforts in a claret and blue shirt.

This follows on the heels of his triumph in the "Morgan on Sport British Football Personality of the Year Award," run by Piers Morgan in the Mail on Sunday. More than 200,000 votes were cast in the competition and 168,933 of those went to Grezza. He beat Craig Bellamy into second with 28,915 votes and Ryan Giggs into third with 9,915.

In Morgan's words: "The common denominator with all three is that whatever you think of them, nobody could ever question that they give 100 per cent to every game they ever play. They are what you call 'commitment' players, the kind of guys who never stop running, tackling, or trying. I'm thrilled that Alexander won, because he personifies the genuine, decent, professional footballer. And let's face it, if ever Burnley fans needed something to cheer them up, then surely it is this week."

Piers then launches into a rant about the treachery and betrayal by Owen Coyle before concluding: "In two weeks' time, in a delicious piece of good fortune for everyone like me who loves seeing traitors meet their victims while the carcasses are still hanging from the crosses, Burnley play Bolton at the Reebok. I hope the extraordinary passion that Burnley fans brought to their voting in my awards for Alexander is matched, if not eclipsed, by their passion in howling their fury at Coyle that day. And I hope come the end of the season, Burnley stay up and Bolton go down."

Hmm, I always thought Morgan was a bit of a prick, but suddenly I am beginning to warm to him.

After all the trauma and upheaval of the last couple of weeks, it's time to get back to the serious business of football.

Time now for the Clarets to put their proud 100 per cent record of 2010 on the line, and where better to test themselves and the new manager than Old Trafford against Manchester United?

The Reds, smarting from their early season defeat at Turf Moor and in hot pursuit of Chelsea at the top of the table, are sure to be a stern test of our unbeaten away record this year. Seriously though, we look ready for a hammering and the bookies certainly think so, quoting us at 15-1 for the win.

What line up will the new manager select? His options are certainly limited in central defence as Caldwell is injured, Bikey is away on international duty and Carlisle is only rated at 50/50 to play. Michael

Duff looks a certainty to start but will there be a place for David Edgar, strangely ignored by Coyle after his pre-season signing?

What can we hope for here? At best most fans would hope that we don't get thrashed and come away with some dignity intact. However, after the events of the last two weeks, who knows what the effect of Coyle's defection and the appointment of Laws will have on the team and its performance?

Defeat at United will surely see us slip further down the table and possibly by the end of the weekend into a relegation spot. If there is a God up there surely now is the time for him to show himself and favour our beleaguered underdogs. We go to Old Trafford praying for the best, but fearing the worst.

Saturday, January 16 and I have a good feeling about today. The morning post brings me an unexpected but most welcome present of £75, courtesy of ERNIE and my Premium Bonds.

Does this signal a change of luck for me and the Clarets? Old Trafford awaits.

Game 21 – Saturday, January 16, 3pm – Manchester United – Away
IT'S the first game for Brian Laws and his first team selection.

Clarke Carlisle is not ready to resume and Brian selects Edgar for his Clarets Premier League debut. He partners Duff in central defence and they have the small matter of Wayne Rooney and Dimitar Berbatov to contend with. Edgar is maybe one of the squad players who is glad to see the back of Coyle as he would probably still have been sat in the stand if his ex-boss was still here.

No sign of negativity either with the rest of the selection as he opts for Nugent and Fletcher up top, so it looks like we are going to give it a go.

Brian Laws comes out to a tremendous reception from the 3,000 travelling Clarets and he goes round to them to acknowledge their support. The crowd of 75,120 is the biggest the Clarets have ever played in front of in league football in their history.

We start brightly and could be ahead in the first 10 minutes as we break quickly from a United attack and have a 3 on 1 situation. Nugent feeds Fletcher, but he agonisingly pulls his shot wide. A bit more composure called for I think.

The first 20 minutes is decidedly end to end. My mobile is kept busy as PNE Ed relays the action from some Irish channel covering the game and I pass it to Stephanie who is working at the local newsagents.

First bit of bad news is on 35 minutes as Fletcher has to go off after being fouled by Antonio Valencia, and he is replaced by Steve Thompson.

But a great save by the Beast on half time takes us in surprisingly but deservedly level. Ed texts to say we are playing well, but I point out its only job half done yet.

The second half continues in similar vein and on 59 minutes comes probably the pivotal moment of the game. Once again we break from defence so quickly that United can't live with it. A great ball through sees Nugent, with terrific acceleration, go clear into the United box and one on one with keeper Edwin van der Sar. As I wait for the commentators to scream "Goal," he puts his shot wide of the post and another great chance goes begging.

Radio summariser and popular ex-Claret David Eyres feels that we have put in a monumental effort in the first 60 minutes, but not for he first time has concerns over the amount of room being given to Valencia.

Then it's bad news, as on 64 minutes Berbatov puts United ahead with a suspicion of a deflection on the shot, and on 69 minutes its 2-0 as Rooney holds off the defence to fire into the corner.

Once again it's a story of missed chances and bad luck, but we continue to keep playing and making opportunities. Van der Sar saves from the impressive Chris Eagles, returning to his old stamping ground, and Thompson's header beats the keeper but hits the post.

Eagles goes off to rousing applause from both the Clarets and United fans and it's no more than he deserves as he has given his all. There is still time for Mears to go close with a free kick and the Clarets to be denied a stonewall penalty for handball.

But at the other end it's comedy capers as the Reds add a late third with a howler from the Beast being largely to blame.

So we lose the game 3-0. It's hardly a fair reflection of our efforts but we are not dismayed. The team and the fans have reacted magnificently to the new manager and he is justifiably proud of them.

In his after-match statement he said: "I have so many major plusses today and I have seen so much I can work with and work on. I am absolutely proud of the lads and the supporters today. I thought we were absolutely outstanding in our commitment, desire and drive and the fans got behind everyone."

Result: Manchester United (Berbatov 64, Rooney 69, Diouf 90) 3, Burnley 0.

Team: Jensen; Mears, Duff, Edgar, Jordan; Elliott, McDonald K (Gudjonsson 73), Alexander, Eagles (Blake 83); Fletcher (Thompson 36), Nugent.

Subs not used: Penney, Kalvenes, Eckersley, Guerrero.

Attendance: 75,120.

Position in Table: 15.

Season record: Played 21, Won 5, Drawn 5, lost 11, Goals for 22, Goals against 43, Points 20.

Sunday, January 17 and there are three crucial games today affecting relegation threatened teams, with West Ham away at Aston Villa, Blackburn at home to Fulham and the new arch-enemy Bolton at home to Arsenal. I pray for three victories for the unthreatened teams but more for Arsenal than anybody else.

Villa kind of let me down in the first one, dropping a point to the Hammers while Fulham fail completely, giving the Rovers a 2-0 win. But joy of joy, Arsenal are the toast of Burnley with a 2-0 win at the Reebok to stop the prematurely celebrating Bolton fans in their tracks.

I don't think I could have stood to see OC's smug, smiling mug in tomorrow's papers and now I won't have to. A draw for the Clarets at home to Arsenal recently and a defeat for the Wanderers in the corresponding fixture, so perhaps Owen has bitten off more than he can chew. Sat in the stands watching our next league opponents is Brian Laws and I hope he is having a quiet chuckle to himself.

Rumours are appearing on the Sunday after the United game of our interest in a young French striker from AS Monaco, Frederic Nimani. Commenting on his position at his club, the player says: "I'm not happy to be on the bench, but I am 21 years old and have time on my side. I have only started two games this season and played in eight games. I have heard about Burnley and that would be a fantastic opportunity for a young player like me. I am waiting to see what will happen in the transfer window."

By Tuesday, January 19, these rumours seem to have gained more substance with reports in the press that we have flown the player over for talks. Almost inevitably it is also suggested that we face competition from…guess who? Yes, Bolton, as well as other interested clubs.

By the same afternoon, Sky Sports News are suggesting a deal is imminent and that the player is currently undergoing a medical at Turf Moor. The deal is said to be a loan until the end of the season with the option to then buy at a fee of €4 million.

The player is apparently 6'4" tall and at that sort of size he will certainly give us a different attacking option. Also, a loan deal will give both parties the opportunity to size each other up ahead of a potential permanent deal which may well depend on our Premier League survival.

By far the best news coming out of Turf Moor is that our three long term injured players, Chris McCann, Martin Paterson and Jay

Rodriguez, are all scheduled to play in tonight's reserve team fixture against Hull City at North Ferriby.

All three have been missing from duty since September, McCann and Paterson with serious knee injuries and Rodriguez with a broken ankle. Their imminent return will give the squad an immediate boost and we hope that they all come through this first run out unscathed.

An in form and fit Chris McCann can certainly expect an early return to first team action, but the cup tie at Reading on Saturday will probably be too soon for all three to be risked.

Wednesday, January 20 sees two important games scheduled for followers of the Clarets, neither of which we are involved in.

The televised game on the BBC this evening is the Carling Cup Semi Final second leg, Aston Villa v Blackburn Rovers. Rovers trail 1-0 from the home leg to the Villains, who must now feel they are favourites for Wembley. It's almost 12 months to the day since at the same stage of the competition we were producing a fantastic fightback before eventually failing at the death against Tottenham Hotspur.

The other game sees Arsenal with the opportunity to go top of the Premier League if they can win by a two goal margin at the Emirates. Their opponents tonight, as they were only last Sunday, are Coyle's Bolton in a rearranged fixture.

Before Sunday's game Bolton trailed the Clarets by two points but with three games in hand, that defeat maintaining the same gap but reducing the games in hand to two. Victory tonight for Arsenal would mean Wanderers stay two points behind, but a win for Bolton and they pass us with still a game in hand. No doubts then about who we want to win this one.

After a long soak in the bath, I turn on the bedroom television anticipating seeing Villa by now comfortably ahead. Imagine my shock to see the Rovers 2-1 up and deservedly so according to the commentators.

There is a text from teacher John who thinks it might be good for the Rovers to win as it will distract them in their league games and work to our advantage. I am not so sure. Working with a number of the blue and white persuasion would mean weeks of their boasting and cheap jibes. No, it's better they lose than that.

I decide to console myself by checking Arsenal's progress to the top of the league on Teletext. A big mistake as I see the score "Arsenal 0, Bolton 2" after about 30 minutes. How the hell can that be?

I text PNE Ed to see how he thinks both these games can be going so horribly wrong, and he is of the opinion that it is going to be a night of Arsenal misfire. The cheerful bugger.

I switch back to live TV in a state of shock to see the turning point of the Villa/Rovers game as Rovers centre back Christopher Samba is adjudged to have fouled Gabriel Agbonlahor in the box to concede a penalty and receive a red card.

I have to say it looks a bit harsh to me as he went to play the ball, but 'rules is rules' and he has to go. If the spot kick goes in it's as good as game over as the Rovers will be one down on aggregate and one down in players. It duly goes in and its game over before half time, I reckon.

A quick check back to Teletext and a glimmer of hope in the other game, as on 43 minutes Tomas Rosicky pulls one back for the Gunners to half the deficit at half time.

Into the second half at Villa and we get the expected onslaught and an avalanche of goals as Villa go 5-2 up, but credit to the Rovers, they don't give up and score twice to pull the tie back to 5-4 before conceding again late on to see the game incredibly finish 6-4, a score which signals the end of their Wembley dreams.

More important to us are events at the Emirates and it's not long into the second half before I get a text saying simply "Arsenal 2." Marvellous. There's loads of time to finish them off now providing there are no more slip ups.

By now I am having multiple text conversations with PNE Ed and the two Johns and am in serious danger of repetitive strain injury to the thumb. The phone goes again with the message "Arsenal 3 (Unprintable word) 2," as John G shows a fine command of the English language to describe his feelings for our now bitter local rivals.

I am feeling so much better now and my joy knows no bounds as Arsenal wrap it up with a fourth, so I go to bed a happy man taking with me the largest whisky in the world. Sweet dreams.

On Friday, January 22, after what seems an age, and with fears growing that the move has broken down or worse still been hijacked by Coyle, the young French striker Nimani signs on the dotted line. It's too late to play in the cup tie at Reading as the seven day rule applies but hopefully all will be clear for him to perhaps play some part in Tuesday's 'Night of the Long Knives' at Bolton.

FA Cup, Round Four – Saturday, January 23, 12.45pm – Reading – Away.

TODAY it's a break from the league and we take our 100 per cent FA Cup record on the road again to Championship strugglers Reading, conquerors of Liverpool in Round Three.

The game is to be covered live on the Internet via the FA website but I follow the early stages on good old Radio Lancs.

We seem to have opted for a strange line up as the returning Chris McCann is selected at left back rather than his customary midfield role. We are packing a five man midfield with Joey Gudjonsson a surprise inclusion whilst Steven Thompson replaces Steven Fletcher as the lone striker. Fletcher picked up an injury in the last game and hopefully is being saved for the Bolton showdown.

Similarly it is reported that Stephen Jordan, the regular left back, is carrying a knock and his natural replacement Christian Kalvenes is unavailable as his wife about to give birth.

After the first 15 minutes of nothingness, I decide to go upstairs and switch on the computer to watch on the FA website. A bit optimistic I fear, as I am met by the words: "We are currently experiencing problems streaming the Reading v Burnley tie. We are investigating now and hope to rectify the situation as soon as possible. We would like to sincerely apologise for any inconvenience this is causing."

Bloody typical. I bet if it had been the Chelsea game they wouldn't have been experiencing problems.

Perhaps it's just as well as the game seems to be pretty dire. Radio Lancs summariser Chris Boden of the Burnley Express suggests that the game wants putting out of its misery and is suffering from a lack of quality on a poor playing surface. By half time I don't think I can recollect a Burnley shot at goal and Reading don't seem much better.

At the break, Brian Laws must be similarly unimpressed and opts to change strikers with Paterson replacing Thompson for the second half. This seems to have a beneficial effect and we start to get more on top at the start of the half. Even the commentators are starting to wake up and declare it a much better game now.

I decide to abandon all hope of the FA website coming up with the goods and go back downstairs to watch Preston v Chelsea whilst listening to Reading v Burnley. It's a bit bizarre really and I find myself believing Burnley are the team in blue doing all the attacking and two goals to the good.

I am brought back to reality as Reading miss from point blank range and we survive by the skin of our teeth. Next it's our turn as the Reading keeper Adam Federici makes a great save from Edgar's flying header and Paterson puts the rebound over the top.

With three minutes of normal time remaining, my Wembley dreams are once more in tatters as Reading score from a 'something of nothing' move and it's all over.

While the league has to be our priority, the FA Cup represented a good opportunity to build confidence, but unfortunately not now.

We have 17 games to make or break our season, starting at Bolton on Tuesday, and for sure we will need a better performance than this if we are to wipe the smile off Coyle's face.

I'm already starting to get a bit concerned for Brian Laws. Two games, two defeats and while one was expected, today's was a winnable game. Next up are Bolton away and then Chelsea at home, and no points from these games will heap massive pressure on Laws, so let's hope we can turn the tide.

Result: Reading (Sigurdsson 87) 1, Burnley 0.
Team: Jensen; Mears, Duff, Edgar, McCann; Elliott, Alexander, McDonald K, Gudjonsson (Blake 85), Eagles; Thompson (Paterson 46).
Subs not used: Penney, Carlisle, Rodriguez, Guerrero.
Attendance: 12,910.

Tuesday, January 26 heralds another monumental evening for the Clarets. Without a win in 10 league games stretching back to October, and with only one point from a possible 30 away from home, we travel again, this time to confront our one time hero but now chief villain Owen Coyle.

On arrival at work I am subjected to aggravation from my long term office partner Alison, a 'non-active' Wanderer by birth. She is building the atmosphere of intense rivalry long before kick off, ably abetted by my other office adversary, PNE Ed. Tomorrow will be unbearable if we fail and I may have to throw a sickie.

215

Good news arrives in the morning with the revelation that new signing Nimani has received international clearance to play tonight if called upon.

There is further encouragement as we learn that David Nugent is still with us and available while we still wrangle over his loan/transfer from Portsmouth. With the anticipated return of Steven Fletcher after injury our striking options are certainly much greater than last Saturday.

Game 22 – Tuesday, January 26, 8pm – Bolton Wanderers – Away.

EVER since Owen Coyle deserted us for Bolton less than three short weeks ago, this game has been hanging over us like a cloud.

There seems to be a need to get this one out in the open, for the fans to show Coyle the full extent of their feelings and at the same time to show their commitment to the cause. Perhaps after this game we can expunge the ghost of Coyle and move on.

We hope that we can do this by turning in a rare away performance of character, flair and goalscoring to show the departed Coyle that he has made a big mistake. However, nagging deep down is the knowledge that our away performances have on the whole been dire and even under OC we have lost at Blackburn, Wolves, West Ham and Portsmouth to name but a few.

Our inability to keep clean sheets coupled with an inability to find the net has cost us dearly on our travels and we secretly fear that tonight could be the same. But our opponents have so far failed to keep a clean sheet in any Premier League game this season and this should give us encouragement.

We are backed by our largest away attendance of the season with more than 5,000 travelling fans making the short journey, and Coyle gets the anticipated hostile reception from his former worshippers.

As a former professional footballer I shouldn't think this bothers him unduly for one minute, but I am sure he too will be glad to get this game out of the way. The game coming so close after his defection means the wounds are still raw.

The Clarets have changes from the side out at Reading with Kalvenes restored at left back, McCann moving back to midfield in place of Big Kev McDonald, and Carlisle returning to central defence in place of the rather unlucky David Edgar.

Up front Steven Fletcher is recalled after injury in place of Thompson and Nugent is back for Joey Gudjonsson, while there is a place on the bench for new loan striker Nimani.

The game is off to a fairly dull start as I listen to the Radio Lancs commentary whilst wrestling again with the Internet trying to pick up a decent streamed link.

It really is the most frustrating way to follow the game as the radio commentary is running at least a minute ahead of the streamed pictures which continually break up and freeze.

After a fairly uneventful first 10 minutes, disaster on 13 as we lose Chris McCann in only his third comeback game after a serious knee injury with, you've guessed it, another knee injury sustained as he landed after going for a header. Immediately I fear the worst for a very promising young player who has been sorely missed since September.

The only midfield option on the bench is Big Kev and he is quickly back into action.

Fast forward four minutes and disaster strikes again as Graham Alexander limps off badly with what looks like a calf injury. After 17 minutes the engine room of the side has been ripped out, and without another midfielder on the bench we bring on Paterson and shuffle the formation.

The injuries seem to unsettle us and we have some uncomfortable moments before the Radio Lancs jinx strikes.

In a quiet passage of play we decide to 'go round the grounds,' so it's off to the Crown Ground, Accrington to see how John Coleman's boys are getting on. It's good news as their run of good form is continuing and they lead 1-0 against Aldershot.

Back to the Reebok and guess what? Yes, there has been a goal and it's not for our heroes. A suspicion of offside then a shot comes down off the crossbar. Did it cross the line?

No doubt if Manchester United or Chelsea had been on the receiving end it would have been disallowed on either or both counts, but not for unlucky Burnley and the goal stands, correctly as it turns out as proved by TV playbacks.

Disjointed by injuries and now a goal down we go in at half time hoping we can salvage something.

Radio summariser David Eyres is convinced that if we can level the score we can go on to win the game as he confirms that Bolton are a very poor side. But what does that make us though as we go from a bad first half performance to a worst second half one?

What's more, the players seem drained of belief and even lacking effort. Confidence is shot at and worse still we seem to be losing our free flowing style and hitting it long. That tactic seems to be confirmed by the withdrawal of wide man Eagles and his replacement by the new boy, the strapping Nimani.

The crowd sense the game is up and the atmosphere goes flat as the fight goes out of the side and the game drones to its inevitable conclusion.

We are beaten 1-0 by Owen Coyle and a poor Bolton side who leapfrog us in the table and we slip into the relegation places for the first time this season.

On top of that, if it could be any worse, Bolton get their first clean sheet of the season and who would you have backed it to come against? Us, of course.

Poor old Brian Laws. Three games, three defeats, all away from home but in two of them, Reading and Bolton, we had a realistic chance of something.

Not a popular choice for the manager's post, Laws now has to contend with a poor start results wise, injuries, loss of confidence and criticism of tactics and selection. Welcome back to Burnley, Brian.

With the team now winless in 11 league games and plummeting, we welcome the potential league champions, mega-powerful Chelsea, to the Turf on Saturday.

To make it possibly even more embarrassing, the TV cameras are coming to screen the game live around the world. It never rains but it pours.

Result: Bolton Wanderers (Lee 35) 1, Burnley 0.

Team: Jensen; Mears, Carlisle, Duff, Kalvenes; Elliott, Alexander (Paterson 17), McCann (McDonald K 13), Eagles (Nimani 66); Nugent, Fletcher.

Attendance: 23,986.

Position in Table: 18.

Season Record: Played 22, Won 5, Drawn 5, Lost 12, Goals for 22, Goals against 44, Points 20.

Wednesday sees heated debate on the fans' websites with much displeasure at the perceived surrender by the team, the long ball tactics, and a real fear that we are fading fast. Spirit in the camp looks from the outside poor and heads are down.

Brian Laws is talking about bringing in new players to boost the squad before the window closes next Monday. By early afternoon, the first is announced as keeper Nicky Weaver, currently out of contract, arrives on a six month short term deal.

Driving home from work Radio Lancs announce a second signing, Stoke City defender Leon Cort, for a fee of £1.5 million. I wait to gauge the fans reactions to these announcements but have a feeling they won't be greeted favourably. Fasten yourself in for a bumpy ride.

How appropriate that a Weaver should be coming to Burnley. The town's history is built on the once mighty Lancashire textile industry and it was one of the most important weaving towns in the world in its heyday. I doubt though that this Weaver has ever set foot in a textile mill and from experience I can tell him that he is probably richer for that.

The goalkeeper's previous short contract with Dundee United in the Scottish Premier League has expired, but by all accounts he has had a successful time with the 'Arabs' and been the regular first choice keeper.

He started his career at Mansfield before joining Manchester City where he played more than 200 games. After leaving City he was at Charlton and so he has no shortage of experience at top level. At 30, he is probably in his prime as a keeper, and is expected to come in as second choice, which makes things look a little ominous for Diego Penny's chances.

Cort, who is also 30, joins on a contract to take him through to the end of the 2012/3 season. Starting out at non-league Dulwich Hamlet, then going to Millwall, Southend, Hull, Crystal Palace and finally Stoke, he now finds himself at the Turf.

Influential in Stoke's promotion to the Premier League, he now finds himself down the pecking order with the Potters and is glad of the chance to come and try to revive our flagging fortunes .Another centre back standing well over six feet tall and reputedly very good in the air, he should improve our performance at set pieces and hopefully chip in the odd goal or two.

On Thursday we hear Brian Laws is not finished yet in the market and hopes to sign two more players before the window closes. One is named as Celtic full back Danny Fox, for whom we are reportedly prepared to pay more than £1 million. Another name rumoured is the

Newcastle central midfielder Danny Guthrie, and again a fee of over £1 million is being touted.

These two names seem to be being greeted with some approval by the shell-shocked fans but we will have to wait and see if anything materialises.

One thing is for sure. With three new faces already in and more possible, there must be some going the other way, if only to free up dressing room space. I think it may be a hectic day on Monday as the window prepares to slam shut.

Full marks to Laws as he is trying to do something in the limited space of time he has had available. The players may not be the ideal choices of the fans, but he is the guy charged with rescuing us from the carnage of the Coyle departure and most level-headed fans are prepared to back his judgement.

On the morning of the Chelsea game, the newspaper is full of revelations concerning sexual relations between Chelsea and England captain John Terry and the partner of one of his ex-Chelsea and England team mates, Wayne Bridge.

The papers are really going to town, exposing all his previous misdemeanours, of which there are several. Our John has been a busy boy between the sheets.

I bet he is really glad now that the game today at Burnley is a televised match and the media and of course the Burnley fans will be following his every move. I think he may well be on the receiving end of some northern humour tonight.

Game 23 – Saturday, January 30, 5.30pm – Chelsea – Home.

HERE we go again with another bizarre kick off time, guaranteed to ruin the true fan's social life while pandering to the armchair fans around the world. I suppose as the armchair fans are paying most of the players' wages we shouldn't grumble.

I am forced into an early tea around four o'clock in order to eat before the game, the alternative being to not eat until eight o'clock by which time I am contemplating a few Saturday night pints. After consuming said tea, an Asda takeaway chicken jalfrezi, Stephanie and myself set off in once again freezing conditions for Turf Moor.

Parking is at a premium and I find myself parking so far from the ground that it's debatable whether we might have been better just walking it in the first place. By the time we arrive at the Turf it's dark and really cold, just the sort of night to play the Southern softies.

It's the first home game in over a month, the last one being Bolton on Boxing Day, and it's Brian Laws' home debut as manager. Lawsy comes out to a rousing reception from the packed home crowd and I'm sure that must have warmed him on this cold night.

There are changes from Tuesday with neither Grezza, McCann nor Michael Duff fit. In comes Leon Cort for his Clarets debut and also big Kev McDonald, Robbie Blake and, back from international duty, Andre Bikey. Elliott and Eagles are posted out wide, I guess to nullify the attacking threat of the Chelsea full backs Branislav Ivanovich and Ashley Cole. The opposition are fielding the bulk of their big names including the disgraced Terry who remains as captain.

There's a bad omen as we lose the toss and have to attack the Jimmy Mac End first, which is not the preferred direction. We are quickly on the back foot as a team of extremely fit and superb athletes, many of considerable stature, are soon into their stride and enjoying lots of possession.

For our part, we are looking organised and whilst not having a lot of the ball, we are keeping compact and not coming under too much threat. We are doing alright although our opponents have the look of serious title challengers and seem in determined mood.

On 27 minutes, we see one of those moments that differentiate the title challengers from the strugglers. From a Burnley free kick which drifted past everybody and into the arms of Petr Cech, we are suddenly unzipped. Cech, spotting we are heavily committed upfield, instantly throws the ball a good 40 yards down his right side to Joe Cole, who is gathering pace towards the Burnley goal.

Crossing the halfway line at speed he transfers the ball across field to Florent Malouda who allows it one bounce before returning it back low into the six yard box for the onrushing Nicolas Anelka. From close range he gives the Beast no chance and in a matter of seconds we are behind.

The sheer speed and accuracy of the move leaves us stunned and it was indeed a fine goal for the neutrals. Not me though. I thought it was crap.

On 35 minutes, we lose left back Kalvenes, himself standing in for Jordan with a knee injury, and he is replaced by Edgar.

A nice break out of defence by Bikey sees the ball flicked into the path of Blake, who is cynically bodychecked by Terry, earning him a yellow card. The Burnley crowd almost to a man take up the chant of "Same old Terry, always cheating" which in the light of his current indiscretions is remarkably accurate.

At half time, we are just the one goal down and having played some good football, most of the fans are reasonably satisfied. This really was a game where we didn't think we'd get anything and that now seems likely to be the case.

The second half starts much as the first ended, with Chelsea having the bulk of the possession but not offering much threat.

Then on 50 minutes a moment of magic and one to savour. Blake chips a pass up to Fletcher who is running to the left of goal with the Brazilian central defender Alex. Fletch flicks the ball over the defender's head and comes inside him, then a fortunate touch off Alex puts the ball right back into the path of Fletch's favoured left foot and he rifles it past Cech to put the Clarets unbelievably level. A goal of the highest quality and thoroughly deserved for a player who works tirelessly and with no shortage of skill.

I look at my watch. Bloody hell, a long way to go yet.

Chelsea, stung by the goal, up the tempo and go looking for the winner, whilst we look to catch them on the break. With 20 minutes to go and the scores still level, my nerves are jangling but we are holding out, just. Ten minutes to go and I am thinking we might just do it, a draw here would be like a win.

But on 82 minutes we concede a corner. The ball is flung in by Frank Lampard and who is rising unchallenged to head it? Bloody Casanova himself. He gets good downward power on the header and despite the Beast's valiant effort he is unable to keep it out.

The Blues hold out to the final whistle without coming under much threat and we are beaten again for the fourth successive time. How cruel again to get so close but come away with nothing.

Realistically, it was a game where we had not much expectation at the outset but ultimately we ran them close. There were many positives, not least the reaction of the crowd who despite recent events were not cowed but defiant. They still believe we can save the day and if that belief can be conveyed to the players, all is not lost yet.

Bikey, once again asked to play in midfield, was man of the match and his performance would not have looked out of place in the opposition team. Edgar had a very good substitute performance in an unaccustomed position, and we had a good debut by Leon Cort against formidable opponents. Fletcher's goal was magnificent and didn't deserve to be part of a losing performance.

Next week we are home again, this time to fellow strugglers West Ham. A repeat of tonight's effort and skill will surely bring some reward from this fixture.

**Result: Burnley (Fletcher 50) 1, Chelsea (Anelka 35, Terry 82) 2.
Team: Jensen; Mears, Carlisle, Cort, Kalvenes (Edgar 35), Elliott, McDonald K (Paterson 60), Bikey, Eagles; Blake (Thompson 72), Fletcher.**

Attendance: 21,131.

Position in Table: 18.

Season Record: Played 23, Won 5, Drawn 5, Lost 13, Goals for 23, Goals against 46, Points 20.

FEBRUARY

Make Or Break?

MONDAY, February 1 sees the closing of the transfer window and so after 5pm today, we have what we have.

Having been very active in the market during January with four players incoming, today is again expected to be busy.

Already we hear that Brian Easton, one of Coyle's summer signings, has returned to Hamilton Academical on loan, being unable to manage more than one game with the Clarets and urgently needing some competitive football. It will be no surprise to see more going out as the squad seems to have a large number of fringe players following the signings and return of the injured players.

First news is that David Nugent will be returning to see out the rest of the season on loan from Portsmouth, and that certainly bolsters the striking department. Also confirmed by early afternoon is the loan of young Chelsea and England under 21 midfielder Jack Cork till the end of the season.

Going out are Jay Rodriguez, on loan to Barnsley to get some much needed games after his recent injury, and keeper Jonathan Lund, now dropped down to fourth in the pecking order, to Rotherham also on loan.

Not a bad day's work and I think that most fans are reasonably pleased that we have certainly made attempts to freshen things up with new faces, and now wait to see how they will be used. At the same time we have managed to hold on to our key players with no moves out for Eagles and Mears as had been rumoured. These two will certainly have a key part to play in our destiny.

On Wednesday, our league position deteriorates as Hull City deny Chelsea victory, the draw meaning they go above us and put us next to the bottom.

On the same night Rodriguez, coming on as a late sub for Barnsley at Preston, scores with his first touch of the ball. His goal completes a 4-1 rout at Deepdale that is sure to have my mate Ed's face down to his knees.

Friday, February 5 sees a Royal visit to the town with newly revealed celebrity Clarets fan His Royal Highness, The Prince of Wales making a trip to see his team. Unfortunately he has come on the wrong day as we don't play till Saturday.

Prince Charles is very active in the town and likes to check on various projects including his own Prince's Trust work and the Weavers' Triangle development. He has scheduled a visit to Turf Moor to see the club's impressive work in community projects as well as visits to Towneley Hall and the new university/college.

On my way home from work, I hear Radio Lancs reporting that Burnley FC chairman Barry Kilby has presented the Prince with his very own Clarets shirt with the letters HRH emblazoned on the back. Sure enough, in Saturday's Lancashire Evening Telegraph is a picture of the

Prince holding the said shirt. You can see by the look in his eye that he can't wait to put it on.

An image runs through my mind of former Tory cabinet minister David Mellor, who reportedly used to wear his Chelsea shirt during extra-marital sex sessions with his mistress. Surely HRH won't be resorting to wearing his in the bedroom? It's far too classy for that, he needs to save it for match days. Perhaps he'll put it on next time he goes to visit his mum at Buckingham Palace to show her how smart it looks worn outside his kilt.

Game 24 – Saturday, February 6, 3pm – West Ham United – Home.
A PACKED White Hart - pub, not lane, that is - and a business that is certainly benefiting from the Premier League promotion gets the match day experience under way.

Although the sign on the door says "Home fans only," I keep picking out some distinctly East End accents, and I don't mean Brierfield. Perhaps they have sneaked in under cover of their claret and blue scarves and they certainly seem to be enjoying the northern beer experience. Two pints are duly dispatched, then it's a quick march to the Turf just in time for kick off.

Playing in a 4-4-2 formation, we are quickly into our stride whilst our visitors are struggling to get out of the blocks.

On 14 minutes, we have a priceless lead as Nugent hares onto a bouncing long ball through the middle by Danny Fox to lob the keeper. The ball seems to take an age to hit the net, but hit it, it certainly does.

The crowd, already well up for this game, are out of their seats and the goal is greeted like a Wembley winner. It's been almost one way stuff up until this point and the lead is well deserved. Can we get another and make for a more comfortable afternoon?

Not likely. Inexplicably we go off the boil and the Hammers seize the initiative. We have several close shaves, none more so than when Leon Cort, with a giant outstretched leg, clears off the line with the Beast beaten, and we go in at the break still ahead.

Half time seems to have settled us a bit and we start the second half on a more attacking note.

A feature of the first half was the delivery of some dangerous dead balls by our debutant Fox, and on 55 minutes this particular skill brings the ultimate reward.

A free kick on the Clarets' right wing sees Robbie Blake and Fox over the ball. Blake defers to Fox who whips in a left foot curling inswinger and we look for the head of a Claret to nod home. But not so as this time the ball sails past Robert Green in the Hammers goal and directly into the net.

We're 2-0 up. Unbelievable. Can it be the first win since Hull City in October?

Two inspired signings by Laws have featured, Cort with his clearance and Fox with his debut goal and assist in the first.

We hope now that the two goal gap will be enough to dampen the enthusiasm of our visitors but no, we go back to a repeat of the first half. The Hammers go for broke and throw the kitchen sink at us. Great saves, intervention by the crossbar, and a goal ruled out for offside. My nerves are shattered, and the bloke next to me is banging his head on the wall at the back of the stand.

Nine minutes to go and, inevitably for us, we concede. Now it's going to be torment for the remainder plus injury time. We get through normal time unscathed except for shredded nerves and tattered nails in the crowd, and then up goes the board saying five minutes added time.

Where did that come from? Still, we buckle down and, roared on by a magnificent home crowd, we hold out despite a last minute rebound off the post.

What joy, what relief. Three precious points, a first win in 13 league games, and back in business.

Were we lucky? In truth, yes, but on how many occasions has the opposite been the case? It's about time. The look of relief and also determination on the faces of the players at the end says it all.

The race is not run yet and the Clarets are back in it. Three points takes us back out of the relegation spots, moving us from 19th to 15th. Even more pleasing is the news that the win takes us above Coyle's Bolton, who can only draw at home.

As almost 20,000 happy Clarets fans wend their way homeward, none can be happier than Brian Laws. Come on you Clarets.

Result: Burnley (Nugent 14, Fox 55) 2, West Ham United (Ilan 81) 1. Team: Jensen; Mears, Carlisle, Cort, Fox (Edgar 86); Elliott, McDonald K, Bikey, Blake (Paterson 73); Nugent (Thompson 88), Fletcher.

Subs not used: Weaver, Duff, Cork, Eagles.

Attendance: 21,001.

Position in Table: 15.

Season Record: Played 24, Won 6, Drawn 5, Lost 13, Goals for 25, Goals against 47, Points 23.

Monday, February 8, and as I drive to work the Radio Lancashire news has me wondering if I have slept through February and March in a state of hibernation and awoke on April 1, All Fools' Day. They are reporting plans by the football club to relocate Burnley Cricket Club to a site on land at Towneley and develop the vacant land at Turf Moor into, wait for it, a university of football.

Now, won't that be something? Preston may have had a museum of football but we are going to have a UNIVERSITY of it. Imagine the scene on University Challenge as our team members are announced as A.N. Other from Burnley studying "The psychology of away day sickness." We should be experts at that. Or maybe "Mental instability among soccer fans." The possibilities are endless.

This idea seems to be a variation on the redevelopment plan for the Cricket Field Stand which, although mooted some time back, has recently been put on ice. I think I'll reserve judgement on this one as I don't think it will happen in my lifetime.

Game 25 – Tuesday, February 9, 8pm – Fulham – Away.
NOT much to report here as my opportunities to follow the game are seriously impaired by the visit for supper of an old friend and veteran Claret fan "Sir" Reginald Clark.

233

Reg is an ex-work colleague of my wife, going back to their days at the Michelin tyre plant in Burnley. He now lives in the wilds of Colne, and we periodically invite him for a meal and a few drinks.

Despite Reg's passion for the Clarets, I feel that it would perhaps not be the wisest thing to spoil the dinner conversation by listening to the Radio Lancs commentary, and what's more it would probably spoil the taste of the food. However I arrange before leaving work to have PNE Ed text me scores as they happen from his soccer studio back in Preston.

With 20 minutes gone and the carrot and coriander soup polished off, there's no text, so I assume all is well. I tell a lie, there is a text. It reads: "Alloa 1-0 Cowdenbeath." Likes to keep you informed, does Ed.

However I don't have to wait long for the expected. "City 1-0, Ful 1-0." He's also a man of few words is Ed.

This is followed shortly after by: "Albion 0 Livings 0, Fulham 2-0, both goals offside according to Sky." He's getting quite verbose now.

At this point, my wife Julie decides to launch into a rant on our inability to work the offside trap. Where did that come from?

Only half an hour gone and it's the familiar story away from home, two goals down and doomed.

Reg and I take the optimistic view that we can still come back and win 4-2, at which point my wife declares that if that happens, and I quote, she will "strip naked and run round the block."

Now I'm as broadminded as the next man but I think that's going a bit far. How the hell would I explain it to the traumatised neighbours? There are some things that are better left unseen, and I think

I'll end the topic now before I get in hot water. However, I am silently praying for an epic comeback, as it's a lovely sub zero temperature night for a streak.

The second half has not long since started before the next text message: "Ful 3-0, City 2-0, Wig 1-1, Pomp 0-1." Resigned to defeat, I console myself that the other results are largely going our way, particularly City's lead over new arch-rivals Coyle Wanderers.

All those scores stay the same with the exception of Pompey, who level it 1-1. Too little too late for them I fear, but we slip one place in the table as Wigan go above us.

Can't really say much about this game due to my lack of information, though the best bit of the game was the food. The chicken breast stuffed with feta cheese and thyme, served on a bed of courgettes and sliced vine tomatoes, was superb.

There is an old saying that if you can't say anything good about something then it's better not to say anything at all. I think that is probably the case with this game.

Never mind. The players will get over it with a four day break to Portugal, while I have to return to work in Haslingden and the waiting North Ender and Roverite. At least Alison the Wanderer will be quiet. Well, quietish. She is a woman after all.

Result: Fulham (Murphy 23, Elm 31, Zamora 54) 3, Burnley 0.
Team: Jensen; Mears, Carlisle, Cort (Eagles 31), Edgar; Elliott (Cork 56), McDonald K, Bikey, Fox, Nugent (Paterson 76), Fletcher.
Attendance: 23,005.

Position in Table: 16.

Season record: Played 25, Won 6, Drawn 5, Lost 14, Goals for 25, Goals against 50, Points 23.

With the squad in Portugal and no game this weekend as it's Round Five of the FA Cup in which we no longer have an interest, Clarets news is very sparse.

I have lost count of the number of stories in the Burnley Express, usually headed "Clarets aim to banish away day blues," that I find it impossible to read them anymore. We get the usual comments about sloppy defending, switching off and missed chances trotted out, and to be honest we got that in the first game at Stoke.

We have now played 13 away games and with only six more to go it's about time something was done. I seriously think that if after those six away games, we still have that solitary point we got at City, it will surely see us down.

Last week's midweek games and victories for West Ham and Wolves see us sitting back in the relegation zone. I get the feeling that there is a growing air of resignation about our fate from fellow fans and neighbours.

Next game up is Sunday's televised fixture at Aston Villa which is a real bogey ground for us. With Villa chasing a spot in the top four and a lucrative Champions League place, I think it's fair to say we will be outsiders with the bookies for that game.

Following on from that is another must win home game against bottom club Portsmouth who are hanging on to their very survival grimly as the financial noose around their neck tightens. Money problems they may have aplenty, and not many league points as they are seven behind ourselves, but they still seem to be playing like they haven't given up and I don't think we will find it easy against them.

While in a quiet moment and in reflective mood, my thoughts turn to what has been the most disappointing part of the Premier League experience for me. Although it would be easy to say that is the regular batterings we get on our travels, I come to the conclusion that it is not.

No, for me the most disappointing aspect is the lack of games. A Premier League season consists of 38 games whilst a Championship season is 46, so we are already eight down. If we then consider that we have not had a home tie in either cup competition and gone out fairly early in both, then I seem to have seen very little actual live football.

We now stand in mid-February and since the season kicked off in mid-August, we have staged just 11 games at the Turf in six months, or 12 if we include the "Save our Stanley" match.

Last season, with our involvement in the cup competitions and the play-offs, we racked up more than 60 games, whereas this time it will be only just past the 40 mark. By the end of this month, we will have played three home games in a period of two months and for a 'home only' attender, this seems a poor return. It seems an age since the last home game and it's still a week and half away from the next.

Even for many of the brave hearted souls who follow the club away from home, many are denied the opportunity due to the restricted ticket allocations granted to the club, the largest so far being around 5,000 plus at Bolton. As there are in the region of 15-17,000 season ticket holders, this must be denying a considerable number of potential travelling fans the opportunity to see their team away from home.

However that seems a positive plethora of games compared to the number of times the reserves have had an outing. We have managed a paltry seven matches this season whilst Hull have had 12.

This is largely as a result of the decision taken some time back to play the home reserve fixtures at the ground of Accrington Stanley to protect the playing surface at Turf Moor. The pitch at Accy seems totally incapable of dispersing water and the lack of under-soil heating coupled with this winter's frequent sub-zero temperatures has meant many postponements.

I think next season will mean a fresh venue for reserve team fixtures but where this will be is unknown at the moment.

Rumours are rife this week that there has been a fall out between midfielder Joey Gudjonsson and manager Brian Laws with Joey upset at being left out of the match day squad recently.

With the first team squad as large as it currently is, there are always going to be instances of unhappy players. We have to trust the manager's judgement and the players left out should knuckle down and try to fight their way back into the manager's plans.

It is also rumoured that Fernando Guerrero, who was described as an exciting talent on his arrival but who has seen very little action recently, is another player not in Laws' plans. It is suggested he may go out on loan to a Championship side for the remainder of the season, but the legality of this arrangement, seeing as he is only a loan player with us, is in some doubt.

On Thursday, February 18, the club announce a new shirt sponsorship deal with Chinese betting company FUN88.

All previous shirt sponsors have been British, with the Cooke oil and fuels firm having their one and only season in the sun as Premier League shirt sponsors. Nice timing on their part.

Chairman Barry Kilby said "This multi-million pound deal is clear evidence of the global appeal of Burnley Football Club as a result of our Premier League status. We had discussions with many top international companies expressing an interest in getting involved with the club.

"But we feel the special relationship we have enjoyed and established with FUN88 will be one that is hugely beneficial to both parties. We look forward immensely to working with them on several exciting ventures over the next two years."

The rumours earlier this year of mysterious Chinese investors weren't far off the mark. This being Chinese New Year heralding the Year of the Tiger, let's hope this deal inspires us to fight like tigers over the next 13 games and preserve our hard won status.

No Saturday game for us this week so its nail biting time as we see what our near rivals can manage before we take centre stage on Sunday. Of interest to us are Wolves at home to Chelsea, Portsmouth at home to Stoke, fast fading Sunderland away at Arsenal, and the clash of two strugglers with West Ham at home to Hull. We have to hope for victories for Arsenal, Chelsea and Stoke, whilst the other game would probably be best ending in a draw.

By tea time, it's well done to our favoured three, all returning maximum points, while in the relegation dogfight West Ham claim the three points, leaving Hull one point above us but having played two more games.

Game 26 – Sunday, February 21, 2pm – Aston Villa – Away.

I AWAKE early this morning, around seven o'clock, bladder distended by the Coniston Bluebird Bitter and cans of Tetley's from last night.

Reluctantly I leave the comfort of my warm bed and make the short trip to the bathroom. Taking a peek out of the window as I go, I see a now familiar sight, a covering of snow on the ground. This has certainly been one of the best winters in recent years for snow but I have to confess that I have seen quite enough of it now.

I creep back into bed to grab a further hour, the plan being to have my usual Sunday morning jog over the golf course before an anticipated trip to the Trafford Centre. At eight o'clock I am up again but not for long, as a glance out the window shows it now snowing heavily and there is no chance of running. My daughter has a trip to York and overnight stay planned and I fear this might be a non-starter.

At nine o'clock, I am greeted by Stephanie's groans as she sees the weather. However, after a quick call from her pal, we note the trip is still on, and it looks like mine is also. Around ten Stephanie departs for York, my wife for church, and I to clean the bathroom. Nothing like a bit of toilet cleaning to get you in the mood.

My mood today seems somewhat upbeat, despite our upcoming away ordeal at the Villa. For some reason I am imbued with a sense of confidence and well being. It must have been something in the Tetley's.

Also coming up, ahead of our scheduled 2pm kick off, is the important Blackburn Rovers v Bolton game at noon. I find myself in a most unpleasant and unexpected position of wanting the old enemy to win a match. It seems like sacrilege but I text the two Johns with the words "Come on you Rovers." I will probably be damned to hell fire for that utterance but we need them to take all three points from Coyle's lot to keep them in the brown stuff.

I have an interesting dilemma of how best to follow the match while at the Trafford Centre.

My thoughts are to get PNE Ed to keep me updated with the scores, but he is becoming extremely unreliable on this front. Last week he tried to tell me that PNE had lost 8-3 at Derby and that Blackpool had lost when they had in fact won. Ed is having a difficult time at work and this, coupled with North End's current dire form, seems to have unhinged him.

I have a cunning plan. I will text Ed and also the two Johns to update me with scores. That way I can evaluate all three as they come in and see if they tally. Brilliant.

Shortly after noon, we leave for the Trafford Centre with the car radio tuned in to commentary from Ewood. It seems a pretty tame affair but is livened up by the interesting phenomenon of the radio picking up different transmissions as we travel.

Approaching Bury I hear the Rovers hitting the post, then almost immediately the Jackson Five cut in with "ABC." Back to the football then suddenly it's a snippet from Steven Lowe's gardening programme.

Onto the M60 and the switching is becoming almost non stop, until I hear with mounting excitement "great ball to Pedersen, Kalinic ….." then something about perennial shrubs. Did he or didn't he? For once I can't wait to hear the dulcet tones of Tony Parkes confirm that Rovers have scored, and score they have. Take that Coyle.

They go off at half time 1-0 up although I'm a little concerned by injuries to Rovers' centre-backs, forcing a defensive reshuffle. However, with a powderpuff outfit like Bolton, there's surely not much to worry about.

As I get in the Trafford Centre, I abandon my wife exploring handbags and jewellery in John Lewis and head for the TV department to see if the televisions are showing the game.

Unfortunately not but a quick text to the boys brings good news from Ed who reports Rovers two up with 10 minutes to play, which is corroborated shortly after by John G. A text follows shortly and the score is now 3-0 and that's game over. All going to plan, now for the biggie.

Back downstairs in John Lewis and my text goes again. Good job I charged the battery recently. It's John G and reads: "Fletcher 1." Bloody hell, what a start.

That's shortly followed by a text from the previously silent schoolteacher John, aka John W: "3-0, and we've just scored". By this I presume he means the Rovers won 3-0, not that we have gone three up.

Silence from Ed, obviously stunned, so I text him: "Super Fletch" but with still no response. However, 20 minutes later comes the reply: "Super Ash," and I guess this means Young has equalised, confirmed by John G's "1-1." The closed circuit TV cameras must be wondering who this loony in John Lewis is, who keeps diving in his pocket every other minute and texting furiously.

Now about 45 minutes into the handbag and jewellery watch, with still no sign of a purchase, I head back to the TV department to see if they are showing our game on Sky. From a distance I can see a football stadium on the multiple screens. Success.

Or is it? As I approach I see they are showing Bristol City v West Brom on the BBC. How could they? Oh well. I will have to continue with the text commentary.

John W confirms: "Villa score 1-1," then Ed with "Thru' Fox's legs, useless," then Ed again with "Pete? You there? Foxy wouldn't get in Nob team. Hesitant, wayward, and slow. Plank – that's his affectionate term for Fletcher - is your best defender."

Ed's now on a roll. "Watch the highlights. Young leaves him for dead." I've had enough of this and send: "Young is not Parkin" and follow it up with: "You don't understand it, it's Premier League football."

This obviously hits the mark as he replies: "Turning it off now seeing as I know nowt about it and its shite." I tell him to watch and learn, and that he will soon understand it. That quietens him down and it's now half time. It's still 1-1, better than I could have hoped for, and I'll settle for that at the end.

By now I'm outside Clinton's Card shop and the dreaded text goes again. It's John W with: "Villa score 2-1," swiftly followed by "3 Bloody 1," then mysteriously an unknown mobile number texts "Villa 3 Clarets 1." That's strange, an interloper.

Seconds later, there's "Its 4", from John W. I begin to suspect a wind up. How could it be?

Nothing from Ed who surely couldn't wait with such bad news, then "4.1" from John G. I then think perhaps John W has implicated John G in the ruse and they are doing me big style.

I text John G and ask how can this be? Have we had three sent off? The reply is: "No just shit, 3 goals in 3 minutes" followed by "5" from John G, and "Now 5-1" from John W.

Bloody hell. My wife goes in Clinton's and it's 1-1. She hasn't come out yet and now its 5-1.

I text back the Johns telling them to block up the goals, and the response from John G is "Shoot the f*****g goalkeeper." Not a man to mince his words, our John.

At this I have to head with my wife for the sanctuary of M&S Café Revive and a restorative cappuccino, at which point John W sends a message saying: "5-2 the comeback is on" followed by John G's "5.2."

Nothing from Ed, he must have died. However, on arrival home there's a belated text. "Took your advice and continued watching. It's you who knows nowt about Prem football." After what has gone on, how can I argue with that?

Against my better judgement, I take Ed's advice and watch the highlights on MOTD2. Contrary to what he told me, I don't see Danny

Fox being left for dead by Ashley Young. That's not to say it didn't happen though as the coverage has been condensed so much that the first half highlights only show about three incidents.

In that time we see Villa's Stiliyan Petrov shoot wide by the proverbial country mile, Burnley go ahead with a well worked Fletcher goal, which our studio pals try to claim may be offside, and Villa equalise. The Villa goal comes from a poorly defended short corner which allows Young loads of time to shoot but which enters the net via at least one deflection off Fox and possibly another.

The second half coverage then treats us to a volley of Villa goals with four in 12 minutes, and the commentators love every minute of it as they justify their pre-conceived notions that the Premier League is perhaps not where the likes of humble Burnley belong. At least one of these goals again benefits from a generous slice of luck from a deflection, but that doesn't seem to matter as we are told each goal seems "almost easier than the last."

A fine move in the last minute involving Eagles and the on loan Jack Cork and finished off by Paterson is passed off as no more than a consolation, which in reality it is.

But what really gets my goat is the studio analysis, or should I say ritual slaughter, of our performance by the smug Alan Hansen, aided and abetted on this occasion by the Croatia manager Slaven Bilic.

Hansen, assisted by the technology of slow motion, playback, and that wonderful ability to draw moving circles on the screen around the players, then graphically reveals all our shortcomings in terms of tactics and defensive failings.

245

Unfortunately in a real match situation the game doesn't slow down so our defence can see that their positioning is all wrong, and there are no circles round the opposition's feet or arrows showing where they are going to run. So as we don't have this technology, it's no wonder we concede so many goals away from home. It doesn't explain why we don't concede many at Turf Moor though.

Even more galling is the contribution of Bilic, who jumps on the bandwagon to have a go, and this from a master defensive strategist who saw his much vaunted side lose 4-1 and 5-1 to England in the World Cup qualifiers. You would have thought they would have learnt from their mistakes in the first game but no, they were worse in the second.

Perhaps he should employ Hansen as his defensive coach, but then again I doubt he would want to actually put his theories to the test in a live situation.

Anyway, gripe over. We lost, we realistically expected to and we didn't disappoint on that score.

So we move on, that one is history and the next game is now the important one. Wigan's defeat at home to Tottenham later in the day meant that with the exception of West Ham, all our relegation threatened rivals lost this weekend, so our overall position is probably no better or no worse than when we set out.

We still have 12 to play with seven at home and it looks like this is where we will have to get the points as the away day jinx looks set to run the course.

Result: Aston Villa (Young 32, Downing 56, 58, Heskey 61, Agbonlahor 68) 5, Burnley (Fletcher 10, Paterson 90) 2.

Team: Jensen; Mears, Carlisle, Cort, Fox; Nugent (Nimani 70), Cork, McDonald K (Elliott 64), Bikey, Eagles; Fletcher (Paterson 82).

Subs not used: Weaver, Duff, Blake, Thompson.

Attendance: 38,709.

Position in Table: 19.

Season Record: Played 26, Won 6, Drawn 5, Lost 15, Goals for 27, Goals against 55, Points 23.

February, in my mind, was going to be a make or break month, so with two defeats and one win as we approach the last weekend, it could be classed as break.

However, as the trend of the top teams consistently beating the strugglers continues, the position at the bottom remains very tight. As we currently stand it looks like a fight to the death for three out of eight teams. West Ham in 13th position have only four points more than ourselves in 19th position so it's still all to play for.

Bottom club Portsmouth are at the Turf on Saturday and this really is a must win game.

Thursday, February 25 sees our visitors hovering on the precipice of at best administration, and at worst liquidation. Informed sources believe Pompey will enter administration by tomorrow in order to suspend the winding up order served by HMRC over unpaid taxes and thereby ensure their survival to the season's end. The price for this will be an automatic nine point deduction and as their tally so far is only 16, it will almost certainly consign them to relegation, leaving two clubs scrambling for survival.

Pompey, reputedly £70 million in debt and currently having their fourth different owner so far in this campaign, are a classic example of the financial mismanagement which is so prevalent in the English game today. They have lived way beyond their means in the pursuit of the impossible dream, seemingly oblivious to the fact that that at some point must come the day of reckoning.

How fortunate we are that in Barry Kilby we have a chairman who would not allow this type of profligate spending to reach a point that threatens the very existence of the club. If indeed we share Pompey's likely fate and are relegated, at least we will be in far better shape financially to recover from the blow.

On Friday, February 26, Portsmouth duly entered administration with the attendant nine point penalty to be confirmed at a date to be decided by the Premier League.

Game 27 – Saturday, February 27, 3pm – Portsmouth – Home.
SATURDAY dawns with me in a strange bed in deepest Yorkshire, having spent a night in Huddersfield as a guest at a retirement party for the sales director of a company with whom we have done business for many years.

Whether it's the rich food from the night before or the full English breakfast at the hotel on Saturday morning I'm not sure, but as I drive back to Burnley I feel definitely knackered. And there's no rest tonight either as it's a friend's birthday celebration at the Indian restaurant for 11 of us.

Still, a couple of pre-match pints and a resounding victory today will soon get the energy levels up and the mood upbeat. Stephanie and I head for the usual hostelry, the White Hart, and on entry find the throng of Clarets, whilst still substantial, noticeably less than usual.

Even more disturbing is no sight of the two Johns, and almost immediately both mine and Stephanie's mobiles start to ring. "Where are you?," asks John G, knowing full well as he has just seen us walk past the Talbot Hotel where he is now ensconced but couldn't be bothered to come to the door and shout as we passed.

The Talbot, after a fairly lengthy closure, is recently reopened and the sign on the door proclaiming "Thwaites Original Bitter £1.60/pint" is certainly having a strong pull.

On entry there's a healthy gathering of Clarets, many of whom it transpires had been using the Sparrow Hawk for pre-match refreshments, but have switched as that pub is itself now closed. With the White Hart now up for sale, it is fast becoming a pub merry-go-round for drinkers in this area, and this is another sad sign of the demise of the traditional pub.

Two pints of Thwaites duly dispatched, we hit the Turf in time for the big kick off.

I must confess to being a bit surprised at the team selection, with last week's man of the match Jack Cork relegated to the bench along with Chris Eagles with these two replaced by Wade Elliott and Robbie Blake. Up front Martin Paterson comes in for Nugent, who is ruled out

249

on the grounds of not being able to play against his own club as a condition of his loan.

I can't help but feel that whilst this is a positive attacking selection for what is a must win game, it may leave us short in centre midfield with only Bikey and Big Kev in that area.

The early exchanges are evenly balanced and the Pompey players to their credit seem to be suffering no adverse reaction to the club's terrible plight. As the game settles down I start to get uneasy feelings about the ease with which they seem to be able to penetrate our defence and the phrase 'a hot knife through butter' comes to mind.

Sure enough, it's not long before the Beast is picking the ball out of his net, but fortunately the scorer Danny Webber is adjudged offside. However, on 25 minutes, there's no such luck as Webber's low curling ball into the box evades everybody but Frederic Piquionne, who steals in unnoticed at the back post to guide it home. We had been warned.

This prompts the Clarets to up their game and within six minutes we are level with what Gary Lineker later described on Match of the Day as a "peach of a goal."

A long clearance by the Beast is headed on by Fletcher into the path of Paterson who, spotting David James off his line, acrobatically lobs the keeper to perfection and the ball drops spectacularly into the net. That's better.

The game is then fairly even to half time with Pompey still looking dangerous in attack and hitting the bar with an effort that probably deserved a better fate.

Half time brings a text from Ed reporting Bolton 1-0 up against fellow strugglers Wolves. One of the two is going to be further in the mire and unfortunately it looks like Wolves at the moment. The concourse TVs show Wigan trailing at Birmingham which is in our favour.

But the mood in the stand around me is not optimistic after what we've just witnessed and I have to confess that I tell my near neighbour that I think we are going to lose this one.

The second half starts in similar vein to the first with the visitors looking dangerous and not long in we see Clarke Carlisle concede a needless penalty for a foul on the dangerous Piquionne. The player was travelling at speed but just entering the box and well wide of the goal so had lots to do, but was gifted a penalty by Carlisle's reckless challenge.

Up steps Jamie O'Hara, facing the Beast and a host of wildly waving Clarets fans in the Jimmy Mac Stand trying to distract him. He hits it hard and low but Jensen is equal to it and gets the ball away to safety.

The crowd to a man stand to hail the Beast and once again he is our penalty saviour. Can this be the turning point of the game?

Suddenly it looks like it might as Paterson is put clear down the right and an inch perfect cross finds Fletcher centre of goal just outside the six yard box. He can't miss as he plants a powerful header... in the top corner? No, in the bloody stand behind the goal. A gilt edged opportunity gone.

Worse still is to come when a Portsmouth attack down the right breaks down as the ball goes out of play for a Burnley throw. Fox takes it and throws the ball to Carlisle who is stood on his own in the penalty area.

Mistake number one I think. Perhaps he should have thrown it down the line, but then again Carlisle was in oceans of space.

However two predatory Pompey attackers suddenly smell blood and start to bear down on our Clarke, and for a second he freezes as he considers his options.

Mistake number two I believe. Why did he not just hoof it back into touch from whence it came?

But no. Clarke then commits the cardinal sin of trying to be a ball playing winger instead of a rough, tough centre back and attempts to dribble his way out of trouble. Disaster as, like we all knew he would, he loses the ball and then completes the trick by downing the striker for penalty number two. What madness. How schoolboyish. What was he thinking?

I am distraught and I bet he is too. At the end of a week when he has enjoyed success in a quiz show on national TV, demonstrating his agile brain power, he now has horrific exposure on national TV as the instigator of our downfall against a team which is probably already relegated.

Can the Beast save the day a second time? Surely that's too much to ask? The answer is no, as O'Hara is relieved of the duty and Hassan Yebda, entrusted with the kick, promptly makes no mistake.

The game's up and despite some late pressure and a sending off for Ricardo Rocha of Portsmouth, it's too little too late and once again we have nothing to show for our efforts. Pompey, as I predicted before the game, showed that although they are the bottom of the league, they are not the poorest team in it.

Questioned on TV later, Brian Laws was asked if the whole administration thing had an impact on the game and the way Pompey reacted. Honestly, and with a knowing look in his eye, he replied that he didn't think it had any impact on the penalties. Did the interviewer?

To be truthful, we played poorly, particularly in defence, but without wanting to be critical, team selection and tactics left a lot to be desired.

The danger is that Brian Laws, not an overly popular appointment with the fans to begin with, is looking more and more vulnerable with every defeat.

The fans have been fantastic in their support this season and the manager and everybody at the club need to keep this goodwill and belief on board. This defeat has made things even more difficult in this respect. For sure, the knives will be out for Brian on the various messageboards tonight.

Bolton went on to win 1-0, while Wigan lost 1-0, leaving Wolves, Wigan and ourselves the major sufferers this time round.

I predicted February as make or break, and one win and three defeats suggests the wheels have come off. Thank God it's almost March.

But the mood of pessimism seems to be growing and we quickly need a result to turn the tide. What better place than at the Emirates against Arsenal next week to get it?

Result: Burnley (Paterson 31) 1, Portsmouth (Piquionne 25, Yebda 76 pen) 2.

Team: Jensen; Mears, Carlisle, Cort, Fox, Elliott (Eagles 63), McDonald K, Bikey (Cork 63), Blake (Thompson 80); Paterson, Fletcher.

Subs not used: Weaver, Edgar, Jordan, Duff.

Attendance: 19,714.

Position in Table: 19.

Season record: Played 27, Won 6, Drawn 5, Lost 16, Goals for 28, Goals against 57, Points 23.

MARCH

Where Did All The Fun Go?

IT'S almost 12 months to the day that the company I work for announced that due to the economic climate, a consultation period would be entered with the intention of shedding in the region of 30 jobs.

What happened in effect was that on April 1, 2009, the whole company, some 100 hundred plus individuals, went into administration – as Portsmouth did - and within a few days 50 per cent of the workforce were made redundant. I was fortunate at that time to be a survivor of the cull and eventually the company, smaller and leaner I believe is the correct parlance, was bought out of administration on July 1 by the current owner.

Today, March 2, 2010, I get that feeling of déjà vu, as I am called to a managers' meeting and handed a brief statement entitled: "Notice of proposed closure of the Twisting/Winding/Stancraft and Merchant Yarn Departments."

The letter goes on to state that: "owing to adverse trading conditions and a never ending battle to compete with prices for products being brought in from the Far East, it has been found necessary to announce that the company is proposing to close the aforementioned departments which could be resultant in approximately 15 positions being made redundant."

Once again, it looks as though I am a survivor but among many friends who aren't is my mate and chief tormentor PNE Ed.

What a bum deal life can hit with you from time to time. People who have given their all in difficult and unpleasant working conditions suddenly thrown out of work with no real prospect of meaningful employment. No big fat payouts for these people, just statutory government redundancy pay and minimum notice periods.

What a lousy day. It certainly puts last Saturday's defeat into context and the spectre of redundancy makes relegation worries fade into insignificance.

On the soccer front, March looks like an interesting month and one where I feel we must achieve a significant points haul if we are to have any chance of survival.

Only one game against a top side, Arsenal away this coming Saturday, then a midweek home clash with the rearranged fixture against Stoke City. This is closely followed by the visit of fellow strugglers Wolves and then an away game at local relegation rivals Wigan, before we end the month at home to arch enemies Blackburn Rovers.

How many points can we get here? I hope for all 15 but I fear it will be more like five.

Today, Thursday, March 4, brings the best office toy I think I have ever seen. A friend of my work colleague Alison emails her a programme called 'Text to Speech' with a free trial download.

The essence of the programme is that there is a face displayed on a screen and several boxes under it. In one of these you can type whatever you want to say in whichever language and then click the box entitled 'say it' and that is exactly what it does.

Added to this are the options to add voice effects such as 'bullhorn,' 'reverb,' 'speed,' 'pitch,' 'flanger' and many more. You can then choose the character of the speaker, ie Fiona, who is Scottish, Daniel from the UK, Tom, who is from the US, Sangheeta from India and many more, who then deliver the text in an appropriate accent, well almost.

This essential tool is quickly distributed by email around the office, and pretty soon the room resounds to comments like "Up yours, Ed" delivered by US Tom in a transatlantic drawl. This is quickly followed by "nob off" and other terms of endearment as the office descends into total anarchy.

I think my favourite was when the unsuspecting Paul, who had come in to cut some paper on the guillotine, was surprised to hear a disembodied mechanical voice in a soft female Indian accent advising him "Mind your fingers Paul" quickly followed by "and your todger." It's a long time since we had such fun at work. Childish, abusive but a hell of a laugh.

I think 'Text to Speech' will be around the office for some time to come. Even Ed, who only yesterday learnt of his redundancy, cheered up enormously and managed several cheap jibes at the Clarets and Brian Laws delivered in a variety of accents and special effects. Aah, simple pleasures.

I click on Clarets Mad in the evening to see if there is any gossip and check who the keyboard warriors have it in for today, and find that summer signing Richard Eckersley is off tomorrow on a month's loan to Plymouth.

The player, who has just belatedly had the fee following his summer move from Manchester United settled by tribunal at £500,000, must be wondering what the hell he has let himself in for at Burnley. Unable to break into the side because of the consistency of Tyrone Mears, his first team action has been extremely limited and he must be questioning the wisdom of turning down a contract at Old Trafford to come here.

Let's hope his spell away will see him get some much needed competitive football and set him up for a real go at winning a place on his return. I think he could still turn out to be a very important player for the Clarets if the fans will allow him time to settle and develop.

Friday reveals that Fernando Guerrero, who was destined according to Coyle to be one of the most fouled players in the Premier League, has had his loan deal terminated and returned to Ecuador.

We'll never know if he was going to be so heavily fouled as he didn't get enough pitch time for anybody to notice him. Fernando's great adventure is over before it got started.

A pity really because the bits I saw of him he looked potentially a real eye-catching player with an air of unpredictability. It looks though that both Coyle and Brian Laws considered him too lightweight to make any impact in the top league in the world and back to South America he goes.

Game 28 – Saturday, March 6, 3pm – Arsenal – Away.

AWAY games I have started to dread.

I am now caught in an uncertainty of not knowing what to do for the best. Should I listen to the radio or not listen as I await the first knife through the heart that signals the start of the avalanche? Home games are easier as you can see the action and get a feel for whether it is going to be our day or not.

I decide, as I knew I would, to listen and try and fit in bits of jobs and domestic chores around the commentary.

The game starts after a thorough clean of the bathroom, with the pre-match discussion as I empty the washing machine.

The Clarets make four changes. Dropped to the bench are Bikey, Elliott and Blake, whilst Fletcher misses the game with a broken hand sustained while training with the Scottish national squad. In come Cork, Eagles and the returning Alexander, and Nugent to replace the injured Fletcher.

Moving on from the washing, it's off with the kitchen radio and on with the car radio as I go for the evening's beer supply and fill up with petrol, the car that is.

On 30 minutes, Radio Lancs kindly gives me the score flash I least want to hear, West Ham 0 Bolton 2.

Almost immediately we go one down. I'm sure they wouldn't have scored if our friends on the radio hadn't distracted my concentration with that scoreline. Inevitably it's a goal described by our chums as "perfectly preventable" as indecision between Grezza and the Beast allows Cesc Fabregas in.

Coupled with the news that Preston are winning at Plymouth, I wonder what has happened to Ed, but bang on cue the texts start coming ie "Heard any scores, Pete" and "Coyle's masterminding a Bolton away win" or words to that effect. I ignore them whist silently cursing West Ham and Spaniards.

I try the pretence of not knowing any scores and claim justifiably that I am chopping onions. More texts and more denials lead to the text "For f**k's sake Pete, how many onions are you having?" I reply that I like onions, and get through to half time with a tear in my eye.

By the second half I've chopped as much onion as I can stand and switch to outdoors on the mobile phone headphones whilst I clean the car.

Still in denial with Ed and under the cosh from early Arsenal pressure my ears suddenly prick up as I hear Carlisle's headed clearance finding the predatory Nugent free in the box. Allowing the ball to bounce he then beautifully lobs Manuel Almunia in the Arsenal goal with a deft shot from the outside of his right boot. Unbelievably we are level with the Gunners in front of 60,000 at the Emirates.

Now I have to break my cover and text Ed: "Good old Nuge." As a PNE fan that is guaranteed to wind him up, as they still seem to think he belongs to them.

It can't last and it doesn't, and not long after we fall a goal behind to a Theo Walcott effort. The game winds to the close with a succession of Arsenal misses, particularly from Nicklas Bendtner who must secretly like us as he always puts his chances wide against Burnley.

Once again the wind up texts come and I go back into the head in the sand routine, claiming I am out of radio contact.

Coming to the end and still only one goal in it, will we get that one chance to make a mockery of the game and level it? The answer is yes, or should that be no, as from a corner the ball drops invitingly to sub Thompson with the chance to drill it through the packed penalty area and in the net.

Does he? Does he hell? He drills it straight over the crossbar and that's our chance gone begging.

To rub salt in the wounds Arshavin, on as a sub for the Arse, manages to drill his shot into the corner of the net with practically the last kick and that's your lot.

Result: Arsenal (Fabregas 34, Walcott 60, Arshavin 90) 3, Burnley (Nugent 50) 1.
Team: Jensen; Mears, Carlisle, Cort, Fox; Paterson (Thompson 74), Alexander (Bikey 65), McDonald K (Elliott 53), Cork, Eagles, Nugent.
Subs not used: Weaver, Duff, Jordan, Blake.
Attendance: 60,043.
Position in table: 19.
Season record: Played 28, Won 6, Drawn 5, Lost 17, Goals for 29, Goals against 60, Points 23.

Sunday sees Everton thrash relegation rivals Hull City 5-1 at Goodison, and Hull stay one place and one point above us from the same number of games. Wolves, beaten at home by Manchester United, sit on the same points as Hull and within easy striking distance if we can run into some form.

On the Monday evening, Liverpool let us down badly by losing to a single goal at fellow strugglers Wigan which puts the Latics five points to the good. The feeling of impending doom is all around and my conversations with many Clarets usually conclude with the words "I think we have had it."

Game 29 – Wednesday, March 10, 7.45pm – Stoke City – Home.
TONIGHT sees the rearranged fixture at home to Stoke City which was postponed in early January due to the icy weather conditions.

It's very unusual for us to play on a Wednesday night but the game has been put back from Tuesday to allow Stoke recovery time following Sunday's cup defeat at Chelsea. Let's hope that has knocked the stuffing out of them, but I doubt it.

They of the long ball and extreme physical presence will form just the type of opposition we don't usually like. It's going to be hold on to your hats and prepare for the aerial bombardment tonight. Stephanie misses the game, being marooned in her student accommodation in Liverpool, so my ears should benefit from the rest.

As I make my way by car to the Turf, Radio Lancashire are speculating on how Burnley should negate the phenomenal long throw weapon posed by Rory Delap.

Jokingly, the suggestion has been made that the advertisement hoardings should be moved closer to the pitch to stop Delap's run up, thereby limiting his distance. Brian Laws confirms, I suspect tongue in cheek, that this has already been done.

On arrival at the ground a look down at the pitch quickly confirms he wasn't joking. Sitting closer than I have ever seen them to the touchlines are the said advertisement hoardings. My fellow supporters confirm that Stoke officials have already signalled their displeasure to the referee and match officials but the boards remain where they are.

Is this unfair and unsporting? Who cares? In our position we have to employ whatever tactics we can to gain an advantage and I don't think for one minute if the roles were reversed our opponents would not do likewise. Not averse to a bit of skulduggery, aren't our adversaries.

As I sit waiting for the action to commence, I can't help feeling slightly negative about our chances. A quick look at the teams confirms the expected physical disparity between the sides as the giants prepare to trample our heroes under foot.

There seems a larger than normal number of empty seats although this is not unexpected for a Wednesday evening fixture. The crowd also seem apprehensive, but the younger elements in the stand behind me are certainly doing their best to lift the atmosphere.

The game gets under way and pretty quickly my fears are realised as our opponents start to dominate with their physicality and their ugly long ball percentage game. Within the first 10 minutes, I count at least three Delap specials that don't seem to be suffering much from the restricted run up. The sight of the guy drying the ball on his shirt at every throw in before he launches it can sure get tedious after a while, and I've only managed 10 minutes.

Our attempts to play are disjointed at best and at times woeful, with Alexander in particular unable to place a pass. Our opponents continue to bully and harry us and we allow ourselves to get sucked into their style of game.

Frequent bouts of head tennis inevitably end with our physically superior opponents coming out on top. Young Jack Cork is traumatised by one bone shattering challenge and never quite recovers from it, passing up one of our better opportunities by trying to play in Paterson rather than go for goal.

On 23 minutes comes the inevitable, a Stoke goal from a long throw in. Delap produces his party piece, Mamady Sidibe flicks on and Sanli Tuncay is first to react, steering a firm header past Jensen.

Our game continues on a downward spiral towards half time and the crowd gets more disillusioned as on the pitch heads start to drop.

My mate John W misses the kick off as it's parents evening at the school where he teaches in Ingleton, but he breaks all speed records to make it in about 10 minutes before half time. He is greeted by cheerful comments like "you shouldn't have bothered," as he sits quietly freezing in his work gear.

To his credit John refuses to be negative and is trying to put a positive spin on things. I suddenly realise that he is right. What is in danger of dragging us down is the cloud of negativity that is starting to descend.

Ashamed of myself, I resolve at half time to try and be more positive in the second half. To assist our chances I decide to put on my as yet untried Clarets hat, to see if it has the magic.

The start of the second half sees the end of Cork, physically destroyed by Stoke's team of Titans, and in his place comes Big Kev McDonald, a much beefier version than young Jack. A bit of an enigma Kev is proving to be, a player with all the attributes but not delivering consistently so far this season.

We start the half much brighter and are playing the ball on the deck now and using the width. Paterson, largely anonymous in the first half, is now starting to make an impact down the right, and Big Kev is quickly into his stride, getting hold of the game and spreading play admirably.

On 52 minutes comes another moment of Turf Moor magic as Paterson is released down the right before checking inside and delivering an almost identical cross to the one Fletcher headed over against Pompey. There's no miss this time as the cross finds Nugent leaping in the centre to power home another superb headed goal.

Game on and suddenly the cloud is lifting as confidence flows back into the players on the pitch and the crowd in the stands. Willed on by the fans we mount several promising attacks and get the upper hand.

Stoke, so overpowering in the first half, are now no longer such a daunting prospect and we have their measure.

Can we find an invaluable winner? Sadly not despite the influential McDonald's close thing and we have to settle for a point.

Coming away from the ground there is a feeling among the fans that the first half was dire but the second has rekindled some hope. Now it's Wolves on Saturday and it's an absolute must win game. The hat will be on from the start.

Result: Burnley (Nugent 52) 1, Stoke City (Tuncay 23) 1.

Team: Jensen; Mears, Carlisle, Cort, Fox (Jordan 77); Paterson, Cork (McDonald K 46), Alexander, Eagles; Nugent, Thompson (Elliott 71).

Subs not used: Weaver, Duff, Bikey, Blake.

Attendance: 20,323.

Position in table: 18.

Season record: Played 29, Won 6, Drawn 6, lost 17, Goals for 30, Goals against 61, Points 24.

Game 30 – Saturday, March 13, 3pm – Wolverhampton Wanderers – Home.

A BREATH of Spring in the air today, and all the pre-match discussions are concerning what clothing to wear. I'm tempted by the sight of the sunshine to go for something a bit lighter and Stephanie is planning on going for the layered look.

Before leaving the house I opt for the safety of the moleskin coat over a thick jumper. It's a wise move as after parking the car we set off for the pub and note that despite the sunshine there's a bitter wind blowing.

A pleasant walk through the park sees us approaching the Talbot in good time and we are greeted by the sight of people sitting outside drinking their pints and smoking in the March air.

Getting nearer I spot that two of these hardy souls are the two Johns, one of whom, John W, is already in the throes of a serious cold and probably now heading for pneumonia.

I arrive just in time for it to be my round. No change there then and having surveyed the ample choice of real ales opt for Timothy Taylor's Landlord, John G sticking with Black Sheep and John W, whose sense of taste and smell are shattered, going for the Carling Extra Cold to show his hardness. I sit outside sipping my beer, holding the glass with hands insulated against the cold by two pairs of gloves and inhaling the delicate aromas of petrol and diesel exhaust. Aah, bliss.

At the ground, a look at the line up shows an unfamiliar centre midfield pairing of Bikey and Alexander so presumably Big Kev, so influential after coming on against Stoke, has picked up a knock. No sign of either him or Jack Cork in the subs either, and we go 4-4-2 with Eagles and Elliott wide and Nugent and Paterson up top.

There's a good crowd with a large contingent of Wolves fans in what for them is an equally must win game which has an uneventful opening. I've adopted my positive philosophy following Wednesday's reflections and the hat and wristband are on from the start.

Not long gone and I get my first twinge of unease as a ball played into space in our half sees Kevin Doyle, the lone Wolves striker, after it. In a moment of madness that only the Beast can conjure he dashes from his goal to meet the onrushing striker.

As Doyle pushes the ball past him, Brian launches himself like a fighting bull at his legs and head butts him in the thigh, stopping his progress. I half expect to see him proceed to gore the now prostrate Doyle but the Beast realises the seriousness of his action and decides wisely to play dead.

Fortunately, after a few minutes the referee decides just to produce a yellow card and I breathe again. The resultant free kick sails harmlessly wide with the Beast flapping wildly at it.

I sense it's going to be one of those days, and I'm soon proved right. On 26 minutes, a ball is played hopefully towards our goal with Mears and Wolves winger Matt Jarvis in pursuit. Mears is favourite to get there first and so he does, but then he attempts to find the Beast with a weak header. Brian this time is slow off his line and Jarvis nips in to poke the ball past him and over the line.

Incredibly we have gifted a goal again. Every time we score it has to be a piece of sumptuous skill, but for the opposition it's a free gift every day. I am beside myself with rage and disbelief, and again we have a mountain to climb.

We try to pick it up again and battle manfully but with not much success. Nugent does manage a shot on the turn which is hit into the ground and bounces up to glance off the top of the crossbar. Fox, who is injured and replaced by Jordan, needs oxygen and a stretcher to get him to the dressing rooms. Half time sees us trudge in depressingly but familiarly one down.

Things can hopefully only get better in the second half, but we don't start promisingly and are on the back foot.

On 47 minutes comes the killer goal and it just about sums up 2010 for us. The ball is played square across our box to the right where some guy with a totally unpronounceable and unspellable name hits a speculative shot. It's going well wide. Oh no, it's not.

Hitting Clarke Carlisle on the back of his heel, the ball changes direction and nestles right in the corner of the net. A gift and an own goal. The singing Wolves fans can't believe their luck but I can.

Cue the last throw of the dice and it's off with Bikey and crowd favourite Eagles. This is met by loud booing from all sections of the ground and the short-lived love affair with Brian Laws is evaporating rapidly. On in their places come Robbie Blake to go left wing, Steven Thompson as the human battering ram up front, with Paterson going wide right and Elliott centre mid.

It's do or die time now and quickly into the action Robbie starts to weave his magic. A mazy run on the left of the box sees him go for goal from a narrow angle only for his shot to cannon back off the near post.

On 73 minutes comes a lifeline as a partially cleared cross comes out to Alexander on the edge of the area, and his hard hit shot goes into the ground and sits up invitingly in front of goal for Thompson to get his head to it and steer home.

Cue the cavalry charge as we throw the kitchen sink at it, leaving glaring gaps at the back as we ride our luck. A must win game it was but boy, would we settle for a point.

Yet it's not to be and once again I leave the ground totally deflated. This has to be the lowest point of the season, and once again courtesy of the self-destruct button. We have been beaten by a poor Premier League side, certainly no better than us.

It's difficult to see a way back from here. We have lost the advantage of the extra home games, have played one more than most of our rivals, and are still in the relegation places. Next week sees us away at Wigan, beaten 4-0 today by Coyle's Bolton.

A statistic from one of the Sunday papers shows we have taken fewer points than any other team against sides in the bottom half and that is a pretty damning stat.

At the bottom there is no game for Portsmouth, Hull lose in the last minute to Arsenal and West Ham are blitzed 4-1 at Chelsea. Wolves and Bolton are the weekend's happy bunnies and doesn't that make you feel sick? So much for the lucky hat and wristband. You know, I never thought that worked anyway.

Result: Burnley (Thompson 73) 1, Wolverhampton Wanderers (Jarvis 26, Carlisle o.g. 47) 2.

Team: Jensen; Mears Carlisle, Cort, Fox (Jordan 39); Elliott, Alexander, Bikey (Blake 54), Eagles (Thompson 54); Nugent, Paterson.

Subs not used: Weaver, Duff, Edgar, Rodriguez.

Attendance: 21,217.

Position in table: 18.

Season record: Played 30, Won 6, Drawn 6, Lost 18, Goals for 31, Goals against 63, Points 24.

On Monday, March 15, Hull City manager Phil Brown is relieved of his duties as the Tigers decide they have to act now to try and save themselves. Good old 'Tango Man,' he of the orange complexion, has been living on borrowed time for a while now and the move surprises nobody.

Whether it will make the slightest bit of difference remains to be seen but with only nine left to play for them it's a last throw of the dice.

The end of March marks the season ticket early bird renewal deadline. This year, following frozen prices in this period over the past couple of years, there is a modest rise of £30 on the cost of my ticket, which I suppose I can't really grumble at.

The renewal period seems to have got shorter each year and March seems particularly early as the current season doesn't finish till May. In my own case it doesn't particularly matter as I have been fortunate enough to manage to stay in work and will be renewing come what may. However I suspect for a significant number of fans, this early renewal date will be an issue.

It's likely that promotion to the Premier League resulted in around 8/9,000 new/returning season ticket holders. If, as is looking increasingly likely, we are relegated, what will be the intentions of this particular section of fans?

If we are down, will they return to Saturday afternoons in the pub/shopping/watching TV? On the other hand, if we survive will they be so inspired they sign up for another ride on the claret and blue roller coaster?

271

There's the dilemma. If they assume we are down and don't renew, they miss the chance of retaining their seats at the discounted prices. If they do renew and we are relegated, they may consider it money wasted. As the saying goes, 'you pays your money and you takes your chance'.

On Tuesday, March 16 Wigan, our hosts this coming Saturday, have a home fixture against Aston Villa who on paper should be favourites.

The Villains, chasing a top four finish and a place in the Champions League next season, seem to have hit a sticky patch and are without a win so far in March. But a defeat for Wigan following Saturday's walloping at Bolton will put them right in the mire, leaving them just four points better off than ourselves.

This surprises me a little as I thought they were one of the better teams we have seen at the Turf, and having beaten Chelsea and more recently Liverpool at home, they should be doing better. However they sit with only one more win and one more draw than us so consistency is obviously not their strong point.

Villa duly do us the honours running out 2-1 victors and setting Wigan nerves jangling.

If only we can topple them on Saturday there'll be only one point in it and they have a similar goal difference, having been on the wrong end of a 9-0 thrashing at Tottenham. Come on God, for once smile on the Clarets and give us that long awaited away victory and some hope.

Wednesday morning at work sees the office 'enemies' in antagonistic mood and fuelled by a nonsense story in the Sun newspaper they are out to wind me up about mercilessly. The newspaper, if that's what it can be called, runs a story claiming that Burnley are already on the look out for a new manager and are on the verge of giving Brian Laws the chop after fearing they have made a big error with his appointment.

This story has then found its way onto several websites including the BBC where my 'colleagues,' who should be engaged in some gainful employment, have picked it up. I point out to them that anybody with a brain the half size of a pea would realise that this is utter rubbish, but they are in vicious mood today. It's at times like this when you wonder how nice it would be to work on your own, but my time will come.

In quick time Barry Kilby rubbishes the story with a statement, which reads: "This is a ludicrous, irresponsible, damaging and inaccurate piece of journalism. We are not in the process of looking for a replacement for Brian and everyone involved with Burnley Football Club is putting every ounce of effort into staying in the Premier League." Well said Barry.

Game 31 – Saturday, March 20, 3pm – Wigan Athletic – Away.
SOMETIMES, though not often, I've found writing this diary a bit of a chore and not the labour of love I thought it would be, and this is one of those times. After the trauma of what went on at Wigan I was unable to write over the weekend and even now on Monday evening it doesn't seem much easier.

Pre-match finds me in the conservatory doing a bit of a spring clean on the blinds in an attempt to stave off having to buy new ones. As I work I switch on the TV to Sky Sports News to see what is happening in the early kick off game.

I am stunned, though I suppose I shouldn't be, to learn that with 15 minutes to go Wolves, our relegation rivals and conquerors from last week, are leading highly fancied Villa 2-1 at Villa Park. How can that be? A team that enjoyed the greatest of fortune and scored two gifted goals at the Turf are doing it again, once more aided by an own goal. Why do we never seem to enjoy that sort of good luck?

I curse our misfortune but am heartened soon after by news of a Villa equaliser and four minutes of added time. Surely time for a Villa winner? But it's not to be and Wolves go away with a prized point for their efforts.

At Wigan's DW Stadium they've just got underway and Brian Laws is forced into changes. Out go Carlisle and Fox from defence and Bikey and Eagles from midfield, and they are replaced by Duff, Jordan, McDonald K and the returning Steven Fletcher.

Chris Kamara is reporting from the ground for Sky and his early observations are very encouraging as he reveals it's all Burnley in the opening minutes and we are going close. On the strength of his optimism I decide to opt for Radio Lancs for a more complete coverage, just in time to hear Preston going 2-0 down at West Bromwich Albion.

Then a lucky let off as Alexander and Jensen needlessly concede a corner and from the resulting flag kick Gary Caldwell, brother of our own Steven, heads powerfully against the angle of bar and post via the head of Wade Elliott, who is well positioned on the line.

Stephanie is doing a stint working in the local newsagents to supplement her meagre student finances so I text her on 30 minutes with the goalless scoreline. PNE Ed is strangely quiet but I know why as news comes through that Nob End are now 3-1 adrift at WBA. Bad news from Portsmouth who, having duly had their nine points deducted for going into administration, now trail to the only other team below us in the table, Hull City.

Still, we seem to be doing OK and the radio commentators report the only threat in the first 40 minutes was the Caldwell header. PNE pull another back before half time to set up a lively second half at the Hawthorns and we go in 0-0 at the break.

How ironic that in Wigan and ourselves we have two teams who have already conceded a combined total of more than 120 Premier League goals this season and yet we have played out a goalless first half.

As the second half wears on it still sounds fairly even and my wife returns from visiting her mother just in time to hear Paterson, put through by Nugent, beat the keeper and hit the top of the crossbar. Will that prove costly? It usually does.

As we enter the last 10 minutes, there are still no goals, Blake is on for Fletcher, and the commentators tempt fate by suggesting what a rarity it is for Burnley to go into the last 10 minutes with none conceded.

Now it's Eagles on for Paterson. Can his pace punish the tiring defence? Results are still not going for us as Hull lead 2-1 at Pompey.

Now it's a great late save from Jensen tipping over the bar and only three minutes to go.

I try to keep the thought that we may have a precious away point and also have denied Wigan maximum points away from my brain but it's getting difficult now. Then Portsmouth level it. Brilliant. Soon it's even better. Portsmouth 3, Hull 2. Just what the doctor ordered.

There are four minutes added time at the DW, and there are chances at both ends with the Clarets throwing bodies in the way of everything.

Three minutes gone of stoppage time, then just as I am about to pour a large gin and tonic to celebrate, unbelievably we concede. Substitute Victor Moses loses Jordan - sounds quite biblical when you put it like that - to get across a left foot centre and there is Hugo Rodellega throwing himself forward to powerfully head past Jensen.

What the hell have we done to deserve that kick in the teeth? Why for once can't God grant us that bit of luck he, or she, seems to reserve for al our rivals?

How cruel can this game get, our hard earned point snatched away at the death and once again by relegation rivals? Brian Laws, is he a poor manager or just bloody unlucky?

Punishing myself with the Match of the Day highlights I watch Hansen with all his usual smugness declare that he can't see Burnley winning the three or four games that they need to and they are almost certainly down.

Much as it pains me to do so I have to agree with him.

Result: Wigan Athletic (Rodallega 90) 1, Burnley 0.

Team: Jensen; Mears, Cort, Duff, Jordan: Paterson (Eagles 82), Alexander, McDonald K, Elliott; Nugent, Fletcher (Blake 69).

Subs not used: Weaver, Bikey, Edgar, Thompson, Cork.

Attendance: 18,498.

Position in Table: 18.

Season Record: Played 31, Won 6, Drawn 6, Lost 19, Goals for 31, Goals against 64, Points 24.

Where did all the fun go? What started out as an adventure full of hope and driven by the simple pleasure of being back where we always thought we belonged has turned sour.

In the aftermath of the Wembley victory, most fans said they weren't bothered if we were to come straight back down. For them the sheer pleasure of seeing us make it was enough.

But clearly most fans I speak to are bothered now, and forgetting the enormity and inequality of the task that faced us, are feeling more than a little disappointed.

The early euphoria generated by winning the first four home games masked the worrying away form. But now the successes at home have dried up and the away form is the worst of any league club with a return of one point from a possible 48.

The fun has gone for sure and the events of January are responsible in no small measure. A confidence sapping sequence of one win in the last 20 league games has drained the players and fans alike. At the half way stage we sat comfortably on 20 points but now 12 games on we have amassed a paltry four more.

With home games to come against 'the old enemy' Blackburn Rovers and then Manchester City, Liverpool, and finally Tottenham, the so-called easy home games have come and gone with scant reward. Away from home we have still to visit Hull, Sunderland, and Birmingham, but to be honest with our away form we wouldn't be optimistic at Darlington or Grimsby.

Tuesday, March 23 sees another puzzling managerial decision as we let David Edgar go out on a month loan to Championship side Swansea. This comes at a time when central defenders Steven Caldwell and Clarke Carlisle are injured, and although we are better placed in this department than I can remember for many years, it's still a strange one.

Clearly Edgar is frustrated at his lack of match action, but on the occasions he has been given first team opportunities he has performed admirably. As a young player only recently signed I would have expected him to be more in the manager's plans than some of the players who are coming out of contract at the end of the season and will surely be moving on. There must be some strategy behind the decision but to me and I'm sure many other fans, it's difficult to see.

Tuesday night sees another relegation 'six-pointer' as West Ham host the improving Wolves. The Old Gold of Wolves comes out on top by a convincing 3-1 margin, much to the disgust of the home crowd who turn on their team.

Wolves' last three away games have resulted in two wins and a very creditable draw, and all these results were against teams in claret and blue, namely West Ham, Aston Villa, and ourselves. This victory allows them to breathe much easier as they move onto 31 points, leaving the Hammers on 27.

Next in 18th and 19th positions are us and Hull, both on 24 points, with Hull having a game in hand. Trailing in behind and almost certainly relegated are Portsmouth on 13 after their points deduction. Barring any serious slip ups it now looks like Pompey and then any two from three, ie West Ham, Hull, and us, for the dreaded drop.

On the same evening Preston are away at Middlesbrough, and that brings us back again to our old friend Ed. As I pointed out earlier, Ed has become increasingly antagonistic to all things claret and blue and myself in particular.

He has now taken to sending picture messages to my mobile of his black Labrador dog Dan's teeth. These messages are usually accompanied with the text "These in ur ass pal." Charming, isn't it?

Ed's problems are not confined to supporting PNE, although now he claims he doesn't care about them as the rugby league season has started and he is following his first love Wigan Warriors. Ed is a casualty of a round of redundancies at the mill and today was the date of his last appeal against his fate. In true fashion, he has fought a magnificent rearguard action, which of course came to nought. However, he will have the satisfaction of not going without a fight.

Our place of work is an old Victorian cotton mill which has seen better days. One of the latest problems is the fact that the troughing over the entrance door was brought down by snow in the frozen winter we have just endured. Needless to say it has not been repaired and lies on the roadway as a symbol of the decay of the once mighty Lancashire textile industry.

After what he describes as a "shit day" fending off disgruntled customers, fighting his case, and generally being harassed, Ed leaves for home at five but not before being deluged by rain water falling from where the aforementioned troughing should be. Coupled with PNE losing 2-0 at Boro and Blackpool winning 5-1, you could say that he was 'guttered.'

Thoughts now turn to the weekend clash with the Rovers and the ludicrous kick-off time of midday on a Sunday.

Once again the transport and ticketing arrangements are a rerun of the military style operation witnessed at Ewood Park in October. The plan is to have all the 2,400 Rovers fans bussed in and inside the stadium by about 10am.

Now, to me, I can't see the point and would have thought it a much better idea to get them there much closer to kick off time although I can appreciate there may be logistical difficulties in that. Still I suppose it will give us the opportunity to sell them more overpriced pies and ale and boost the coffers.

What the game will bring in terms of a performance is anybody's guess as derby games are notoriously unpredictable and the form book often goes out the window. Let's hope so in this case.

I have heard, not for the first time, the comment that relegation would be bearable if we could just beat the Rovers. Not for me it wouldn't and what a short sighted viewpoint that is. Let's beat the Rovers and use that as the launch pad for a renewed survival battle.

Game 32 – Sunday, March 28, noon – Blackburn Rovers – Home.

SATURDAY is a relaxing day with no game and just our rivals' results to look out for.

Hull upset the applecart with a 2-0 home win over Fulham to go three points clear of us with a game in hand. Fulham were always going to be the sort of team that would capitulate, as they are comfortably in mid-table with nothing to play for domestically but with a good run in the Europa Cup underway.

But Gianfranco Zola's sorely troubled Hammers lose at home to Stoke, their second home reverse this week and a sixth straight defeat, to give us added encouragement ahead of the derby game.

Sunday dawns, and the fact that the game falls on the day that the clocks go forward coupled with the early kick off means many fans will still be half asleep when the action starts. It's a fine day with sunny spells but a cool wind takes the edge off the temperature and has the coat being buttoned up in quick time.

This at the start of the season was the most eagerly awaited game but recent events have soured expectations and there aren't many optimistic fans making their way to the Turf.

We have to park so far away from the ground that it's questionable whether we might have been better off leaving the car at home and walking the whole way. We are down at the ground in good time but I have that intangible feeling of impending doom which I am trying desperately to dispel.

The crowd are doing their best to lift the atmosphere but it sounds a bit half-hearted in contrast to the party atmosphere being generated by the Rovers fans. A look at the line ups once again confirms the physical disparity between the sides as the Rovers giants, led by the colossus that is Chris Samba, dwarf our minnows.

We opt again for a strangely wingless wonder type of formation with the only sort of pretence of a wide man being Martin Paterson down the right. Fletcher and Nugent are going up front against the 'twin towers' in the Rovers central defence and we attempt to pack the centre midfield with Elliott, Alexander, and Big Kev.

From the off it's apparent that the greater physical strength of our opponents aided by a stiff breeze at their backs is going to give us problems. I remark to my mate John W that it would be nice to see a game with no schoolboy errors, but he like me thinks it will only be a matter of time before we see one.

Not long to wait before our central defence is split down the middle with a simple through ball that sees Martin Olsson fire home, but not before the assistant referee comes to our rescue with a an offside flag.

Early warning there then but is it heeded? No.

Shortly after comes the same trick, a simple ball through a non-existent defence and out comes the Beast to take the ball from Olsson's feet only for the B*****d to produce a perfect dive worthy of young Tom Daly, our Olympic hopeful, to earn the referee's reward of a gift penalty.

Now this signals real trouble as the Beast is surely the last man and if the referee deems it a penalty and it was right in front of the goal, then surely Jensen has denied him a goal scoring opportunity and he has to walk? Incredibly not, as the spot kick is given but no punishment for the Beast. How can that be?

David Dunn duly despatches his gift into the net and we are one down and on the showing so far already beaten.

We continue to blunder our way through the first half, creating nothing and contriving to make a pretty inept looking opposition look dangerous without trying. We have one close shout for a penalty as the lumbering Samba takes out Elliott on the edge of the box with a cynical bodycheck, but our friend the ref sees this one as outside. Shortly before half time we lose Jordan to injury to be replaced by Danny Fox and we go off at the break to a muted stadium except for the delirious Rovers fans.

Texts from Ed watching on the box confirm Olsson's dive but TV suggests his offside goal was marginal. I tell him that we will get them in the second half with the wind in our favour, but I don't really believe it for one minute.

The second half starts a bit brighter and we, as we quite often seem to do, are starting to play some football on the deck and looking more attractive but no more effective. We start to enjoy some spells of possession and retain the ball a bit better as the Rovers settle for sitting on their slender lead. Presumably Big Sam has seen the limit of our threat and reckons one goal will be enough.

With only two substitutions left through the injury to Jordan, it's no surprise to see Blake on for Paterson after 59 minutes. Robbie and Chris Eagles are probably the only two players who are capable of pulling this one out of the fire, and Eagles also joins the fray on 71 minutes, replacing the departing Alexander.

We continue to push forward without any assistance from a truly shocking refereeing performance from Mike Dean who wages a one man anti-Burnley campaign out on the field. At the other end we are rocked by a thunderbolt crashing down from the underside of the crossbar, once again from today's villain Olsson, which is hastily cleared. Ed reckons TV replays show the ball has crossed the line, but he would say that wouldn't he?

We go close ourselves with a great ball in from Fox that flashes across the goal line with firstly Elliott and then Fletcher failing to poke it over the line. But again it's too little too late and we trudge off beaten by the old enemy and I have another week of constant ribbing to face at work.

The match statistics show just six goal attempts with only two on target and it's now abundantly clear where we are heading.

March, with five games in the month, three of which were at home, seemed to be the month that would decide our destiny. Unfortunately we have lost four and drawn one of those games and we are as good as sunk.

Like I said, the fun has now all gone and sad to say I am beginning to dread the remaining six games as the side drains confidence and belief with every defeat. At home we have to face Manchester City,

Liverpool, and Tottenham, all of whom are desperately pursuing points in their quest for a top four finish and a Champions League place.

What prospects there for us then? On this form none and potentially some severe beatings. It's all gone pear shaped and how.

On Friday, I renewed my season ticket and tomorrow I will do the same for Stephanie. We are bloodied and battered but in the words of the Chumbawamba song, "We get knocked down but we get up again".

Leaving the ground and making my way back to the car, we are treated to an outburst from a so-called fan who loudly informs us that he will not be going anywhere near the ground again whilst Brian Laws is the manager.

Well, that's very good of him to tell us that but who bloody cares? This is exactly the type of cretin that promotion to the top flight has encouraged. Where were these guys when we struggled in the lower reaches of the league? Nowhere near Turf Moor, that's for sure, and next season they will be gone as fast as they came and good riddance to them.

More to my liking are the words of my mate John W in an email he sent me shortly after a moaning session concerning our plight. I quote: "This time last year where were we? Going nowhere and achieving nowt. Along comes Owen and his ambition and suddenly we are somebody. What's changed? You? Me? The Clarets? Your expectations of the place we hold in football's pecking order?

"Accept a day in the sun and that we will soon be returned to lower league footie. Look at Bradford, Leeds, Norwich, Charlton, Southampton, to name but a few. I'm proud to be a Claret and always will be. Sometimes that means you have to accept the harsh realities of footballing life. Like we won't win anything and we won't dine at the top table for more than a brief moment.

"So stop bloody whingeing and cheer them on to defeat with pride and a little defiance. After all, they're your team. Lecture and sermon over. Honestly Pete, I think this last 12 months has been fantastic and I don't want it tainted by people booing like they did at the end of the last home match."

Well said John. Keep the faith Clarets, we have been in far worse places than this.

Result: Burnley 0, Blackburn Rovers (Dunn 20 pen) 1.
Team: Jensen; Mears, Duff, Cort Jordan (Fox 43); Paterson (Blake 59), Alexander (Eagles 71), McDonald K, Elliott; Nugent, Fletcher.
Subs not used: Weaver, Carlisle, Cork, Thompson.
Attendance: 21,546.
Position in table: 19.
Season record: Played 32, Won 6, Drawn 6, Lost 20, Goals for 31, Goals against 65, Points 24.

I sleep fitfully on the Sunday night with the events of the game and its consequences running through my head. I never thought that as a grown man with responsibilities I would lose sleep over football, but that's what this game does to you when it gets in your blood.

When I get up on the Monday morning I am quickly reminded of what I don't like about the Rovers derby game. Once again we are treated to news reports on Radio Lancashire of trouble after the game and 40 arrests. Blackburn fans have destroyed a section of seating in the stands and the toilets. There are reports of a bottle aimed at Brian Jensen and also missiles thrown by the Burnley fans.

The FA have launched an investigation into the incidents which, following the coin throwing incident by Clarets fans at Wigan last week, paints us in a very poor light. How bloody mindless and pointless.

Sat on the row in front of me yesterday was a young man of about 18 who I had never seen there before. Not scruffily dressed and sporting no team colours, the sound of the first whistle turned this guy into a ranting lunatic who leapt out of his seat frequently, often for no apparent reason, to hurl invective and vitriol in the direction of the Rovers fans who could neither see him nor hear him. I hope it made him feel better. It didn't appear to and in fact only confirmed to me that he must have some sort of mental problem. Perhaps I'm getting too old.

Messageboard posts confirm the tide of public opinion turning against Brian Laws and calling for his dismissal. Initially not a popular appointment but with the majority of the fans prepared to get behind him, things now seem to be rapidly deteriorating for him and his management team.

Quite simply, huge swathes of the support feel that he cannot get the wins we need in this division and doubt that he can in the Championship. There seems to be player unrest although only Joey Gudjonsson has gone public with it, and the place from the outside seems a million miles away from the start of the season.

Pressure is mounting on Kilby after only three months of Laws' regime. What will be the chairman's reaction? He has had to deny that an alternative was already being sought but the question will surely be raised again shortly.

We look quite capable of losing the last six remaining league games and where will that leave team and supporter morale ahead of a major summer rebuilding job?

APRIL

Going, Going, Gone

WHEN and why did the national media stop loving us?

During the fantastic play off run and the aftermath of Wembley we were the darlings of the media. Every day seemed to feature a national newspaper story on how plucky little Burnley had overcome all the odds to earn a shot at the big time. The press marvelled at our free-flowing attacking style and determination to win every game.

But today it's difficult to find a paper with a good word for us, and the emphasis is now on recent crowd incidents and our "shambolic defence." What terminated our special relationship with the media, and are we still 'everybody's second favourite team?'

I think not. The same journalists that built us up have now not been slow to ridicule us and highlight our shortcomings. It's now unlikely many would want to claim us as their second team as nobody wants to be associated with failures and that is what we are now being portrayed as.

The swell of public support has turned towards poor old Pompey who lived beyond their means in a financial football fantasy land that inevitably crashed around their ears. Burnley, who attempted to live within their budget and did everything legitimately, paying their players and creditors on time, are now viewed as a club that had ideas above its station, or at least that's the impression I get. Perhaps it's paranoia setting in.

Did the love affair end with the departure of Coyle or had it already happened? Has Brian Laws' less charismatic personality turned the media away from us?

The reality I think is that after the initial novelty wore off, the press got back to its fascination with the 'big boys,' and the Wigans, Boltons, Blackburns and ourselves went back to being the sides that make up the numbers.

Slowly but surely the magic of our promotion ebbed away and with every passing away defeat we became a bit more ordinary and faceless. Without Coyle a lot of our mystique disappeared. The guy who had led us from nowhere to the promised land had jumped ship and we replaced him with an honest, likeable but less inspirational figure.

More worrying to Clarets fans is what happened to the sense of unity, the 'oneness' amongst team and staff, and also between team and fans, the bond that made the impossible possible. Now we have the 'togetherness' theme associated with the season ticket sales drive, but in reality there is little of that unity apparent now.

There are rumours of disaffected players and every defeat drives a bigger wedge between manager and fans, who become more and more disillusioned and fearful of the future. This rift is also damaging the support for Barry Kilby whose dignity throughout the whole Coyle affair won him the admiration of the fans. The awful form and points return achieved under Brian Laws is now seriously calling into question the chairman's wisdom in his choice of the manager.

March 31 signalled the end of the season ticket renewal discount period, though the club decided to extend the deadline for online applications for a short period due to technical difficulties with the website.

On April 1, Burnley announce a figure of almost 10,000 season ticket renewals in the discount period, which in the light of our present parlous state is a very commendable figure and an encouraging show of loyalty from the fans. This at least gives some encouragement that if the likely relegation occurs we will at least be playing to reasonable crowds next season.

Game 33 – Saturday, April 3, 5.30pm – Manchester City – Home.

TODAY'S game is against top four hopefuls City, they who have the dubious distinction of being the only side to grant us an away point.

With their mega-million pound team assembled at a cost in excess of £200m and their previous liking for handing out wallopings to us, I fear it will make for a difficult early evening for sure.

A bad back, which has plagued me for some days now and which I inform my work colleagues has been caused by carrying them on it, prevents my normal Saturday morning gym outing. My wife and daughter go without me and on their return I am reprimanded for not informing my wife that there is a home game today, something she has learned from the Sky Sports screens in the gym. I'm sure I told her some weeks back but I've been married long enough to know not to argue and accept the admonishment.

At lunchtime my work colleague Alison, the Coyle Wanderer, texts me to ask how my back is and says she can recommend a good physiotherapist if I want to dig in my pocket. I tell her I am still in pain but will suffer rather than that.

She also asks what seat I am in for the game, as her husband is a City fan and her daughter Emily, who is a fledgling Blues fan, is coming with him. They have seats in the James Hargreaves Upper which she informs me are Row Q.

I text back to say she should be careful as they are animals on Row Q, to which she replies: "What row are you on then? I always said you were a pig." I think that's set the tone for the game.

It slowly ticks round to the afternoon and Stephanie and myself decide we will defer teatime until after the game as she is working till four and doesn't want to "bolt" her food.

That's the other thing with Premier League kick off times. They don't half mess up your meal times and natural body rhythms. That means eating about 8pm which should be the start of beer time.

As we approach the ground, the now familiar feeling of apprehension starts to come over me and, judging by the strangely quiet procession of fans to the ground, over them too.

My apprehension turns to trepidation as I see the starting line ups and realise it looks like we are going to match them up formation wise, going for an attacking 4-4-2.

City will field a midfield of Adam Johnson, Patrick Viera, Gareth Barry and Craig Bellamy supporting strikers Carlos Tevez, and Emmanuel Adebayor. We will confront these with Eagles, Alexander, Big Kev and Robbie, fronted by Fletcher and Nugent. In boxing parlance, a bit of a mis-match.

I text Stephanie, who is occupying my seat on Row E, from my lofty eerie on Row Z: "Hammering likely today."

How prophetic, or should that be pathetic. I can't believe my eyes as we crumble from the start to go three goals down in seven minutes. Our defence is non-existent as City pass and move their way through it like ghosts. Embarrassing is not the word as every attack seems likely to yield a goal.

Adebayor starts the rout on four minutes after they have already hit the post. How did we even last so long? Bellamy joins in on five and Tevez gets in on the act after seven as City, without breaking sweat, steamroller us under foot.

This is too much for a number of fans who up and leave the ground, presumably as they have been told their tea is ready.

To call the defending amateurish would be an insult to amateurs and an almighty rout is on the cards. The crowd that are left are stunned and some are exceedingly angry, and on 20 minutes Viera makes it four.

Then gradually, the atmosphere in the James Hargreaves starts to change as the fans, slowly at first but with increasing vigour, find their voice. It's the moment for me when the crowd realise the dream is over, the Prem experience is ending, and it's as if a huge weight has been lifted. The fans have accepted our fate and now they're going to enjoy what's left of it as they try to lift the 11 lads out on the pitch.

Gradually the chanting and singing spreads to all corners of the ground and a party atmosphere is generated. A chant of "We're going to win 5-4" goes up to be followed shortly by another gift for City as they go five up. Undaunted, the crowd come back with: "We're going to win 6-5."

The team leave the field at half time to rousing cheers in contrast to the booing and contempt aimed at Brian Laws as he trudges off. Can he survive this and what's more will he want to?

During the interval, God himself, or herself, decides to intervene and sends a deluge of rain to soak the pitch. The ground staff foolishly start forking the pitch to cries of "leave it alone" as we pray for an abandonment.

Unpredictable as ever, Lawsy makes two changes and off go Big Kev and Robbie, certainly no worse performers than any other in the first 45, to be replaced by Jack Cork and Wade Elliott.

The constant rain is certainly making the pitch a great leveller as our inability to move the ball is matched by City's. You would have thought that for all that money they'd be able to play on a bog.

The crowd, now thoroughly enjoying themselves as mass hysteria sets in, takes up the chant "This pitch is dangerous" to the tune of, take note culture lovers, La Donna E Mobile, followed by "off, off, off" as we seek abandonment.

On 58 minutes, Vincent Kompany adds number six to become the fifth goalscorer and my thoughts are drifting to the nine goals Wigan conceded at Spurs. Are we going to go one better?

Fortunately not. The water is taking its toll and the ball mostly sticks but occasionally flies, to make any attempt at serious soccer futile.

The Clarets are toiling away manfully as they attempt to plough through a paddy field and on 71 minutes Steven Fletcher scores a fine goal to cap a battling performance from the striker. Is this the start of the great comeback? Game on.

The teams continue to slug it out in a combination of football and mud wrestling till the referee eventually calls time. Well, at least we got a draw in the second half.

Once again the team leaves the field to cheering and applause but the manager is left in no doubt as to what most of the fans are now thinking.

Result: Burnley (Fletcher 71) 1, Manchester City (Adebayor 4, 45, Bellamy 5, Tevez 7, Viera 20, Kompany 58) 6.
Team: Jensen; Mears, Duff, Cort, Fox; Eagles, Alexander, McDonald K (Cork 46), Blake (Elliott 46); Nugent, Fletcher (Paterson 81).
Subs not used: Weaver, Bikey, Carlisle, Thompson.
Attendance: 21,330.
Position in Table: 19.
Season record: Played 33, Won 6, Drawn 6, Lost 21, Goals for 32, Goals against 71, Points 24.

Once again, my night's sleep is ruined as I wake in the early hours of Sunday morning replaying the whole nightmare again in my head.

After getting up I text friends and foes with the message: "Have those horrible men in black shirts gone away yet? Is it safe to come out?" There are many replies but I think the most accurate comes from John W who texts: "Don't worry about men in black. Tigers, black cats, and even cockerels scare me." Not bad as Hull City, Sunderland and Tottenham Hotspur are amongst our remaining fixtures.

What went so badly wrong on Saturday? Was the team selection and formation too attacking considering the strength of our opponents? Should we have gone to pack the midfield to try and nullify our visitors' threat and frustrate them in the hope of nicking something? It seems incredibly naïve to think that we could match them man for man.

Has Brian Laws lost the respect of the players? Certainly the rumours of player discontent are rife and are growing. It's also suggested that Robbie Blake and Kevin McDonald left the ground shortly after being substituted at half time, and even that Big Kev went to the nearby 110 Club to rendezvous with family and friends. Surely this can't be right?

What the hell is going on? The club seems to be falling apart at the seams and stories of indiscipline and insurrection are being rumoured daily on the messageboards. Some decisive action needs to be taken quickly to restore both discipline and morale or the next thumping is just around the corner.

It's Friday, April 9 and on a personal note it's been a good week for me as I have enjoyed a long Easter vacation which included Good Friday and all the following week.

Trips to St Annes, Skipton and York, complemented by the opportunity to do some much needed jobs around the garden have made a pleasant change from the daily grind. By today even the weather is feeling decidedly spring-like as the temperature hits double figures.

A good week for me but I doubt it has been for Brian Laws as pressure on his position mounts. Confirmation of the Kevin McDonald debacle comes via the national media to further tarnish our image. Big Kev is forced to offer an apology in the form of a statement which is so eloquently worded that I can't help but suspect that it has been ghost-written on his behalf by the club media people in an attempt at damage limitation.

His statement read: "I now realised it was naïve, disrespectful and totally wrong of me to leave the ground at half time on Saturday. It was a gross misjudgement and instead I should have remained at Turf Moor to support my club and team mates. I acknowledge that I showed a lack of respect to all the fans that were at the ground and who pay good money to watch their team play.

"I would like to apologise to the players, management and supporters and I have accepted my punishment. In closing, I would like to reassure all supporters that I am fully committed to helping the team as we fight to stay in the Premier League."

No details were given as to what the punishment he received was, but conjecture in the press suggests he was fined one week's wages, amounting to £5,000. Bloody expensive trip to the pub, that one Kev.

Towards the end of the week stories again emerge in both the Daily Mail and the Mirror that Brian Laws is in line for the chop, and that failure at Hull City on Saturday will bring about his downfall.

The Mirror article claims the run of only one win in 14 games has led to a "private admission" from Burnley's hierarchy that the appointment has failed. The article hints at dressing room unrest and rows with senior players Robbie Blake and Clarke Carlisle, which have weakened Laws' position.

The McDonald affair is said to have added to the disquiet among the board, and hints that a short term appointment to the end of the season may be in the offing. Sounds to me a bit like the Mirror putting two and two together, but who knows? There's usually no smoke without fire.

On Thursday, it's reported that Christian Kalvenes has left the club by mutual consent and returned to his native Norway to begin a new life in accountancy. Sounds like life has become too stressful for Christian and he has decided to opt for a more stable occupation. Who can blame him?

Just to round the week off nicely for Brian, our old friend Joey Gudjonsson comes forward to "put the boot in." In a story run on Sky Sports he claims: "He lost the dressing room long ago. I think all the players have lost faith in him, the performances say all that has to be said."

Well, losing a dressing room. That doesn't sound good to me. In the past I have lost my comb and small coins down the back of the settee, but to lose something as large as a dressing room? No wonder the players have lost faith. All they've lost are matches, and they're not very expensive.

Oh well, having said all that it's Saturday again tomorrow and we can look forward to our next Premier League outing at almost equally desperate Hull City. However our hosts now have a three point advantage and a game in hand on us, having won last time out. There's no doubt which of these two clubs are going to be up for this one and you can almost feel them thirsting for our blood to enhance their improving survival prospects.

After last week and this week, I fear the worst and Saturday could well be another painful day for all connected with Burnley FC.

Game 34 – Saturday, April 10, 3pm – Hull City – Away.

THE day of the match, it has to be said, starts beautifully with lovely, warm sunshine and an almost summery feel to it.

That's good news for my next door neighbours Albert and Margaret whose daughter ties the knot today. Albert and his sons-in-law are all devoted Clarets and for sure will have one eye on the scoreline as their own ceremony kicks off at three o'clock.

My afternoon will be made up of domestic chores and nail biting and I opt to cut the front lawn for the first time this year. Entering into the spirit of summer, I go for the T-shirt and shorts look, with the lucky Clarets wristband on the left wrist, writing facing down.

Radio Lancs give the team news and it's no surprise to see McDonald omitted from the squad completely, although he has travelled, presumably to sample the hostelries of Hull and report back to the other lads. Also out are Blake and Eagles as we quickly ditch the 4-4-2 formation with Lawsy belatedly realising we can't play with only two central midfielders. In come Cork, Elliott, and Paterson.

As I make a cup of tea, why am I not surprised to hear us go a goal down in the first three minutes? According to our friends at Radio Lancs it's courtesy of "abysmal defending." No change there then.

Not sparing my feelings, they continue to inform us that we are being ripped apart, and that against a better team it would be like the City game. I decide to go out in the garden to see if that will bring a change in our fortunes, and after all I have put my shorts on.

Soon after we hear of a head injury to Michael Duff and prolonged treatment, though our radio friends reassure us that won't be a problem as we have three centre halves, Carlisle, Caldwell, and Bikey, on the bench. In their opinion that's too many for a game we have to win.

I sort of detect a growing confidence within these guys, Scott Read and Chris Boden, to have a go at Laws' tactics and team selection. They obviously think his days are numbered and so he's now fair game.

To be fair to them, they reckon it's a terrific game now after our dodgy opening with the play flowing from end to end. On 24 minutes a dangerous free kick to our hosts, just to the left of the D, sees Jimmy Bullard put it over the top. Phew.

Then comes a great save by Jensen from the lumbering Jozy Altidore with Bullard putting the rebound over again. Is that the turning point?

The Clarets are coming back into the game and on 35 minutes Paterson, with a turn and shot following a ball in from Mears, levels the score. That quietens the majority of the KC Stadium but revitalises the long suffering but always enthusiastic visiting fans.

Now we've fully recovered from the start and the commentators reckon half time is coming too soon for us as we gain the ascendancy. We're in at half time at 1-1 and all to play for second half.

The news from the only other Premier League fixture is not so good as Sunderland are drawing 0-0 with relegation rivals West Ham. Still, plenty of time yet. Come on the Mackems.

Shortly after half time, Hull lose left back Andy Dawson, who is stretchered off, then Duff misses a sitter as West Ham go one up.

It's 4.15 and time for the Grand National so I reluctantly ditch my headphones and forsake coverage from Hull for the duration of the race. It's not bad, and Stephanie's horse Hello Bud comes a creditable fifth, mine is Character Building which comes in seventh, while my wife has Backstage which I believe is still, as the race commentators say, "crossing the Melling Road." I think it must be waiting for a gap in the traffic.

Race over, I dash back to my earphones and am amazed to hear our friends say it's relatively comfortable now at 3-1. They don't seem to be having a go at any one so I assume, shortly to be proved correctly, it's 3-1 to us.

Would you credit it? As soon as my back's turned, the Clarets go goal crazy and - dare I think it? - an away victory at the 17th attempt might just be about to happen.

We need Sunderland to get something at West Ham but we can't do anything about that. There are 15 minutes left now and if we maintain the two goal difference, it will move us up above Hull to 18th.

Substitutes start to appear as we run down the clock, with the returning Caldwell on for Duff and Bikey on for Fletcher. In the words of Victor Meldrew, "I don't believe it." Then its five minutes added time and Thompson on for Nugent.

We are heading for our first away win in the top tier of English football since 1976, and our first double of the season against hapless Hull. As I sip my hard earned G&T and look forward to a great night, the icing on the cake arrives as Wade Elliott makes it four from a free kick.

What a fantastic and unexpected response after all last week's trials and tribulations. Football never ceases to amaze me.

Our hosts must have been so confident especially after their early goal, but they ended up on the end of a Burnley-style thrashing. Bloody brilliant.

As I meet up with Albert and family at the bar in the Oaks to celebrate the wedding, we agree that in the words of Lou Reed, it's been a "Perfect Day." Bring on the beers.

Result: Hull City (Kilbane 3) 1, Burnley (Paterson 35, Alexander pens 64, 70, Elliott 90) 4.

Team: Jensen; Mears, Duff (Caldwell 85), Cort, Fox; Paterson, Elliott, Alexander, Cork, Nugent (Thompson 90); Fletcher (Bikey 86).

Subs not used: Weaver, Carlisle, Blake, Eagles.

Attendance: 24,369.

Position in Table: 18.

Season record: Played 34, Won 7, Drawn 6, Lost 21, Goals for 36, Goals against 72, Points 27.

It's Tuesday evening before I get a chance to see the goals which I recorded on MOTD, but the wait only enhances the experience. What a great turn and finish by Pato, two supremely taken penalties from Graham Alexander, the undisputed 'King of Penalties', and an exquisite free kick from Wade.

The sight of Brian Laws jumping for joy and with a grin like a Cheshire cat was heartwarming. All the fans I spoke to on Saturday night were so pleased for Lawsy that after such a torrid week he had achieved something Coyle couldn't, an away win. Even if they had reservations about the guy, they were delighted for him, and who could begrudge him that one?

Really, we had no right to deserve anything there. One of their players managed more letters in his name than our entire back four put together, Vennegoor of Hesselink amassing a total of 20, whereas Mears, Duff, Cort, and Fox could only manage 16 between them. It just goes to show that being a man of letters counts for nothing in football.

Gudjonsson's latest verbal assault on Brian Laws earns him a two week suspension by the club pending a full investigation of the incident. I think this is the last we will see of Joey, even at reserve team level. The player's contract expires at the end of the season and it's now impossible to see him being offered an extension.

His outburst, reported on Friday, seems to have had little effect on team morale at Hull where the Clarets showed great spirit. That tremendous result can only have improved the mood of determination and togetherness that started to reassert itself on Saturday, and which will hopefully be evident in the remaining games to come.

The 'Fat Lady' has barely started her vocal warm up exercises but the vultures have already started to circle. Sky Sports run a story headlined "Burnley keen to keep top talent," in which they state we have warned off possible suitors who may be after our star players over the Summer.

The article quotes chief executive Paul Fletcher as insisting the club will not be looking to cash in on their prize assets, whatever division we end up in. They name Steven Fletcher and Chris Eagles as top targets, whilst also suggesting Tyrone Mears and Clarke Carlisle may be coveted by other clubs.

Coyle is identified as being interested in Fletcher and also Wade Elliott. Paul Fletcher's response in the Lancashire Telegraph is: "It's part and parcel of Burnley as a club. People will think we are rich pickings for the wealthy teams but we intend to keep hold of our best players whether we are in the Premier League or Championship. We've got four games to go and we've still got a reasonable chance of staying up."

Game 35 – Saturday, April 17, 3pm – Sunderland – Away.

IT'S another away day on Saturday and again a lovely day as the sun shine downs on Harle Syke, God's country. Now what we need today is for the sun to shine down on those boys in claret and blue as they step out at the Stadium of Light and try to repeat last week's result.

We sit four points adrift of safety, but with our abysmal goal difference it's effectively five points with only 12 to play for. We really need something today although defeat won't relegate us whatever happens to our rivals.

The team news is not good with an enforced change. Nugent misses out with a hamstring injury and is replaced by Eagles with a similar formation as last week, ie a 4-5-1 switching to 4-3-3 when we attack.

Our Radio Lancs friends today are Phil Cunliffe and summariser Chris Boden, and the game starts with a familiar "started sluggish" from our duo. This soon changes to "highly encouraging" but even from my position in the back garden, I'm not convinced. I can hear the crowd in the background on the radio and they seem to sense easy pickings.

There's also an element of revenge in the mix here as Sunderland manager Steve Bruce was rejected by Burnley as a youngster, having come down on trial at the same time as current Burnley boss Brian Laws, who was offered an apprenticeship.

Add to that the Clarets handing out of a 3-1 mauling to the Black Cats on September 19[h] in those heady days when we used to win home games, and I sense trouble.

Sunderland, now safe in mid-table after a sticky patch either side of Christmas, have plenty of fire power and are starting to turn it on us. We have a shot from Kenwyne Jones hitting the post and then a great save by Jensen from a John Mensah header.

The radio boys inform us Sunderland are really stepping it up and applying a lot of pressure, so it comes as no surprise when they take the lead on 25 minutes with a goal from Fraizer Campbell.

I can't sit and take any more of it as Sunderland continue to pile it on so I make a start on painting the garden fence posts. It's to no avail as on 41 minutes it's 2-0 with a goal from Darren Bent, his 23rd of the season. In the words of our chums we are "dead and buried," and we go in at half time two down.

I'm a bit late getting tuned in for the second half but am relieved to hear it's still 2-0. We have made a change at half time with Steven Thompson on for Martin Paterson, who I don't think I can remember being mentioned in the first half.

It's a bit brighter this half and at 4.25pm, 23 minutes into the second half, we manage our first shot on target in the game. The fightback is on.

With nine minutes to go, Blake is on and within two minutes the "little magician," as he is described by Phil Cunliffe, conjures an opening for Thompson who makes no mistake and it's 2-1.

With four minutes added time we give it our best shot, but it's not to be and we go down again to our 16th away defeat from 18. The scoreline probably flattered us and once again we really were just not good enough, but that is no disgrace in this league and the lads did put the effort in.

With Hull getting a draw at Birmingham we slip to second bottom. With time running out we now probably need to win the last three games, at home to Liverpool and Tottenham and away at Birmingham, and even then it might not be enough.

Oh well. On to the next game and let's hope Liverpool's exertions in Europe this week leave them a little battle weary for the Turf on Sunday next.

Result: Sunderland (Campbell 25, Bent 41) 2, Burnley (Thompson 82) 1.

Team: Jensen; Mears, Duff, Cort, Fox; Paterson (Thompson 46), Elliott, Alexander, Cork (Blake 81), Eagles; Fletcher.

Subs not used: Weaver, Carlisle, Caldwell, Bikey, Jordan.

Attendance: 41,341.

Position in Table: 19.

Season record: Played 35, Won 7, Drawn 6, Lost 22, Goals for 37, Goals against 74, Points 27.

After Saturday's results, what looked already an unlikely escape got even more improbable following an incredible turn round at Wigan on Sunday.

The Latics, with a four point advantage over us but with a similarly poor goal difference, trailed by two goals to nil entering the last 10 minutes at home to Arsenal. That would have been a good result for us as it would leave the gap at four points and worsen their goal difference.

Then, incredibly, Arsenal crumble in the final minutes to concede three goals and dump us further in the mire. That's the sort of season Wigan are having. When you least expect it they come up trumps and they have previously upset the form book with wins against Chelsea and Liverpool at the DW Stadium. They now go seven points clear with nine to play for and look out of reach.

That leaves just Hull and West Ham as the teams in our sights and West Ham have a game at Liverpool on Monday night.

Sad though it sounds, I am heartened when I pick up Monday morning's paper to see that the Liverpool goal machine Fernando Torres has had a knee operation and is out for the rest of the season.

Now I don't mean the lad any harm and hope he makes a full recovery in time for the upcoming World Cup, but if there is one guy I didn't want to see lining up against us on Sunday, it's him. Of course there is another one in Steven Gerrard but I suppose it would be too much to ask for Rafa Benitez to rest him at the Turf.

Let's hope Torres's absence is not too big a burden for Liverpool as they try to overcome the Hammers tonight.

No worries. Liverpool without Torres easily overcome a poor West Ham side and they keep our rivals in reach if we can manage to win some games.

On Wednesday, April 21, a letter from the administrators to the creditors of Portsmouth FC highlights the extent of the financial lunacy that has taken place there. The club is reported to have debts of £119m, almost double the figure estimated when they became the first Premier League club to enter administration back in February.

On the plus side they are still owed money from outgoing transfers amounting to about £14m.

However the letter reveals £38m owing to former owners, and more than £9m to players' agents. They also owe £500,000 on the loan signing of Jamie O'Hara and £3m for the transfer of Kevin Prince Boateng, both players coming from Tottenham Hotspur, managed by former Pompey boss Harry Redknapp.

The total unpaid tax bill is £17.1m, and the list of unsecured creditors made up of local businesses and services runs to 15 pages with a total of £5m owed. These are the real losers in this situation and are likely to receive only 23p for every £1 they are owed, as the footballers and football creditors get paid in full from the proceeds of any sale of the club.

Interviewed on TV one of these creditors, the local newsagent, who was owed a figure something in excess of £100, explained how he had no alternative but to stop the supply of papers to the club. I began to feel really sorry for the guy but then he blew it when he claimed that as a result of the administration he would not be able to have a holiday this year. Now come on, where did he think he was going to get a holiday for £100? It wouldn't pay for a day trip to Blackpool.

On the same day, Hull City chairman Adam Pearson pointed the finger of financial mismanagement at his predecessor Paul Duffen, accusing him of overspending and creating a "doomsday scenario."

In his programme notes prior to the evening game at home to Aston Villa he said: "Of course the future is very tricky, it's bound to be when you consider the figures. The club desperately needs to stay in this league."

He went on to say: "The club under Mr Duffen spent money it did not have." Summing up his view of the over-ambitious spending he was quoted as saying: "This is not ambition or 'giving it a go' or 'living the dream.' It is, in my personal view, poor business sense."

At last a realist along the lines of our own Barry Kilby, but will it be too late for Hull, saddled with a wage bill of around £40m and with £6m wasted in agents' fees? On Wednesday evening they entertain the Villa in their game in hand and duly lose 0-2. Oh dear.

Arriving home from work on the Friday preceding our 36th 'must win' game of the season at home to Liverpool, I am greeted by a Rovers supporting neighbour. I know that lowers the tone of the area and devalues property prices but I can't exactly burn his house down.

This sadly misguided individual, who finds himself transported to Burnley by an accident of marriage, feels he has to chip in with "Could be all over this weekend, Pete." I can't let him get away with that and give him back twice as much as I take.

When I was young I could never accept relegation or defeat until it was mathematically impossible to escape. It's funny but although we all age physically, mentally we're still as daft as we were when we were teenagers, and so where there's life there's hope.

As he disappears up the road I continue my outward show of bravado until he is out of hearing. The ironic thing for this guy is that coming from the Blackburn area all his family are Roverites but his son, born and educated in Burnley, has followed his mates and is a Claret. Good lad.

Saturday's results leave us knowing exactly what we need to do to survive, and we have a veritable mountain to climb. Hull City are virtually gone following a 0-1 home defeat to Sunderland, whilst West Ham claw their way towards safety with a 3-2 home win over Wigan.

That means we now have to win the last three games and hope that West Ham only collect one more point from their last two, or that Wolves and Wigan lose both theirs. It's a big ask considering we've only won seven out of 35 so far.

Today we go up against Liverpool knowing our fate could be decided by 5 o'clock. Doomsday looms.

Game 36 – Sunday, April 25, 3pm – Liverpool – Home.
SATURDAY was a lovely, sunny, warm Spring day but it's not repeated itself as I rise on Sunday morning and see there has been light overnight rain and it's cloudy.

I have my usual Sunday morning jog over the golf course in an attempt to rid my system of last night's beer, and then I'm set for the afternoon's date with destiny.

My daughter and wife head for town to meet up with my mother-in-law to make a three generational attack on the clothes shops and I arrange to meet Stephanie on the way to the ground from the pub.

The weather is showing signs of improving and before leaving I receive a text from Stephanie telling me to go easy on the clothing as it's now really warm. Heeding her advice I settle for a light fleece over a T-shirt, dead casual.

As I leave the car to walk to the pub I look up at the sky and think it doesn't look too promising, but carry on anyway as it starts to spit with rain. Approaching the point of no return, ie whether to go back and get a coat or press on, I opt for the latter.

Mistake, as just as I get past the Queen Vic the heavens open and there's no shelter. I could swear my pants are made of tissue paper as I absorb water at a frightening pace, and so I leg it for Thompson Park and try to shelter by the park ranger's building.

Great start this. Not even made the pub and soaked, with an afternoon of sitting in wet clothing ahead. Remind me not to listen to Stephanie in future.

Eventually I make the Talbot and two pints of Tetley's later set off to rendezvous with Stephanie once more in heavy rain. Fortunately she rescues me on TK Maxx's car park with her umbrella, and soon I'm safely at the ground and not too wet, my trousers having the ability to give up water as rapidly as they absorb it and my fleece steaming slightly. It's show time.

We go with the same starting line up as at Sunderland with the exception of the returning Nugent for Eagles. Liverpool are without Torres and start with Dirk Kuyt up front, supported by Ryan Babel and Maxi Rodriguez out wide. Unfortunately Gerrard has not been injured or rested and plays as Liverpool continue their quest for a top four finish and a Champions League place.

We start quite steadily and there is no hint of a City-style collapse in the early stages. Neither team is making much impression on the other and for once our defence looks quite solid.

I think this may be down to the fact that Liverpool don't look all that good. Chances at either end are scarce although the Reds force a few early corners which come to nought.

Encouragingly, the home crowd seem well up for it today and are giving the team great encouragement with no hint of concerted criticism of Brian Laws, although there are as always the odd dissenting voices.

The first real attempt on goal for us doesn't come till past the 20 minute mark with an effort from Fletcher. Within a couple of minutes following some good play down the right and a great teasing cross in from the right by Paterson, Fletcher heads a good chance over. We are starting to build some momentum now and still look comfortable at the back.

Once again we seem to be getting nothing from the referee and I come to the conclusion that some of the big name players in the Premier League are untouchable as far as the officials are concerned. Gerrard is one such player as any sort of a tackle or challenge on him earns a free kick whereas he can get away with the same without penalty.

Half time comes and it's still 0-0 and a fairly encouraging first half performance sees a good round of applause as the players leave the field. To a neutral in the crowd it would have been difficult to differentiate which of the sides was the struggler and which the Europa Cup semi finalist.

During the interval, I make the big mistake of suggesting to John W that we can get something from this game, and he wisely counsels caution by telling me to shut up.

Too late I fear as about five minutes into the second half we give Gerrard the luxury of too much space on the edge of the box and his shot nestles in the corner with the aid of a huge deflection. Not long after that, our goose is well and truly cooked as Gerrard hits an unstoppable 25 yarder into the opposite corner, a strike of true class applauded even by the home fans.

The crowd continue to give magnificent vocal backing to the team even as we go 0-3 down to a goal from Maxi Rodriguez as Danny Fox goes missing and the Beast is once again in no man's land.

Chants of "going down" from the now happy Scousers are met with a better retort of "going bust" from the Clarets, as the home fans remind our visitors their reported debt is in excess of £200m.

We chase the game and sacrifice a midfielder to bring on Blake and go 4-4-2, with Nugent joining Fletcher up top. Eagles replaces Paterson and finally Thompson for Nugent. Fletcher hits the post with the ball rebounding to safety, although there is a strong suspicion of handball as he controlled it in the build up.

The game is up and we are doomed, but God can't resist one last sickening twist of the knife as he allows Babel a goal from the last action of the game.

Biblically, we are told that God was not all that happy with Babel as it was during the building of the infamous tower that mankind got a bit too big for his boots and was creating the tower as a symbol of people power. God in punishment caused the people to speak in many tongues, creating confusion and scattering them to different corners of the earth. Just a different corner of Turf Moor would have done on this occasion, but no.

What a shame that the dream should end like this. It was never a 0-4 game and without Gerrard there was nothing between the teams. In truth, the fans knew it was all over some weeks back, I suspect during the City game, but to their credit again stayed to roundly applaud the team from the field.

The harsh truth is that over the season we were nowhere near good enough, but as reasonable people, we know why and accept that. As long as everyone can hold their heads up and say they did their best then that's all we can ask for and again today this was certainly the case.

So the relegation issue is settled with the three teams now down with two games to go. Oh well, no pressure in those then.

Result: Burnley 0, Liverpool (Gerrard 52, 59, Maxi Rodriguez 74, Babel 90) 4.

Team: Jensen; Mears, Duff, Cort, Fox; Paterson (Eagles 71), Alexander (Blake 64), Elliott, Cork, Nugent (Thompson 77); Fletcher.

Subs not used: Weaver, Caldwell, Bikey, Rodriguez.

Attendance: 21,553.

Position in Table: 19.

Season record: Played 36, Won 7, Drawn 6, Lost 23, Goals for 37, Goals against 78, Points 27.

So the Premier League experience is over, but for how long? Will it be a quick return or the hard slog?

Did it end in tears? No, it ended in a magnificent show of defiance, support, and solidarity, at least by the fans.

Inevitably, quickly after the game the subject of Brian Laws' future is raised on the fans' messageboards. Ambiguous comments by the chairman and chief executive in media interviews seem to in one sense to confirm his position but yet not totally. The chairman's statement that he will sit down in a week or two with Brian and discuss the situation seemingly adds fuel to the speculation.

A report in The Lancashire Telegraph intimating that there is a clause in the manager's contract by which failure to reach 29 points could trigger dismissal seems a bit far fetched to me. Even if such a clause existed, who would be disclosing that sort of information?

It's difficult to gauge what the general support thinks regarding Brian as inevitably those making the loudest noise are those who are critical, whilst the moderates form the silent majority. But I guess that even among the moderates there is a fairly even split as to whether he should go or stay.

Whatever is going to happen it needs to be clarified quickly as decisions have to be made on players coming out of contract and potential transfer targets need to be worked on.

Reaction amongst my work colleagues seems rather subdued. I must confess that I was expecting a hard time on Monday morning from the various factions, but only the token Man United fan, who I doubt has ever seen them play, seems to have an appetite for mickey taking.

Things are quieter in the office anyway as the reluctant Rover Jilly has departed on maternity leave, and on Monday, April 26, produces her own eye-watering bundle of joy, a daughter Esme, weighing in at 8lb 13oz.

PNE Ed is rapidly approaching his termination date, redundancy that is, and leaves on Friday, April 30. He is still reeling from Wigan Warriors' defeat at Bradford on Friday night, when after leading 24-6 at half time, they were overhauled 26-36 at the finish. It's going to be quiet after Ed's gone, even though he is a pain in the ass!

That leaves just Alison, the Coyle Wanderer, who I suspect is too ashamed of her team's underhand dealings to take full advantage of the situation.

Thursday evening, April 29, and I receive a text from John W as I am engrossed in domestic chores, ie cleaning the bathroom. This is largely a futile exercise as tomorrow Stephanie will return from Liverpool at the end of her second year studies to take up her one woman assault on the said room. From its pristine condition it will rapidly be subjected to globs of conditioner randomly distributed around the room along with hairs the length of which I can only dream of. Water will be liberally sprinkled to create a wet room effect and an array of weird and wonderful potions will fill the storage spaces.

I digress. Back to the text, and in it John W is urging: "Come on Fulham, get Burnley into Europe."

Now I must confess I do recall seeing some article somewhere that suggested we may qualify for next season's Europa League by some convoluted series of results allowing us in via our Fair Play League position. I had obviously dismissed it as highly improbable, but here it was again coming back to the fore.

Continuing my foray into the depths of the lavatory I dispelled it from mind until at 21.36 another text: "Fulham now 1-1, another goal we're in Europe," followed at 21.38 by "Fulham score we're in boys!" At this point I respond: "Dream on," which then brings about a phone call explaining that we are seriously in contention if Fulham win, and that it must be true because it was on Sky Sports News.

Now I'm praying for a Fulham victory, which they duly manage. What lovely Cockney geezers they are. Oh, what memories. Johnny Haynes, Jim Langley, Alan Mullery, George Best, Rodney Marsh. Now they are on the verge of doing something truly wonderful for the Clarets, and we will be forever grateful.

It seems John W was a bit premature and that Fulham have actually to win the competition by beating Atletico Madrid in the final in Hamburg, coupled with us staying in our current position in the Fair Play League and one or two other things to fall into place, but it is a definite possibility.

I know on occasion in this diary I have been critical of God's neglect of the Clarets this season, but if he, or she, pulls this one off it will be one of his/her greatest stunts yet. Relegation and a place in Europe. How ironic would that be?

It may also be very influential in retaining 'want away' players or indeed attracting potential transfer targets. Let's not get carried away, but you bet we'll be cheering on Fulham in the Europa Cup Final in May, and on Friday, April 30, the Clarets Mad website confirms that we have been granted a UEFA Licence for potential entry into the same competition in 2010/11.

Also confirmed on the same day is the news that Clarke Carlisle, a player out of contract this summer and strongly linked with a move to Bolton, has signed a new two year contract to stay at Turf Moor. Clarke is currently out injured and is unlikely to feature again this season. Let's hope he can come back after the break in his most commanding form.

More good news from the reserve team fixture on April 30 is the return to action of Chris McCann, who came on as a substitute just before half time. The influential midfielder, out for most of the season with a serious knee injury picked up in September and more recently cartilage surgery, has been sorely missed. Let's hope Chris is now on the road to a complete recovery ready to make a major impact on next season's promotion campaign.

As April draws to a close we look forward to the Bank Holiday weekend and a welcome day off on Monday. My wife and I will on Saturday head for Horncastle, Lincolnshire at the invitation of friends who have just purchased a holiday home there.

The Clarets will go on to Birmingham to play the last away fixture of their Premier League season.

This game, that only last week seemed totally meaningless, now takes on a different twist. Not important now are the league points, but highly important are the Fair Play points. Let's keep it clean lads.

MAY

The Wheel Turns Full Circle

Game 37 – Saturday, May 1, 12.45pm – Birmingham City – Away.
SATURDAY, 11am, sees the car packed and Julie and I en route to stay with friends in their newly acquired holiday home near Horncastle, Lincolnshire.

Before leaving, I text John G and John W to ask them to keep me updated with scores as I have no idea where the afternoon will take me.

No updates from PNE Ed this time as yesterday was his last day at work and not only had he to surrender his company car but also his company mobile. I hope the miserable sod invests in one of his own soon as this situation is excluding the opportunity for hostile rivalry and intellectual jousting.

Stopping at Ferrybridge services on the M62 to eat our butties before heading off down the A1, I am slightly confused by a number of football fans strolling around the service area in black and gold colours, with scarves displaying the nickname of The Pilgrims. On closer inspection they turn out to be Boston United fans and a considerable number there are too. We count seven coaches and many cars, a good turn out for a non-league outfit and they're certainly up for it.

Having availed myself of the toilet facilities, I decide to take a quick peek at a newspaper on the stand to see if I can see where this merry throng are heading. Can't see them anywhere but what does catch my eye is the fact that we are already underway at Birmingham as we kicked off at 12.45. Didn't expect that, thought it was a 3 o'clocker.

A quick check of the watch and I see we are already about 25 minutes into the game and I head rapidly back to the car to see if we are still in Radio Lancashire range. The radio commentary is obviously at the edge of its range but I can pick up that it sounds ominously as though we have just conceded another comic cuts goal in the style that only the Clarets can muster.

Before Julie has the opportunity to get in full swing with a complaint about having to listen to more of that for the next hour and a quarter, the texts start rolling in. First to the trigger is John W with: "Cock up in defence, own goal by Jensen," to be followed seconds later by John G and: "Mears own goal," and Radio Lancs crediting the goal to Cameron Jerome.

Oh well. Clear as mud that and a mental picture forms of the ball ricocheting around the Burnley box like it was a pinball machine with both our defenders, their strikers and even the goalie claiming the glory.

I switch the radio off, not wishing to suffer any more damage to my morale from the commentary or from the wrath of she who must be obeyed.

At 1.28pm and just heading down the A1, there are incoming texts again, although not immediately decipherable for Julie as she has to read it as I drive.

Once again John W beats John G to it with the cryptic message: "Choochoo its 2 more on the way," followed by John G's rather simpler "2 nowt." In view of the time delay in the texts, I can only assume John W is following an analogue signal and John G a digital, either that or one has quicker thumbs.

A few minutes later and off goes the phone again, unfortunately once again to be read by Julie. I say unfortunately as the tone of the information is worsening from John W. It reads, after editing: "1/2 embarrassing time, what a f*****g shower of s**t." Straight to the point that in plain Anglo Saxon.

We continue south-eastwards now, engaging in a game of bluff with the Sat Nav system which is dreaming up imaginary roundabouts on the A1 and telling me to take junctions that don't exist. I suppose I should pay for a map update on the thing, but it sort of goes against the grain.

We seem to have been going ages with no texts and I start to assume that the aforementioned shower must have passed. Then, against the first half form, John G pulls one back, getting in first with: "2-1 Thompson." Oblivious to his second place this time comes John W with "Thommo scores 3 mins to go." Now that has Julie going as she tries to decipher whether he means ie has Thommo scored three or are there three minutes to go? I assure her that the former is indeed very unlikely, although I believe that goal does take his total to three in the Premier League this season.

Not to be undone, the almost forgotten Stephanie rounds off the afternoon with: "Lost 2-1 think we got one yellow." That's my girl, spotting the importance of a good performance in the Fair Play stakes, whereas the importance of it completely bypassed the other two roving reporters.

So we finish off a sorry tale of Premier League away performances with our 17th defeat from 19 games. Say no more.

Incidentally I later find out that Boston United of the Unibond Premier were on their way to Bradford for their play-off final, with the reward of a step up to the Blue Square North for the winners. Coming from a goal down they overcame Bradford Park Avenue to clinch promotion. Well done to them.

Result: Birmingham City (Jensen 29 og, Benitez 41) 2, Burnley (Thompson 87) 1.

Team: Jensen; Mears, Caldwell, Cort, Fox; Paterson, Elliott, Alexander (McDonald 85), Cork, Nugent (Blake 65); Fletcher (Thompson 68).

Subs not used: Weaver, Duff, Bikey, Rodriguez.

Attendance: 24,578.

Position in Table: 19.

Season record: Played 37, Won 7, Drawn 6, Lost 24, Goals for 38, Goals against 80, Points 27.

On returning from a very enjoyable weekend in Lincolnshire, I read Tony Scholes' match report on Clarets Mad, which confirms our chronic failing of comic defending whilst praising the efforts of the fans for their light hearted commitment to the cause.

Notable songs and chants from the fans included: "That's why we're going down" on conceding the comic capers goals, and "Going down, we're having a laugh." Old favourites such as "Jimmy Mullen's Claret and Blue Army," and "Eli, Eli, Eli" were aired, which must have had the Brum fans and probably some Clarets scratching their heads.

With five minutes to go 'Wandering Kev McDonald' was entered into the fray, presumably having satisfied Brian Laws his rehabilitation was complete following his recent second half beer outing. Entering the arena he was greeted by chants from the fans of "It's your round." However it appears that Kev didn't see the funny side, presumably preferring to forget the whole affair.

On Wednesday, May 5, news comes from the club that Joey Gudjonsson's contract has been terminated with immediate effect following his recent suspension after comments made about Brian Laws' management. Joey's departure comes as no surprise to anybody. His contract was about to expire anyway and he appeared unlikely to be offered an extension.

To be fair, Joey never really hit the heights at Burnley and his fabled long range shooting ability only really showed on one occasion that I can remember, a 35 yard screamer against Preston. His departure is number two of the promotion heroes following Christian Kalvenes and by the end of this summer I expect there will be many more gone.

Friday, May 7 is a historic day in Burnley's political history as for the first time in 75 years the town does not have a Labour MP. Gordon Birtwistle, leader of the local Liberal Democrats and former mayor of the town, has won the seat after some heavyweight campaigning and the targeting of the seat as winnable by the Lib Dem hierarchy. I can't count the number of leaflets that landed through my door not only from Gordon but also the likes of Lib Dem leader Nick Clegg.

However as I drive to work listening as usual to Radio Lancs, I am hit by a bolt from the blue. Presenting the early morning show is good old Graham Liver, a dyed in the wool Rovers fan, who in commenting on Gordon's victory has to add that "he's a Rovers fan as well."

Now come on. Are you trying to tell me that the good folk of Burnley have just elected a B******d fan as their MP? Nowhere in all the volumes of leaflets did it state that. Sure it told us of all the good things Gordon had done for the town and particularly how he opposed the closure of the A&E department at Burnley General Hospital and its transfer to Blackburn. But not that important fact.

It's a con. How many votes would he have lost had the electorate been aware he was a Rover? It makes departing Labour MP Kitty Ussher's expenses fiasco seem minor.

I'm on my guard now. What next? Transfer of the football club to Deadwood Park? Not an auspicious start for our new man.

Game 38 – Sunday, May 9, 4pm – Tottenham Hotspur – Home.

TODAY it's the last game of our Premier League season, and in a way I'm not sorry. Things since Christmas have gone downhill and the run of poor results have left me drained and shell-shocked.

I think it was in a piece for Clarets Mad that Dave Thomas, the esteemed writer of previous Clarets diaries, said: "We may well have banked the Premiership money but sadly, this season cannot end soon enough."

On this Sunday morning I can readily agree with those sentiments. The atmosphere feels flat and I have no eager anticipation for this game as once again it has the potential for another embarrassing defeat for the press to gloat over. Our visitors today are sure to be in party mood having clinched a top four slot and the prized Champions League place courtesy of a win at Manchester City in midweek.

We need a clean break now, a chance to regroup, and hopefully come again. Today is the closing of the Premier League chapter and with it comes the opportunity to go out with a whimper or a bang. Which will it be?

For good measure, the Premier League have foisted on us another bizarre kick off time of Sunday at 4pm. What the hell is wrong with 3pm?

Still, it's not a bad day and I can go without coat. I'm beginning to feel more like it already. Stephanie misses the game this week as she has started a summer job at M&S's Boundary Mill store. I think the last home game she missed was the win against Manchester United. That could be an omen.

I'm at the ground just in time for kick off and see we have a different centre back pairing of Caldwell and Bikey. For me, this is the position Bikey was signed for and should have played at all season. His aerial ability and general physical strength is a great bonus there and he can play the ball out of defence better than any of our other centre backs.

Looking at the size of the opposition, strength and aerial ability are going to be required in abundance. Once again it's a total physical mismatch with the likes of Crouch, Kaboul, Huddlestone, Bale, Dawson, and King to name but a few of the giants lining up against us.

Spurs have done us the honour of naming a formidable team and are pretty much at full strength, with England pair Peter Crouch and Jermain Defoe up front, backed up by the likes of Aaron Lennon and the Croatian Luka Modric.

From the kick off, normal service is resumed almost immediately as we go a goal down inside the first three minutes. A simple ball inside Fox sees the pace of Lennon take him clear. His cross is not particularly great but in our own inimitable style we fail to clear it and it comes out to Gareth Bale, who at the moment can do no wrong, and he promptly lashes it home.

Oh no. Visions of City all over again. The crowd do their best to keep the lads' heads up but we are making little headway against a very good and very strong Spurs side.

On 32 minutes, we allow the impressive Modric to waltz his way into the box and crash an unstoppable effort past the Beast. It's 2-0 and that looks like it for a chance of a good send off from the Premier League. How many more? That's now the question on most fans' minds.

Then shortly before half time, a lifeline. There's a fine piece of skill from Fletcher as he flicks the ball through and there is Elliott running clear in the area. Come on Wade, thump it past him. He does so, not totally convincingly, but the ball nestles in the back of the net. That cheers us all up as the teams go off for the half time break.

Rejuvenated by the half time cuppa, the Clarets start the second half in attacking mood and soon have our illustrious visitors pinned back.

The Spurs fans, so noisy in the first half, are now showing the first signs of apprehension and rightly so as on 54 minutes, a great cross in from the right by the never-say-die Paterson finds Jack Cork unmarked in the box, and he steers his header just inside the post.

Delirium. What joy. What a comeback.

But there's more to come as the Clarets continue to take the game to Spurs and on 71 minutes we are unbelievably ahead. More magic by Fletcher on the left side of the box gives him enough room to produce the perfect low cross for Paterson to steer home.

It's not all one way and Lennon hits the post for the visitors and in a separate incident Caldwell heads against his own bar, but God has decided that today is for little old Burnley.

The crowd are baying for Robbie Blake, who it seems highly likely will be making his last appearance and on 79 minutes they get him as he runs onto the pitch to a standing ovation. What a popular player Robbie has been and how sorely he will be missed.

Blake is quickly weaving his magic and how everybody of the claret and blue persuasion would love him to score. However, it's not Robbie but another popular sub, Steven Thompson, who sends Turf Moor into raptures as on 88 minutes he manages to get a touch on a Wade Elliott shot to steer the ball into the net and put the Clarets 4-2 up.

How typically of Burnley to go two goals down then stand the game on its head with a four goal response.

News filters through that Hull can only manage a draw and we move above them in the final table and claim an extra £800K in prize money. What an afternoon, and how reminiscent of the optimism and joy of the early season games. If only we could have reproduced this against Wolves, Portsmouth and the Rovers.

The players come out for a lap of honour and most of the 21,000 crowd stay to applaud the team for their efforts this season. Many of those players will not I fear be here next term, and we may lose some 'adopted sons' like Robbie, but that is the way in football. Players and managers come and go but the fans are the true heart of the club. They are unwavering in their support and most will be back again next time.

Thanks to this bunch of players for giving us our taste of the big time, our 'Season in the Sun.' They may not have been the most skilful, most powerful or the paciest players in the Premier League but they didn't fail us in terms of effort and it has been a truly memorable experience, with some magic moments.

At least tonight I can watch MOTD without having to cringe behind the settee.

Result: Burnley (Elliott 42, Cork 54, Paterson 71, Thompson 88) 4, Tottenham Hotspur (Bale 3, Modric 32) 2.
Team: Jensen; Mears, Bikey, Caldwell, Fox; Paterson (Eagles 90), Elliott, Alexander, Cork, Nugent (Blake 79); Fletcher (Thompson 86).

Subs not used: Weaver, Duff, McDonald, Jordan.

Attendance: 21,161.

Final Position in Table: 18.

Season record: Played 38, Won 8, Drawn 6, Lost 24, Goals for 42, Goals against 82, Points 30.

So the year had almost gone full circle from where it all began with the play offs and Wembley.

We entered May 2009 as a Coca Cola Championship side and we leave May 2010 going back to the same league. But boy, what a year we had in between and I am privileged to have been around to witness it. In the words of Alastair Campbell, "Don't cry because it's over. Smile because it happened."

With the dust settling on the last game, I think this is probably the right time to bring my epic to its natural end.

As I write, there are persistent rumours about the manager's position and players both coming and going. The last kick of our Premier League season is over but as soon as one season ends, the next begins. Players coming out of contract need to be either jettisoned or offered new terms, incoming targets need to be identified and pursued, and hostile bids for our 'star' players need to be rebuffed if possible.

In truth, the book could go on forever, but I couldn't, so now is as good a time as any to break.

EPILOGUE

SO that was our Premier League experience, and on reflection how was it for me?

The euphoria after Wembley enveloped the whole town and raised its profile, giving everybody a huge boost. We all thought we knew how difficult life in the Premier League would be but it held no fears for us as under a manager who had assumed God-like status and with our indomitable spirit, we were ready to take on the world.

And anyway, we all said: "If it's only for one season it doesn't matter, we did it."

Despite the opening day loss at Stoke, we were still on a high for the first home league game of the season and who better to face than reigning champions Manchester United? Who can forget Robbie Blake's unstoppable volley, Brian Jensen's penalty save, and the wall of sound that erupted from the stadium, shaking it to its foundations?

A magic night, unbelievable. It was Roy of the Rovers stuff that only happens in boys' comics, but here it was happening for real. What must Sir Alex Ferguson have thought seeing his side go down to little old Burnley? And, as it turned out, perhaps the defeat that cost them the title this time.

A fluke? No such thing as a few days later we were at it again, this time dispatching highly rated Everton, and again the stadium reverberated to perhaps not the biggest crowd in football but certainly one of the most passionate and adoring.

Then a series of tough away fixtures and some moderately hefty defeats, albeit against three of the top teams, started to cause some concern. These, followed by an early exit in the Carling Cup at Barnsley which also saw long term injuries to key players, were soon forgotten as the impressive home run continued.

The first four home league games in the Premier League were all won, a record for a newly promoted club. The team that everybody had considered cannon fodder showed it had some firepower of its own.

Disappointing defeats at arch enemies Blackburn after taking an early lead, followed by the first home reverse to Wigan, took off some of the shine.

However, we were then back to winning ways at home, beating Hull City followed by gaining our first away point at Manchester City. In purely monetary terms, we had no right to be on the same pitch as City but we stunned them with two early goals before typically conceding three then saving it at the death.

The away defeats continued with monotonous regularity and suddenly the home wins started to turn into draws as we shared the points in the next four. The feeling was that we had started to lose momentum but at the halfway point of the season, we sat in 13th position with 20 points, a very respectable haul.

Then came the turning point following the FA Cup win at MK Dons. We were sold down the river by the man we all thought of as God.

What a sickening blow, and what a dirty trick to walk out with the job half done and take the backroom staff as well. How could he, after all the speeches about building something here, turn his back on everything and everybody at the club he professed to love?

At that moment, in my eyes and I think in the eyes of many other people in football, Owen Coyle lost all credibility. I think in reality, Coyle sensed the wheels were coming off and in a misguided sense of self-preservation, jumped ship in order to keep his reputation intact. He may have preserved his status by saving Bolton but he has lost the moral high ground he so loved to inhabit. He has shown himself as no better than the rest and can hardly quibble when any of his players decide to quit at the first sign of a few dollars more, or a safer ride in the Premier League.

How ironic that the job I guess he most craves, Celtic, became available so quickly after he pledged himself to Bolton. He couldn't do it again, could he?

After a short period of frenzied activity, in stepped Brian Laws to a club reeling from the blows. Not a popular choice among the fans and with a less than distinguished recent managerial history. What chance had he?

The optimists hoped for a miracle, the pessimists threw in the towel, and the rest of us watched in ever increasing despair as the season took a fatal downturn. The team and supporters suffered an understandable loss of belief as results and games ebbed away and we slid down the table. Reports of infighting in the squad, player unrest, and almost as importantly the will of the fans to drive the team on, particularly at home, all contributed to the gathering air of gloom around the place.

Must win games came and went without the win, and then the final humiliation, the home drubbing by Manchester City.

Funnily enough this game, to my mind, marked a turning point. The home crowd, realising that the dream was over, decided to go down fighting and once again got behind the team, if not the manager, 100 per cent.

The atmosphere at Turf Moor once again improved tremendously and even in the heavy defeat against Liverpool, the fans stayed right with the team.

It was almost a relief when the season ended, but at least we went out the way we came in, with all guns blazing. Down we are, but out we are not, and we live to fight again.

We claimed after Wembley that we didn't care if it was only for one season. However the truth is that after tasting what we craved for so long, we clearly did care and the relegation hurt badly.

I think what hurt most was that at the halfway point salvation was within reach, but because of the turmoil of January, we fell away. A points return of only 10 in the second half of the season was never going to be enough.

There's no doubt that the step up from Championship football to the Premier League is huge. For a club of such limited resources as Burnley, survival is therefore an almost impossible task.

However, we almost made it and without the Coyle saga I believe we would have done.

We go down stronger than when we came up both financially and in terms of squad quality and depth. We proved Premier League status can be achieved without breaking the bank, and we almost maintained it.

The so-called experts who wrote us off before a ball was kicked are now no doubt congratulating themselves for their foresight. Who needs them? They only have eyes for the big boys, but the Premier League consists of 20 clubs, not six.

We gave hope to the lesser lights that it can be done. As I write, Blackpool have followed our lead and their Premier League ride is about to begin. Good luck to them.

So having said all that, have I enjoyed the Premier League experience? Well, the answer is yes and no.

What I didn't like was the lack of games, which was exacerbated this time by the lack of any cup ties at Turf Moor following our early exits from the competitions. Already four home games short on a Championship season, we seemed to have a lot of blank weekends.

In addition, I didn't like the variable kick off times. For me, football is a social occasion and quite often the only chance I have to catch up with old mates and enjoy a couple of pints before the game. The traditional Saturday 3pm is ideal for me, leaving Sunday free for family pursuits. I won't be sorry to see the back of lunchtime, teatime and Sunday soccer, played at times to suit the Asian viewing figures of Sky TV, not the paying punters at the ground.

I won't miss the heavy defeats, although to be fair despite every pundit imaginable belittling our defensive efforts, we have not suffered the seven, eight and nine goal hammerings handed out to 'better' teams than us.

Along with that goes the genius of the TV pundits. Their mastery of slow motion technology and computer graphics have proved invaluable in simplifying a game that is in reality played at break neck speed at the top level. Oh, what a gift it would be to have such wonderful hindsight in advance of the action.

Another downside was the apparent refereeing bias towards the top clubs. The 'Big Four' seemed to pick up all the 50/50 decisions whilst in some games we struggled to even get throw ins awarded to us.

And finally, the cheating, diving histrionics of some of the Premier League's top imports I won't miss for a long time.

What was great to see for the first time in many years was the stadium packed to the rafters for every game. The fantastic atmosphere generated by a full Turf Moor has to be experienced to be appreciated, and I think the setting of the ground in the heart of the town, and with spectacular scenic views from my seat in the JHU, added to the appeal.

Premier League football raised the profile of the club and the increased media coverage meant we were always in the news. The chance to see highlights of every game on MOTD was a real boon, although I had to switch the sound off when the pundits appeared.

The games also produced a number of fantastic goals both for and against. Goals such as those scored by Nicolas Anelka for Chelsea, for its pace and precision from goalkeeper to finish, and Modric for Tottenham at the Turf, for his sheer technical ability, will be long remembered. Other collector's pieces were of course Robbie's stunning strike at home to Manchester United, and Steven Fletcher's individual brilliance in the home game against Chelsea.

Another plus was the chance to see the top players in the best league in the world gracing the Turf Moor pitch. It was also great to see some of our older players get a last chance at playing at the top level, none more so than Graham Alexander and Robbie Blake.

So yes, overall I did enjoy the Premier League experience and having been there once, I know now it's the only place to be.

Way back at the end of May 2009 and elated by the Wembley success and our incredible achievement, I set out on the long and sometimes arduous journey that has become this diary.

The intention was to write a book in celebration of the events of May 25, 2009, a date that will be etched forever in Clarets history, and record a log of our Premier League season.

It was never meant to be a factual regurgitation of the season's details as the statisticians and journalists can do a much better job of that than me. It was intended to be one fan's view of the everyday things that add up to make a football season, and how this interacts with daily life.

I hope it has reflected the highs and lows and whilst being a largely personal account, I'm sure many other fans have experienced the same emotions throughout the year.

For the most part it has been a joy to write but at some times, particularly after heavy defeats and amid the growing disharmony, it has felt a bit of a chore.

Would I do it again? You bet, but only when we next get promoted back to the Premier League.

UP THE CLARETS!